SEVEN MI

D0117407

TRANSFORMING CORPORATE DATA INTO BUSINESS INTELLIGENCE

Vasant Dhar
Principal, Morgan Stanley
Professor of Information Systems
Stern School of Business, New York University

Roger Stein
Vice-President, Quantitative Analytics
Moody's Investors Service

Prentice Hall, Upper Saddle River, NJ 07458

Editor-in-Chief: Richard Wohl
Senior Acquisitions Editor: Jo-Ann DeLuca
Assistant Editor: Audrey Regan
Editorial Assistant: Marc Oliver
Marketing Manager: Nancy Evans
Managing Editor: Katherine Evancie
Manufacturing Buyer: Alana Zdinak
Senior Manufacturing Supervisor: Paul Smolenski
Manufacturing Manager: Vincent Scelta
Production Editor: Carol Lavis
Design Director: Patricia Wosczyk
Cover Design: Suzanne Behnke
Composition: Graphic Sciences Corp.
Cover Art: Boris Lyubner

 Copyright © 1997 by Prentice-Hall, Inc.
A Simon & Schuster Company
Upper Saddle River, New Jersey 07458

Printed in the United States of America
10 9 8 7 6 5 4 3 2

ISBN 0-13-282006-4

Prentice-Hall International (UK) Limited, London
Prentice-Hall of Australia Pty. Limited, Sydney
Prentice-Hall Canada, Inc., Toronto
Prentice-Hall Hispanoamericana, S.A., Mexico
Prentice-Hall of India Private Limited, New Delhi
Prentice-Hall of Japan, Inc., Tokyo
Simon & Schuster Asia Pte. Ltd., Singapore
Editora Prentice-Hall do Brasil, Ltda., Rio de Janeiro

This book was simultaneously published under the title "Intelligent Decision Support Methods: The Science of Knowledge Work."

DEDICATION

To Curran, Sonya and Erica.

To my parents who taught me to work hard, be fair and stay curious, and
to Jeff and Janet for keeping me honest.

Contents

Preface

Sen-ri no michi mo ippo kara.
Even the journey of 1000 miles begins with the first step.
Japanese Proverb

Why did we write this book?

We felt we had something useful to say about making some powerful technologies really *work* in business. These technologies have been motivated by a variety of underlying reference disciplines such as biology, neurology, psychology, statistics, and computer science. The field of Artificial Intelligence (AI) provided a sort of glue in integrating the ideas from these underlying disciplines by comparing them in terms of their power for solving various types of problems.

One motivation for writing the book was for business people who often asked us to explain to them in simple terms how these technologies could be used profitably in business. Technical books on AI, decision theory, and statistics are much too technical or abstract for business people, while others are too superficial to give them a good solid understanding of the technology. Clearly, we needed to bring the technology down to earth without losing its essence. This is one need we've tried to fulfill. We've also provided detailed case studies showing how some organizations have utilized these technologies to improve key business processes.

We also were motivated by technologists who understood the technology well enough, but were unclear on how they could apply it to business problems. How could they explain the techniques in a clear and simple way to business people? Is there a methodology they could use to compare techniques from a business standpoint? Are there classes of business problems that map onto these techniques? These are the questions we've addressed for the technologists.

In short, we've tried to reduce the sophisticated models to their essence, and at the same time adopt a pragmatic business orientation in describing when and how to use them.

The modeling techniques on which we focus in this book have emerged over the last few decades: the symbolic approach (rules, case-based reasoning, and fuzzy logic), the connectionist approach (neural nets), the evolutionary approach (genetic algorithms), and the inductive approach (machine learning). At the same time database technology, "data warehousing", and online analytical processing (OLAP) are making it easier to get at organizational data. This is significant because the difficulty in fluid access to corporate data has been a big barrier to data intensive decision support. Collectively, the tools that we describe in this book allow organizations to access, view, understand and manipulate their data more easily to make decisions. They are essentially a set of "search engines" that can leverage organizational data.

These techniques derive their power only when more fundamental technologies are in place: telecommunications networks, database systems and desktops. The figure below shows how these fundamental enablers have matured over the last few years. With these enablers in place, organizations have an unprecedented opportunity to harness the power of intelligent search engines.

The figure also highlights one reason that previous attempts at exploiting intelligent techniques were not altogether successful. The information infrastructure was simply not mature enough. Computing power was expensive; networks were neither reliable nor did they provide adequate bandwidth. Database technology was immature. Consequently, access to corporate data was slow and limited. Finally, desktop technology was still in its infancy. Computers were only available to those who had access to special terminals and knew the right commands. It doesn't make sense to build a skyscraper starting with bricks. You've got to be able to construct larger subassemblies in order to build useful systems quickly and easily.

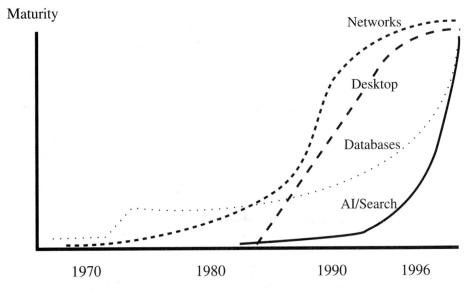

FIGURE PREFACE.1 Technological Maturity

But the primitive state of the infrastructure was only part of the problem. As the figure shows, AI/search technology was also highly inadequate a decade ago. People misperceived which types of problems computers could solve well and which types they couldn't. Early successes with expert rule-based systems that could do pattern recognition, solve calculus equations, or play chess led researchers to predict that machines with full human reasoning power were only a decade away. Unfortunately, it turns out that solving equations and playing chess, although very difficult for humans, happen to be activities that lend themselves to clear algorithmic descriptions and thus are tasks that software systems can be programmed to do quite well, as long as adequate computing power is available. On the other hand, recognizing faces and understanding simple sentences turns out to be very difficult for computers, even though most human children do these things with no problem. Early AI programs had tremendous difficulties in situations where there were subtle distinctions or ambiguous conditions.

And what about business applications of AI during the early days? Although rule-based expert systems were the focus of most AI development, businesses were unable to take advantage of this technology to as high a degree as they had hoped. Why?

While most businesses have lots of *data*, most have only limited amounts of the valuable *expertise* required to feed a rule-based system. Rule-based expert systems need human business experts to teach them about business. It can be very expensive to have a highly paid expert spend months helping to develop an expert system. Ironically, rule-based systems couldn't capitalize on the transaction data that businesses had in plenty. Instead, they required high-priced expertise that businesses had in short supply.

A decade ago, other technologies such as neural nets were still largely gestational, having been prematurely stifled in their development because of harsh critiques by some AI gurus. Genetic algorithms were a fringe phenomenon. Most people hadn't even heard of fuzzy logic. Machine learning was in its infancy. Case-based reasoning hadn't even been envisioned. All of these technologies began to come into their own during the eighties and nineties.

We now have a much richer bag of tricks at our disposal, whose effectiveness can be realized using mature networking, database, and desktop technologies. Each one models a different aspect of human reasoning and decision making. Each technique has a different objective and different character. Collectively, these techniques offer the business community a broad set of tools capable of addressing problems that are much harder or virtually impossible to solve using the more traditional techniques from statistics and operations research.

In what way are the different characters of the techniques useful?

Some of the techniques, like rule-based expert systems and fuzzy systems, are based on "top-down" representations of knowledge where a model developer gives a computer explicit expert knowledge about how to solve a problem. For such models, problem solving involves designing systems that follow an encoded reasoning process. One can also use these as pattern recognition systems that sit on top of databases and monitor their data content, triggering alarms or other kinds of processing whenever the patterns are matched by the data in the database. Such systems can be extremely useful in attention focusing.

Other approaches like neural networks take a "bottom-up" approach. These models are given no knowledge about how to solve a problem. Instead, neural networks themselves learn through trial and error how to build models. Similarly, other machine learning algorithms take as input large amounts of data and discover rules or relationships that exist in the data. Given the explosion of raw data in this electronic age, such techniques are highly useful to business organizations.

Another approach comes from the "evolutionary" natural selection paradigm. Techniques that have emerged from this area, most notably genetic algorithms, work by allowing various potential solutions to compete simultaneously for the chance to solve a problem. Survival of the fittest then determines which solutions ultimately "bubble up" to the top. This approach has applications ranging from pattern discovery to combinatorial optimization.

Yet another problem solving approach based on "analogical reasoning," that is, using "similar" past situations and answers to solve problems. Models developed with techniques such as case-based reasoning find solutions to problems by looking for similar problems that have been solved in the past and then modifying the past solutions to these problems to account for differences between the past and present situations. This approach has a highly flexible feel to it, allowing new knowledge to be added incrementally to a system with additional experience. This approach is highly useful to organizations that deal repeatedly with variations of a problem, such as customer services.

But technologies are useless unless they are accompanied by a framework that makes it easy to compare or combine them. In order to demonstrate the practical usefulness of the technology, we have provided a business oriented methodology for helping a decision maker systematically map techniques onto problems. It involves a consideration of the organizational and technical issues that are important in developing knowledge based systems. We have found the methodology useful in our own work. In retrospect, whenever we used it, we had greater success than when we did not.

In describing our approach, we have also tried to demystify the technology. We explain the techniques in such a way as to give a thorough introduction to their workings and application, while rooting this discussion in the reality of the business world. Our treatment is highly "visual": All key concepts and examples are presented using highly descriptive graphics. The visual presentation is also intended to make it easier for technologists to *communicate* these ideas with business people.

While our treatment is "demystified," it is nonetheless a thorough investigation of the technology, designed to give the reader a working foundation for understanding the techniques. Our goal is to put the reader in a position to understand *how* a technique can be applied, *why* it works, and *what concerns* might arise as a result of its use. People seeking technical depth shouldn't be disappointed.

One last point. Intelligent systems don't necessarily lead to more intelligent organizations. Technology provides the maximum leverage when it is well integrated into a well designed business process. To drive home the practical significance of the various techniques that we discuss in this text, one section of the book is devoted to case studies. It contains seven extended case studies illustrating the application of each technique. The cases, drawn from various application areas, demonstrate how each of the techniques covered in the book was considered or applied in order to address a business problem, given the context of the organization doing the development. The case studies discuss what the business process looked like before and after a system was introduced and in what ways that system strengthened the process. Ultimately, the true benefit of smarter systems derives from their repeated application in a larger business process.

Despite the usefulness of the methodology and the power of the various techniques we discuss, there are no magic bullets. There is no framework, methodology, or technique that eliminates the need to think critically, creatively, and with curiosity about problems you are trying to solve. Intelligent systems are usually components of larger systems, and ultimately, organizations. We have written this book to help you integrate intelligent solutions into your organization. Its goal is to empower you to increase your firm's intelligence about how it deals with its customers, suppliers, and internal business processes.

ACKNOWLEDGMENTS

This book would not have been possible without the help of some very special people.

Andrew Kimball read and re-read this entire text several times. We thank him deeply for his tireless reviews, his countless suggestions, and his endless patience. Without Andy's help this would have been a far less readable text and we would have struggled far more in writing it.

We also thank Kevin Parker, Mike Dellomo, Douglas Lucas, Ted Stohr, Ken Laudon, Herbert Simon, Stephen Slade, Joe Sniado, William Ries, Bill Rosenblat, Ritu Agarwal, Mark Silver, and Fred Powers for helpful reviews and comments at various stages of the project. We thank Barbara Sporn for suggesting the "visual" approach that we adopted for presenting the material. Each picture replaced more than a thousand words.

For case histories and background, we thank Ganesh Mani of LBS Securities, Tej Anand of AT&T, Gary Kahn of Coopers and Lybrand, Constantin vonAtrock of INFORM GmbH, Andrea Danyluk and Foster Provost of NYNEX, Trung Nguyen of Compaq, and Rod Ermish of U S West.

Much of this material was refined and developed as class material taught by the authors at NYU. We thank MBA and Ph.D. students, who attended these lectures, for their comments and suggestions on the material.

The proprietors of several restaurants were more than accommodating in letting us spend hours in their establishments while we worked on and debated portions of the book. We would like to thank the owners of Rectangles, Café Reggio, the Village Crown, John's Pizza, and the Olive Tree Café for their hospitality.

VASANT DHAR
ROGER STEIN

1

Information Systems

Past, Present, and Emerging

I know of no commodity more valuable than information.
—Oliver Stone, spoken by Gordon Gekko in the movie *Wall Street*

What a long strange trip it's been. . . .
—Jerry Garcia

The field of information systems (IS) has undergone dramatic changes since its inception several decades ago. In this chapter, we discuss how these changes have affected business and how changes in business have affected IS. We explore a taxonomy for understanding the various branches of IS, and then briefly introduce the material that follows in this book.

INTRODUCTION

Twenty years ago, the term *information system* in a business usually meant an *electronic data processing system*. The goal of such systems was to deal with large volumes of commercial transactions quickly, with few errors, at low cost. The workhorse of electronic data processing systems was a mainframe computer.

Information systems (IS) have come a long way since those early days. Mainframes still process the bulk of most business transactions and they have become even faster. But the real growth area in IS has been in *distributed systems*. Unlike mainframe systems that concentrate all their processing power in a single large computer, the processing power in distributed systems is spread out across many smaller computers and desktops.

How did this shift help businesspeople?

A key characteristic emerging from the trend toward distributed processing is that computing has become much more interactive. Early mainframe systems processed user requests in what was known as *batch mode*. This meant that the user would submit to the mainframe a list of all the tasks (programs) needed. The user's request would be put into a processing queue with all of the requests from all the other users. When a user's turn came, the entire request would be run at once. This meant that programs needed to be written to run without any user involvement since the user couldn't interact with the program once it was in the queue.

Now, since each workstation or PC has its own processor, much more of what the computer does can be customized to the needs of the individual user. Users can interact with their own private processor to execute the commands they need as they need them executed, instead of all at once. Workstations now have graphical user interfaces and are often networked with other computers, making it easier for a user to access remote databases and other devices. This allows users to be more spontaneous in how they use computers and the data they store.

The trend toward more interactive systems has been a gradual one. In the mid-70s IS departments began developing new types of systems called *decision support systems* (DSS). DSS made a sharp distinction between the earlier genre of transaction processing systems that crunched through lots of data and kept accurate records, and those systems that were designed to support business decision making in a more interactive manner. Not surprisingly, the origin of the DSS concept also coincided roughly with the emergence of interactive workstations, although decision support systems really began to come into their own with the maturing of workstations and powerful personal computers.

The shift toward decision support also reflects the changing nature of the work in business organizations. Increasingly, work is becoming "knowledge oriented." People have to work with information—gathering, summarizing, and interpreting it—in order to make decisions. There has been an explosion in the volume and variety of electronic data available to businesses, and, correspondingly, a huge need for systems that help businesspeople make sense out of these reams of data. This has led businesses to develop systems that are smarter about how they condense and interpret data for the end user.

Early DSS were quite rudimentary. In fact, many were nothing more than simple systems developed using spreadsheet software (which was novel at the time). The more sophisticated DSS also used optimization models taken from *operations research* and *management science* (OR/MS). These systems incorporated techniques like linear programming and they had front-ends that made them more user friendly. These front-ends made it easy for the decision maker to run models and do "what if" kinds of analyses.

Why was this so useful?

"What if" analysis was particularly powerful because the standard OR models that ran on mainframes only spat out a single "best" solution; that is, they were completely automated. They didn't permit the user to explore solutions interactively. With the introduction of more user-friendly and interactive front-ends, the decision maker could explore a wider range of possibilities and exercise more judgment in making decisions.

Since these early beginnings, decision support systems have become increasingly sophisticated, making use of models from a variety of disciplines including artificial intelligence. Systems that use artificial intelligence techniques are sometimes referred to distinctly as *knowledge-based systems* (KBS).

We don't find the distinctions between DSS and KBS to be terribly useful since the type of model used by a system, be it a simple spreadsheet model or a complex neural network, is irrelevant from the decision maker's standpoint. The user just needs help doing analysis to make good decisions. We think of a DSS as *any* kind of system that supports decision making, regardless of the type of internal model that the system uses.

That said, this book is about smarter kinds of intelligent decision support systems that make use of techniques that have emerged from the field of artificial intelligence over the last two decades. Interestingly, these techniques have all reached a high level of maturity. What this means is that we now have an unprecedented opportunity to build powerful decision support systems with minimal effort and cost, *if we go about it sensibly.* This text presents a framework for helping with this task.

There are literally dozens of books on the more traditional types of DSS, which use spreadsheets, mathematical optimization, numerical analysis, or simulation models. While these will continue to remain a mainstay for many problems, the growing number of "knowledge workers" in organizations will require systems that "know more" and "do more" in terms of accessing, summarizing, and interpreting information. Knowledge workers will depend more and more heavily on these systems to help them make decisions faster or with a greater degree of confidence. This is the future of information systems in general, and decision support in particular.

A TAXONOMY OF MANAGEMENT INFORMATION SYSTEMS

Figure 1.1 shows a general taxonomy of management information systems (MIS) along the lines we've been discussing above. The taxonomy breaks information systems in general into transaction processing systems and decision support systems.

The major purpose of a transaction processing system is *accurate record keeping*. Every transaction that the business conducts is recorded, primarily for bookkeeping, billing, and audit purposes. These systems deal with the bread and butter of a business. For example, a large bank would have a transaction processing system to record every customer's activity with the bank. Such systems are usually highly automated, where the choices that the system makes are simple, like deciding on how much cash to let you withdraw from your bank account on a particular day.

Because a major goal of transaction processing systems is accurate record keeping, such systems are also set up to make very simple "decisions" about whether the data they get are valid. For example, the bank's system might check to see whether the account number on a transaction is a valid one and whether the name on the account matches it.

Transaction processing systems do this type of validation before recording transactions so that the database is as "clean" as possible, and more generally, to ensure that people get paid only what they are supposed to be paid. They are also designed to be able to do things like "roll back" a transaction, which involves canceling a transaction and undoing its consequences. The logic involved can be quite complex because of the need to keep accurate and up-to-date records.

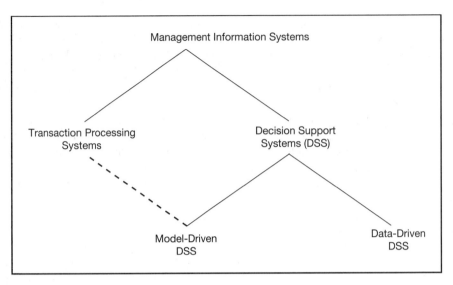

FIGURE 1.1 A Taxonomy of Management Information Systems

The second class of information systems, decision support systems, includes systems designed to support businesspeople and managers with decision-making. DSS are used as part of a process where a human is in the loop making the decision. Whereas a transaction processing system handles routine daily activity, a DSS typically supports decisions that have longer-term implications and require some human judgment. The need for human judgment arises when a particular problem is too "unstructured" for the DSS model to capture all the nuances of the decision-making situation.

In the late 1970s and 80s, the term *decision support system* was used exclusively for systems that used some sort of model into which data could be fed to let a user do "what if" and other kinds of analyses. An example is a model that lets the manager of a retail sporting goods chain see the impact on profitability for a product in response to various price changes for that product. Such a system would have a model that would relate the input (the price change) to outputs (revenues, cost of sales, and so on). Similarly, a DSS for a fund manager might let him or her vary input parameters such as the volatility of interest rates and compute their impacts on the value of a given portfolio.

These days the term *decision support* is used rather generically, but it is useful to think of DSS as being divided into two basic branches or types. The first type continues along the lines of the older DSS and involves primarily "model-driven" support systems. The value of such a system is largely in the *quality* of its model. Its analysis capabilities are based on a strong theory or model, coupled with a good user interface to make the model easy to use.

For example, the portfolio manager's system might take in historical data about an investment portfolio's contents and use an econometric model to compute and graph variables like the expected risk of the portfolio and how this risk varies in response to certain market parameters. The decision maker can use this system to make a judgment about the "goodness" of the portfolio based on the outputs of the system and the investment objectives.

The second type of decision support systems are more "data-driven." In such systems, most of the value added is in the data. The model is usually quite simple, computing information like averages, totals, and maybe data distributions. The idea is to allow the user to easily condense large amounts of data into a form that is useful to manage the business.

For example, a sales manager may want to know how much of each of his products was sold by each salesperson in each region. He can then reward or mentor salespeople according to the numbers, reassess the overall sales strategy, and so on. The value of the system is largely in its ability to summarize large amounts of data.

With the maturing of networks and database technologies, data-driven decision support is achievable to a much greater degree. Unlike the more traditional reporting systems, the goal of such systems is to free the user from painfully specifying the requirements and then painfully waiting for months while they are coded. Rather, the user decides in *real-time* how to slice through the data: by customer, geography, time, and so on. This is a dramatic break from the traditional approach in which various pre-defined perspectives on the data would be coded into a system. The current drive towards "data warehousing" reflects the growing importance of interactive data-intensive types of decision support systems.

It is useful to think broadly about the "data" that feed a DSS. In most cases, such as the example above, the data come from a database system consisting of structured transaction data. However, organizations are also swimming in data from hundreds of different sources: news stories, internal projects, group meetings, and so on. Much of this goes unseen despite the fact that there's a lot of potential value in it. There is a huge requirement for decision support systems to make sense of these diverse types of data.

You may be wondering about the dotted line on the bottom left of the figure between transaction processing systems and model-driven decision support. This highlights a hybrid kind of system, which is very much like model-driven DSS, incorporating a sophisticated model, but with one important difference: There is no human in the loop.

This type of system is used when the time required to make decisions is short and/or the system makes equally good or better decisions than a human. This type of system performs what you might think of as *decision automation*. Such a system might sit on top of a transaction processing system and evaluate each potential transaction. If a potential transaction is approved, the data are passed on to the transaction processing system. Otherwise the transaction is rejected. In such systems, the sophistication of the DSS model enables it to take over the judgmental part of the decision process.

For example, a system that approves credit card transactions might be fully automated, without a decision maker in the loop. In this sense, it is like a transaction processing system, trying to determine whether a potential transaction is legitimate or fraudulent. But its decision about legitimacy might be based on a complex model that uses expert knowledge, more in the spirit of a decision support system. As businesses become more "real-time" oriented and leverage their data in the process, they will develop more of these kinds of systems that combine transaction data and complex decision models.

In general, as the information infrastructure of organizations continues to mature and data quality and access improves, there is an increasing need for more sophisticated model-driven as well as data-driven types of decision support systems. Putting such systems into place requires two things:

1. an understanding of the range of tools and techniques available to model business problems
2. a business-oriented methodology for developing decision support systems

This book focuses on the two requirements simultaneously. In the next chapter, we discuss the central concept around which the methodology is motivated. We propose that the central purpose of a decision support system is to increase the "density" of relevant information that it presents to the user. We use the term *intelligence density* to refer to this concept.

Chapter 3 presents the methodology for operationalizing the concept of intelligence density. The methodology shows how you can map solutions to the business objectives and the constraints of a specific organization.

Chapters 4 through 10 focus on the techniques using the business-oriented methodology of Chapter 3. To bring the methodology squarely into a business context, we present an appendix of seven case studies from organizations. Each of these cases shows how the methodology and techniques can be applied to analyzing problems and to finding effective solutions as painlessly as possible.

Intelligence Density

A Metric for Knowledge Work Productivity

I'm not interested in developing a powerful *[artificial] brain.*
All I'm after is just a mediocre *brain . . .*
—Alan M. Turing

The major drag on performance is the limited number of
hours in the day. You run out of time.
—Jim Little, Morgan Stanley & Co.

Once upon a time there were two companies. Airhead Industries and Jetstream Un-
limited. Airhead and Jetstream manufactured and sold do-it-yourself PC computer
kits. They both faced a similar problem: A cursory analysis of their technical support
databases revealed that about 60% of the support calls they received from do-it-
yourselfers were passed on to engineering personnel because it took the technical
support staff too much time (usually more than 20 minutes) to assess and resolve the
problems. As a result, the engineering staffs of both organizations were overloaded.
In addition, the calls were proving to be a distraction to the engineering staff, whose
primary responsibilities involved product development, not support . . .

Airhead Industries elected to remedy its problem by doubling its technical sup-
port staff.

Jetstream, on the other hand, decided to analyze its database further and inter-
view its staff. The firm examined its technical support database and corrected incom-
plete and erroneous records. Jetstream classified the types of support problems into
various categories, charting the relative frequency of each type. The firm's IS depart-
ment interviewed engineering experts to ascertain how they dealt with various types of
problems. The engineering staff determined that most of the calls did not, in fact, re-
quire an engineer once the problem was properly identified. Unfortunately, most prob-

lems were not identified correctly. Jetstream formalized the expertise, categorized its problems into prototypical cases, and put this information into an interactive system that was made available on-line to the technical support staff within a month. The volume of Jetstream's transferred calls dropped to 5%. . . .

What can we make of the two companies' approaches to solving their problems?

Airhead chose to treat a symptom.

In contrast, Jetstream's solution is far more *knowledge intensive* than the Airhead approach. Jetstream does a more thorough analysis of its database. It leverages its highly skilled engineers' expertise by collecting it, codifying it, and quickly making it available to its less skilled support personnel. As an organization, Jetstream Unlimited *learns* about itself and about its industry and customers.

Knowledge-intensive approaches to solving problems are applicable to every industry. For example, consider a securities firm that uses intelligent systems to detect patterns in historical price data so that its analysts can make better investment decisions, or a mail-order company that uses intelligent systems to analyze demographic information to better target high-probability prospects, or a consulting company that makes important facts about its past consulting engagements easily accessible and usable by its professionals around the globe. All of these organizations are knowledge intensive: They *transform* raw data into something useful—knowledge—and *deliver* the knowledge to the part of the organization where it can be used most effectively.

What makes this kind of transformation and delivery possible?

Skilled employees, of course. But skilled employees are stretched for time, especially as the business environments in which they work become more complex. It is almost impossible for any one employee to understand, evaluate, and act on all of the information available in a practical amount of time.

Can computers help? Yes. But computers and networks are becoming a commodity. They are necessary *just to enter* the competitive arena. Increasingly, firms are looking for higher value-added uses for their computing infrastructure. Organizations today need to be able to leverage the expertise embodied in their employees and locked up inside their large stores of data. Much of the focus now is on developing smarter decision support systems. These systems need to increase the value of data and allow organizations to learn from them.

For example, consider a toy manufacturer with a large database of orders. The fact that one of the firm's customers, Toy Town, placed an order for 15 Messy Paint kits is a relatively meaningless piece of data. To add value, the manufacturer's DSS might organize this and other pieces of data into a more informative format, say, showing the overall sales of Messy Paint kits in the Southwest region, and comparing this to the other regions.

Alternatively, the DSS might look for patterns in the sales of products. Perhaps the purchase of Messy Paint kits is accompanied by a purchase of Tidyboy Smocks in 83% of all cases. The toy manufacturer might then interpret this and other information to decide that an effective campaign would be to package Tidyboy Smocks with Messy Paint kits to reduce production and operations costs. Knowledge and action are the results of this interpretation.

As you transform the raw materials from data to knowledge, your ability to use these new value-added materials to make useful decisions increases. The efficiency and quality of the decisions your organization makes also increase by using these more concentrated decision materials. In effect, the decision content of these materials becomes more *dense.*

INTELLIGENCE DENSITY: A MEASURE OF ORGANIZATIONAL INTELLIGENCE AND PRODUCTIVITY

Adding value to data enables an organization to "know more" about something—its industry's environment or "terrain," circumstances under which its products do or don't sell well, the movements of its competitors, and so on.

An organization can increase its intelligence in the same way that an army unit gathers "intelligence" about the movements of the enemy. A radar-tracking system or a satellite-imaging system that tells a military unit about the enemy's movements is providing intelligence. So is a monitoring system that analyzes that satellite and radar information and comes up with a useful summary.

In this book, we are not so concerned with making the computer "intelligent" in the human sense as we are with using it to provide more intelligent *solutions.* Statistics, decision theory, and operations research all provide methodologies that are similarly motivated and have been used extensively to build decision support models for problems that can be described mathematically. Our focus on the less traditional techniques in this book reflects their growing usefulness for less well-structured problems, where traditional techniques tend to break down or require excessive effort.

To characterize the intelligence provided by a particular analytic decision tool, we use the term *intelligence density.* Intelligence density (ID) is a heuristic measure of the "army type" of intelligence. Think of it as the amount of useful "decision support information" that a decision maker gets from using the output from some analytic system for a certain amount of time. In other words, how much of the book, chart, status report, financial statement, or computer output do you have to examine before you can make a decision of a specified quality; or, inversely, *how quickly can you get the essence of the underlying data from the output?*

While there is no general method for measuring an amorphous concept such as "the amount of decision support information," there's a useful concept in economics of *utiles* or utility units. Utiles are simply units for comparing different types of consumption (i.e., "one whiskey will give me the same amount of pleasure as two vodkas").

Conceptually intelligence density can be viewed as the ratio of the number of utiles of decision-making power gleaned (quality) to the number of units of analytic time spent by the decision maker. Said another way, ID measures how many utiles per minute a particular output gives us.

Thus, if a decision maker can consistently make the *same quality* decisions and come to the same conclusions after examining Source A for 3 minutes as he or she could after examining Source B for 30 minutes, Source A can be said to have 10 times the intelligence density as Source B. Similarly, if the time required to make a decision were fixed and unchangeable, and a decision maker made decisions that were consistently determined to be twice as good (by some qualitative or quantitative measure) after examining Source X as those made based on Source Y, we could say that Source X had twice the intelligence density as Source Y and we would prefer to use it for that reason.

In effect, if an organization can either *decrease* the time spent making specific decisions and doing specific analysis without a loss of quality, or *increase* the quality of analysis performed in a fixed time frame, its resources can be used more effectively.

Intelligence density is the postindustrial or information age equivalent of what we think of as productivity. Just as you can give a manufacturing organization a bigger factory or a faster die-casting machine, you can give a data-intensive organization higher intelligence density materials thereby making its information systems and decision making more knowledge intensive.

An excellent metaphor is the phenomenon that occurred in the financial industry with the advent of the electronic spreadsheet. Prior to this innovation, a financial analyst who wanted to, say, make projections about the impact of different sales growth scenarios on a particular firm would (a) copy by hand the income statement, balance sheet, and cash flow data into a ledger; then (b) perform the appropriate arithmetic and accounting operations for a scenario; (c) repeat steps a and b for each scenario; and, finally, (d) perform the analysis. The frustrating thing was that the brute force calculations required to do the work in a, b, and c took the lion's share of the time, but the actual *analysis of the end results,* d, which took a *much* shorter time, was what the analyst was really getting paid for!

With the advent of electronic spreadsheets, though, things changed. Now an analyst can experiment with new scenarios as fast as they can be typed. Once the initial data are entered and the spreadsheet is set up (one time only), the analyst is free to experiment extensively. All of the extra time that the analyst *would have* spent calculating ratios and adding columns by hand can now be spent doing analysis and making better decisions. While many would consider a spreadsheet to be a rather primitive tool compared to some of the ones we will discuss later on, the spirit is the same: You need tools that show you the important things quickly.

This metaphor of squeezing out the tedium and leaving the essence is an important component of intelligence density. High intelligence density materials allow developers and decision makers to concentrate more of their time on the higher value-added portions of their work, rather than worrying about the lower value-added and more mundane aspects. Those organizations whose members are able to take advantage of high intelligence density materials to produce, measure, and improve their output have a competitive advantage.

Figure 2.1 shows how you can increase the intelligence density of a firm's raw data. It is important not to forget that the data we are talking about are not necessarily a bunch of numbers in a database but could be any one of the various forms that data might take in an organization.

The data by themselves are not very useful. The trick is to condense them. This means that you need to first figure out how to get at the data. For electronic data, this means figuring out where they are located, how to query them, and so forth. For

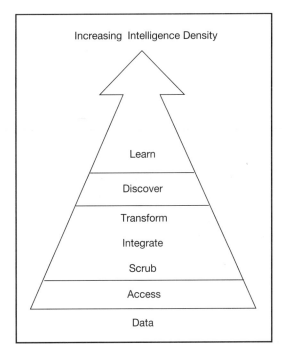

Increasing Intelligence Density

Learn

Discover

Transform

Integrate

Scrub

Access

Data

FIGURE 2.1   Steps for Increasing Intelligence Density

human expertise, this means figuring out who has the experiences you want to tap into and how to contact them.

Once you get your hands on the data, you need to scrub them. This means that you might have to deal with inconsistent or conflicting data, sloppy record keeping, and so on. If you clean the data up, you can next integrate them with data from various sources to build up a more complete picture of the business.

The problem with bringing together a lot of types of data is that there is usually too much detail. You get buried in the minutiae without being able to see the bigger picture. To improve the situation, you can transform the data into compound or aggregate units. Statistics, ratios, totals and subtotals, trends, and so on. are all examples of how you might want to transform data to get a better picture of what they mean.

But what if you want to do more than just look at the data and analyze them interactively? What if you want to learn about new relationships in the data or use automatically the knowledge about the data to help solve business problems?

The next level of intelligence density boosting takes advantage of many of the model-based approaches to DSS that we will discuss. In addition to using data-driven systems to make *examining* your data easier, you can use them to generate data to *feed* more sophisticated model-based DSS systems that discover new relationships in data or apply known relationships in new ways.

What do we mean by learning from discovered relationships? Let's go back to Jetstream and Airhead. What's the difference between the firms?

Jetstream was able to reduce wait time on customer calls from an average of 30 minutes to just under 5 minutes, thus increasing its customer responsiveness. In addition, the general quality of the responses has become much more uniform and of higher caliber since the engineer's expertise was made available on-line for the technical support staff.

Furthermore, now only the most complex calls (about 5% of the total number of calls) are passed on to the engineering department. As a result, the productivity of that department has correspondingly improved. In fact, some of the calls they get involve such sophistication that they are very useful for R&D! Since the engineers are no longer overloaded with calls, they are able to concentrate more on the calls they do get. Instances of the same caller repeatedly inquiring about the same error has declined to about 25% of the original.

On an organizational level, Jetstream gained a rich understanding of the problem resolution process because, as part of the development of this project, it needed to track, classify, and learn about the quality and quantity of its historical responsiveness. Jetstream is now able to predict better the volume of calls it will get regarding various types of support problems, and how these problems relate to a diversity of factors from new product lines to seasonal usage. Jetstream is now able to better plan staffing, new product releases, and research projects based upon this knowledge.

Airhead, on the other hand, got eight new employees.

Consider again the steps that Jetstream took. Figure 2.2 shows how the firm moved its data through each of the steps we've been discussing. Note how each of Jetstream's actions helped the firm move up the ladder of intelligence density. When the firm finished its system, it not only had tools to let its staff work more efficiently, it also understood its business to a much greater degree.

MAKING THE RIGHT TRADE-OFFS

Getting to the right solution was far from easy for Jetstream. It forced the firm to define explicitly which business requirements were critical and which weren't. It demanded that the firm understand the capabilities of the various modeling techniques. Jetstream needed to pick solutions that covered the important business needs. The firm needed to compare various approaches from a technological and business perspective, analyzing the trade-offs among the different solutions.

What kinds of trade-offs?

For starters, Jetstream had to determine what was required from a business perspective in order to make the support solution successful. For example, the *accuracy* of the advice to Jetstream's customers had to be high. Even though Jetstream's old way of doing things kept customers waiting, at least the clients were confident that they would get pretty good advice at the end of the call. If the quality of advice from the new system dropped, Jetstream would *lose* customers. That was unacceptable.

Likewise, the *response time* had to be quick. Jetstream's management determined, for example, that it would be unacceptable for the support staff to keep customers waiting for too long while the staff resolved problems. If the new system kept

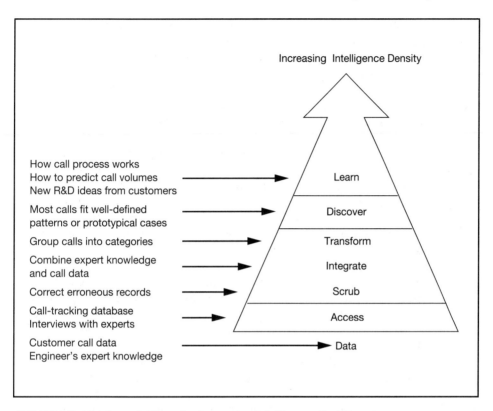

FIGURE 2.2   Jetstream's Steps for Increasing Intelligence Density

the customer on hold for long periods of time, it would accomplish nothing over the current way of doing things, at least from the customer's perspective.

And what about the depth of advice the system was able to help provide? Customers were used to engaging in a dialog with the expert, sometimes steering the conversation to other, possibly related subjects. An expert could deal with this. The expert could explain the problem in simple English and explain how it could be fixed. Would a sales rep using the new system have sufficient knowledge about customers' problems to even describe the customer's problem correctly to a computer system? Could a system provide depth in its reasoning comparable to the expert? Could it justify *why* it was recommending a particular action? That seemed important. In order for Jetstream's customers to feel comfortable with the support, they had to feel that reps on the phone understood the dynamics of their problems and were confident about the advice they were giving.

These factors, accuracy, response time, explainability, and others like them, are the ultimate *determinants* of intelligence density. In developing and evaluating alternative solutions, an organization needs to ask how well a proposed course of action meets the constraints specified for such dimensions.

We should underscore that accuracy, response time, and explainability were dimensions that Jetstream determined as being important. For an organization with different objectives, the important dimensions could be very different. For example, while Jetstream needed to be able to explain its system's recommendations, a trucking company that develops a system to generate optimal routes and schedules automatically for its truckers might not require this level of explanation if it only cares about optimality of the schedules. On the other hand, for the trucking firm, even a response time (waiting time) of 1 hour from the system might be acceptable. Requirements specified in terms of the dimensions of intelligence density will always be problem specific.

Jetstream also had to think about the logistics and organizational resources needed to build the system. Presumably, it had enough recognized experts who could be counted on to articulate clearly the knowledge that would go into the system, but what about the programmers and technical people? Did they have sufficient expertise in building similar systems? Did they have sufficient knowledge of the relevant tools? How would various solutions line up with Jetstream's existing call logging and tracking systems?

Logistic organizational constraints tell the solution providers what resources they have at their disposal. The availability, experience, and technical expertise of staff will determine which solutions to consider. Some approaches might take a longer time to develop than others. Or a certain methodology might require large computers, and an organization might not have access to those machines when its staff actually *uses* the model (when visiting a client's office, for example).

Finally, Jetstream had to take all of these competing constraints and somehow decide on which problem-solving technique would work best. Each technique has inherent strengths and weaknesses. Some techniques make it easy to explain their outputs. Some give very fast answers. Some require consultation with experts in a particular field during development. Some need lots of data. And so on.

Effective solutions require generating a good match between the intelligence density requirements of a problem, the logistic constraints within which to develop the solution, and, finally, the compatibility of a proposed solution method with these two factors.

This all involves compromise. The trick is to try to create solutions that require as little compromise as possible. You don't want to whittle away the real problem requirements too much, otherwise you end up either solving the wrong problem or solving the problem in the wrong way. You need to be realistic about the resources at your disposal and what you can accomplish with them; otherwise you simply won't be able to deliver anything. And you need to understand what each of the various techniques can and cannot do; otherwise you'll spend a lot of time learning this—the hard way—instead of delivering a solution. If a solution stretches any of these three factors too far or compromises them too much, chances are all of the reaching and stretching will result in a less than satisfying solution. You might be able to pull it off, and occasionally people do, but the deck will be stacked against you. You're taking an unnecessary risk.

The next chapter lays out a methodology that is helpful in avoiding the downside risk. In the following chapters, we explain the various problem-solving techniques by applying the methodology to each of them in the context of real-world case studies.

The Vocabulary of Intelligence Density

Now, if the estimates made before a battle indicate victory, it is because careful calculations show that your conditions are more favorable than those of your enemy; if they indicate defeat, it is because careful calculations show that favorable conditions for a battle are fewer. With more careful calculations, one can win; with less, one cannot. How much less chance of victory has one who makes no calculations at all!
—Sun Tzu, *The Art of War*

The following anecdote is told about a seasoned golf pro playing with three younger players on a difficult course. The pro had won a famous tournament on the course thirty years earlier. When the group approached a particularly notorious hole, one of the younger players asked the pro, "Thirty years ago, when you shot a birdie on this hole, how did you do it?"
The pro replied, "See those trees over there? I hooked the ball over the tops of those trees and onto the green."
Each of the three young players tried to "hook the ball just over the tops of those trees" and each had his ball fall squarely into the wood.
"Wait a minute," said the last of the young golfers to the pro, "We're all pretty good strong golfers, and we couldn't even come close! How were you able to hook over the same trees thirty years ago?!?"
The pro smiled, "Thirty years ago, those same trees were a lot shorter."
—Anonymous

Avalon said solemnly, "We are merely outlining the dimensions of the problem, Mr. Washburn."
"And doing it all wrong," said Gonzlo.
—Isaac Asimov, "Middle Name"

INTRODUCTION

1. *A Case of Poorly Defined Business Objectives and System Requirements:*
   A large bank commissioned the development of a system that would take over the back office function of processing letters of credit (LOC), which banks

issue for commercial clients as guarantees of payment. The system was supposed to categorize LOCs into acceptable and unacceptable categories, depending on whether the letter had logical errors in it or exposed the bank to unacceptable risks.

A rule-based expert system[1] was developed and tested. The results of the testing showed that the system was accurate about 90% of the time. At the final review meeting with top management, a senior business manager wanted a "yes" or "no" answer as to whether the system should be deployed.

None of the businesspeople could give the manager a straight answer.

All the manager got were conditional answers, which was not satisfactory. The meeting digressed into a discussion about the consequences of the errors. Would the bank lose important business as a consequence of the system's errors? What would be the average size of a loss due to an error? Should the system be used in a decision support mode where all applications would be scanned by clerks after being processed by the system? And so on. In effect, the real definition of business objectives and hence the system's accuracy requirements started only after the system had already been designed, implemented, and tested! The bank had not adequately considered the system's accuracy requirements and their implications.

2. *A Case of Bad Problem Formulation and System Inflexibility:*

A national railroad company wanted to install an intelligent diagnostic system on all of its locomotives. The system was supposed to enable the train operator to diagnose and correct mechanical problems quickly.

A research team spent several man-years of effort interviewing experts on how they diagnosed faults in locomotives. The experts described their reasoning sequentially: "first I check for traction; if there is traction, I check to see if there's a short; if there is a short, I throw open the switch to release traction and see if the short goes away; if it doesn't go away, then I try and release the brake . . ." The research team decided that the problem area was small (apparently with only a few hundred symptoms), and the reasoning process seemed clear and simple enough for it to be specified literally as described by the experts.

They used flowcharts showing the logic sequence as articulated by the expert. After a few months of interviewing experts . . . they were still at it. Only now, they found that each time the expert told them something new that the expert had neglected to mention earlier, they spent the whole day trying to figure out how to modify the logic, and everyone ended up feeling uncertain about the integrity of the knowledge at the end of the day! Their approach had failed to consider adequately issues of scalability and flexibility.

3. *A Case of Low Scalability and High Complexity:*

A trading firm wanted a system to predict foreign exchange movements. The system was supposed to analyze the past patterns of exchange rates for var-

---

[1]This type of system uses pre-programmed rules of thumb to solve problems. Rule-based expert systems are discussed in Chapter 7.

ious currencies and highlight those that looked likely to increase or decrease in value significantly over the course of the month.

A research group chose a fuzzy logic-based system[2] to do the task. Basic trading rules were encoded and developed for the system. Using the basic rules, combined with the manually interpreted information, early tests of the trading system showed promising results.

However, when the system was actually scaled up to a realistic environment, it got more and more complicated. In the end the system could only predict accurately for the previous month, and only if experienced currency traders also input their opinions!

Why did the system fail to produce useful results? Because the knowledge representation, in this case fuzzy rules, couldn't capture the range of situations that affect exchange rates. The developers had to spend many hours interviewing experts and the resulting knowledge was far from complete and accurate. The problem complexity didn't favor a "top-down" approach. The research group had not considered adequately the degree to which its system would need to scale up from a simple prototype to a practical system operating in a complex environment.

DIMENSIONS OF PROBLEMS AND SOLUTIONS

How can you avoid having your projects end up like the ones above? Is there a method you can follow that can ensure that you're on the right path?

We think there is.

The method needs to cover the problem requirements (like accuracy) without overextending the organization's resources (like development time or cost). A good solution does not compromise the problem requirements and does not overly "stretch" the limits of the organization in doing so.

Other than the obvious things like immediate costs and benefits, what "dimensions" should you consider in formulating and evaluating alternatives?

First, you need to satisfy model output *quality* requirements. A solution must satisfy basic things like accuracy and response time. More generally, the quality of the outputs should be adequate to meet your organization's needs.

Second, you need to consider longer-term cost drivers. Like what it will cost to maintain, extend, or modify the system. These types of constraints will help determine how useful the system is in the long run. The system must be *engineered* correctly.

Third, you need to ensure that the quality of the organization's resources is sufficient to undertake the proposed project. These dimensions deal with human resources and infrastructure.

---

[2]Fuzzy systems use rules expressed using linguistic variables like "hot" and "cold" or "inexpensive" and "costly" rather than specific numerical values. Fuzzy systems are explained in Chapter 8.

Finally, you need to ensure that the organization can support the *logistical* requirements of the project. These considerations impact things like development schedules and budgets.

The first set of these factors, those dealing with model quality, is listed in Figure 3.1. They answer the following questions:

- Does the system need to provide optimal solutions in terms of accuracy or "goodness"?
- Does the decision maker need to know how the answer was derived?
- Does the system provide responses within a reasonable amount of time?

```
• Accuracy
• Explainability
• Speed/Reliability of
  Response Time
```

FIGURE 3.1   Quality of Model

Business examples:

A bank needs a back office system that processes and classifies letters of credit into "acceptable" and "unacceptable" categories to be able to classify at least 85% of the letters correctly to make business sense. (accuracy)

A mortgage application evaluation system must give some indication of what factors it used to determine that a mortgage applicant scored poorly so that this can be explained to the applicant or be used as the basis of further inquiries by the mortgage officer. (explainability)

A point-of-purchase credit card fraud-detection system must be able to return the results of its evaluation in under 5 seconds so that using it will not overly inconvenience store owners or cardholders. (response time)

The second set of factors shown in Figure 3.2 relates to how well the solution is *engineered* when it is developed:

- How flexible is the system in allowing the problem specifications to be changed?
- How scalable is the system?
- How easily can the system be embedded into a larger system or the existing work flow of an organization?
- How compact is the system?
- How easy is the system to use?

```
• Flexibility
• Scalability
• Compactness
• Embeddability
• Ease of Use
```

FIGURE 3.2   Engineering Dimensions

Business examples:

A system designed to rank financial investment alternatives according to risk and return needs to be updated over time to allow for new investment instruments and financial strategies. (flexibility)

A system that designs shipping routes for a cargo freight firm needs to be able to generate good routes regardless of whether there are 10 or 200 cities being served, or 3 or 30 ships in the fleet. (scalability)

A system that aids marketing personnel in interviewing clients and suggesting products needs to be compact enough to be installed on a laptop computer and taken on client calls. (compactness)

A system that determines how much a client should be billed for a particular service based on information about the client must be able to share information with the firm's client information database and its current billing and accounting systems. (embeddability)

The third set of factors listed in Figure 3.3 addresses issues relating to the *resources available* in the organization required to attack the problem. These are *organizational* dimensions. They require you to assess the complexity of a problem, and the amount of "work" you need to do to *understand* a problem, organize the data required to model it, and model it correctly:

- Are there good, *high-quality* electronic data available?

- Are there *a lot* of electronic data available?

- Is the organization far enough up the learning curve?

- How subtle and easily understood are interactions between the problem variables?

- Tolerance for Noise in Data
- Tolerance for Sparse Data
- Learning Curve
- Tolerance for Complexity

FIGURE 3.3 Quality of Available Resources

Business examples:

In developing a particular type of stock trading system using neural networks,[3] developers estimate that they will need at least 60 months of accurate historical data, normalized for stock splits, and so on. (tolerance for data sparseness and noise)

A consultant suggests that you need to develop a system using a genetic learning algorithm for data mining. You have never done it before, which means you'll need to do a lot of background work and learning first and implement a small-scale prototype system to understand how the GA would mine the data. (learning curve)

In talking to a portfolio manager about choosing securities to acquire or discard, you find out that the manager first runs a simple test involving three financial parameters

---

[3]Artificial neural networks are systems that automatically "learn" relationships from raw data. The developer only needs to tell the system how to learn, but does not need to put problem-specific knowledge into the system. Artificial neural networks are explained in Chapter 6.

on all securities in the database, then additional tests involving two more variables, and finally, a ranking phase based on preserving a specific profile of the overall portfolio. Is it reasonable to decompose the portfolio selection problem like this? (complexity)

Finally, the fourth set of factors shown in Figure 3.4 relates to the *logistical constraints* within an organization:

- What is the access to experts, or conversely, how independent are you from them? In particular, are experts readily available for advice and testing?
- Are the computing infrastructure resources adequate for the problem?
- What development time can the organization afford?

- Independence from Experts
- Computational Ease
- Development Time

FIGURE 3.4   Logistical Constraints

Business examples:

In developing a stock-picking rule-based expert system, you need to realize that you need access to an experienced trader for at least 4 hours a week over the course of several months in order to specify the process by which stocks are selected, and for validating the system's results. (access to experts)

If you decide to use a genetic algorithm[4] for data mining, you will have to load hundreds of megabytes of data into memory at one time; this will require access to a very large mainframe or a massively parallel computer. (computational ease)

Based on initial discussions with experts, in developing a hybrid rule-based system to spot exchange rate patterns, you estimate that the system will consist of roughly 500 rules, which will probably require 6 to 8 months to extract from experts, validate them, and organize them to develop a production version of a system. (development time)

THE STRETCH PLOT: A VOCABULARY FOR REQUIREMENTS AND ANALYSIS

The interesting thing about the four sets of dimensions is that they serve as a *vocabulary* for expressing system requirements as well as for comparing solutions. In other words, the vocabulary is a checklist of the objectives and constraints of the various stakeholders in the organization—top management, users, and technologists. The vocabulary helps you *describe* the problem and to compare how various alternatives stack up in addressing requirements.

---

[4]Genetic algorithms are systems that solve problems by using a kind of "survival of the fittest." They try many different solutions and allow the better ones to survive. Genetic algorithms are explained in Chapter 5.

Interestingly, the dimensions of this vocabulary fall into the quadrants of a plot, as shown in Figure 3.5. We refer to this as a *stretch plot* since in practice you end up stretching some of the dimensions when making trade-offs on requirements or system features.

The dimensions in the top half of the stretch plot relate to the system itself and reflect requirements of the end product being designed, while those in the bottom half deal with the organizational environment in which the system will be developed and used. The dimensions in the left-hand quadrants of the stretch plot relate to quality issues, whereas those in the right deal with practical constraints in system development and use.

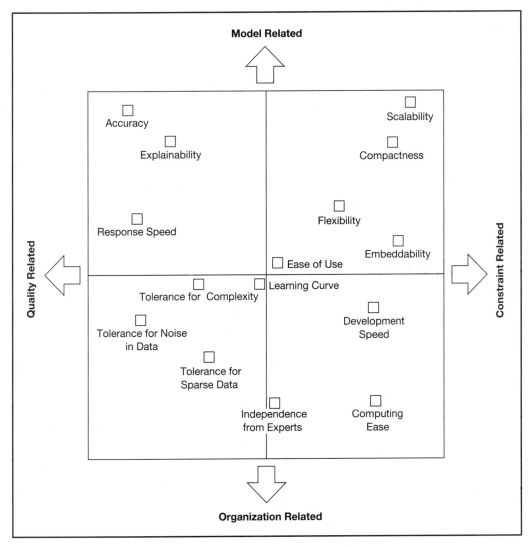

FIGURE 3.5   The Stretch Plot: A Comprehensive View of Intelligence Density

Together the dimensions form a "committee of critics." Each of the committee members has an ax to grind. Each is concerned with a separate aspect of the development process or the organizational impact of the system. Each critic will try to influence the outcome of the final product. Each of the critics must be satisfied to some degree or another in order for the project to be a success.

The useful thing about such a committee is that it forces you to consider early in the life cycle the set of issues you'll have to deal with during the course of the system's development, use, and maintenance. Depending on how concerned you are with the issues that each critic raises, you will weigh more or less heavily its influence on the decisions that lead up to selecting a technique and strategy for solving a problem. The final system will be the result of careful consideration of these issues. As is often the case with committees, it will almost always also involve compromises.

For example, the end user of a customer support system (say, a customer service representative) might want to be able to explain the diagnoses and recommendations of a system easily to customers. The *explainability* critic would represent these demands. But the user may also need the system to produce answers quickly, say within 30 seconds, so that customers don't have to wait a long time on the phone. The *speed* critic asserts itself to advocate this dimension. Taken together, these two critics might narrow down considerably the range of techniques that you could use to build a system.

You can think of each technique and each problem as having certain rubbery "shapes" that are determined by the various critics. The ideal solution will match a problem to a technique without allowing the competing critics to stretch beyond the snapping point. In other words, you must try to match your solutions to the problem without "stretching" the technique, the environment, or the requirements for the solution too much.

USING THE STRETCH PLOT

How did we decide on the critics in the stretch plot?

We based the stretch plot on our own experiences and those of other information systems professionals. What we tried to do was concentrate on the critics that are most general to the broadest variety of problems and techniques. But the critics we've described above are not exhaustive. In particular, critics like *management comfort, internal resistance to technology projects,* and *external marketability* are often important.

Fortunately, each of these would also fall into one of the four quadrants. *Internal resistance,* for example, would go into the lower right quadrant: an organizational constraint. The framework is robust enough to accommodate a wide variety of additional dimensions.

Are all critics created equally?

No, some are more equal than others. Not every critic is important for every problem. For example, if you are involved in a project in which the data were plentiful and of very high quality, the data quantity and data quality critics cease to influence development decisions (except that you may decide to rule *in* certain techniques you might normally have excluded!).

So how do you know whether or not a critic will be important?

You need to perform a stretch plot analysis. Each problem and each technique has its own stretch plot "landscape." You reveal the landscape by asking questions about the problem or solution. For any given problem, you can look at the landscape formed by your problem specification and see the importance of each critic. Figure 3.6 shows what such a landscape might look like for a typical problem. The height of a bar indicates its importance for the problem.

In this case, it was important that a solution have HIGH explainability. In contrast, scalability was not as important, and so you would tolerate any solution that provided only LOW scalability.

What is happening is that you are defining the boundaries of your solution. For example, you would be more inclined to rule out solutions that did not provide HIGH explainability, but you would be less concerned if they did not have HIGH scalability.

We've defined the dimensions in such a way that if the value required for a critic is HIGH, it is harder for a technique to satisfy it. For example, it is harder to find techniques that satisfy HIGH explainability than it is to find techniques that have

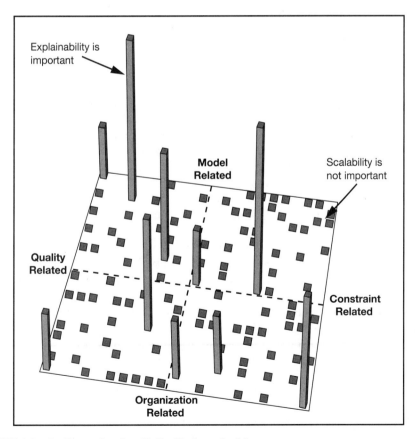

FIGURE 3.6   An Example of an ID Profile for a Problem

LOW explainability. Why? Explainability is always a desirable trait. All things being equal, you'd rather have it than not have it. By definition, HIGH explainability also satisfies LOW explainability.

The upper half of the stretch plot of Figure 3.5 can be used to describe two things: When you are talking about a problem, it describes what the *system will provide* to the organization. When you are talking about a potential solution technique, it describes what is demanded by the organization (requirement). The more demanding the organization is, the harder the problem becomes for a technique. The challenge is one of finding a solution that meets or exceeds the requirement.

The dimensions on the lower half of the stretch plot give you the complement. They describe what the *organization provides,* and how the technique stacks up on that dimension. The idea is that the organization constrains the availability of factors, and it is up to you to design a solution that makes the best of what you have: It satisfies the constraints.

The four types of dimensions are important to any systems development effort. In fact, as we mentioned earlier, you might want to define other dimensions for yourself. Beware, however, that the *meaning* of some of the dimensions depends on the problem context, while others are much more obvious.

For example, when people discuss scalability for a database, they are generally concerned with how the database performs as the amount of data in it increases. Factors like storage space and the time it will take to update the database after a new piece of data is input are usually central to this discussion. However, when you consider the issue of scalability for, say, an expert system, you are more concerned with issues of knowledge engineering; for instance, how easy will it be to extract rules from an expert as you scale from a dozen rules to several hundred? How will these new rules interact with other rules? In this case, storage and time requirements necessary to *execute* a larger system are secondary compared to the knowledge acquisition bottleneck problem involved in *maintaining* the system.

Another property of the critics is that some critics are technique specific (that is, they favor or discourage certain types of techniques regardless of the problem at hand) and some depend on both the problem and the technique (they will favor or discourage certain techniques depending on the nature of the problem). This makes life easier.

For example, let's say that you are trying to classify mortgage applications into good and bad risks. Assume that you also want to be able to explain to prospective borrowers why they were or were not granted credit. The explainability critic becomes important.

What if you solved the problem using a neural network? While neural nets can be very good at classifying things, you also need to consider that neural networks are generally unable to provide good explanations as to how they decide on the classifications. On the other hand, rule-based systems are very good at explaining their results.

In fact, what you will find is that neural networks are *usually* difficult to explain, while rule-based expert systems are *almost always* easily explained. Thus, the explainability of systems developed using a certain technique tends to be *independent* of the problem you're solving. The *explainability* critic is largely *problem indepen-*

dent. This is useful to know since it immediately suggests or rules out certain techniques if explainability is to be an important feature of a system.

In contrast, other critics can depend on the *interaction* between the problem *and* the technique being considered. For instance, rule-based systems have fairly quick development times for moderately sized problems provided there is a good theory for how to solve the problem. This type of expert system does, however, require far more time for complex, poorly understood systems. Neural networks, in contrast, do not suffer as severely in this respect. On the other hand, as we will discuss, much of the neural network development time is often spent identifying the correct variables and preparing meaningful input data for training and testing the net. This also takes time, but in a different way.[5]

The point is that from the *development speed* critic's perspective, the right choice of technique depends on the number of variables, the quality and quantity of data, the existence (or lack thereof) of a theory, and so on. Thus the influence of the *development speed* critic varies both with respect to problem characteristics and technique. It is problem *dependent.*

SUMMARY

The preceding dimensions provide a concrete way of operationalizing the concept of intelligence density. The checklist provides a handle for bringing to the surface the important questions involved in imposing structure on an initially ill-defined problem. The framework makes explicit both the organizational and technical objectives and constraints. It reduces the risk of getting trapped into developing a solution that uses a favorite technique or an apparently obvious solution that could turn out to be a bad choice from a business standpoint.

In the next chapters, we describe a toolbox of techniques for solving problems. Along with each technique, we present an analysis of its strengths and weaknesses with respect to the stretch plot. In the case studies in the latter part of the text, we present a series of cases that demonstrates how the stretch plot can be used in a practical manner to plan and solve real business problems.

---

[5]Throughout this book we will discuss these features of techniques and explain why some techniques demonstrate certain characteristics while others do not.

Appendix to Chapter 3:
Dimensions of Problems and Solutions

Intelligence Density Dimensions: Quality of System

Accuracy measures how close the outputs of a system are to the correct or best decision. Can you be confident that the errors (results that are *not* accurate) are not so severe as to make the system too costly or dangerous to use?

Explainability is the description of the process by which a conclusion was reached. Statistical models explain the output to some degree in the sense that each independent variable influences or "explains" the dependent variable in that it accounts for some portion of the variance of the dependent variable.

Other systems, where rule-based reasoning is involved, show explicitly how conclusions are derived. Yet others, such as neural networks, generate opaque mathematical formulas. These are sometimes referred to as "black boxes" because for the user they are the mathematical equivalent of the magician's black box: Data go in at one end and results come out the other, *but you cannot (easily) see the rationale behind the conclusion.*

Response speed is the time it takes for a system to complete analysis at the desired level of accuracy. The flip side to this dimension is *confidence* in the sense that you can ask how confident you are that a certain period of time, within which the system must provide an answer, will be *sufficient* to perform the analysis. In applications that require that results be produced within a specified time frame, missing that time frame means that no matter how accurate and otherwise desirable the results are, they will be useless in practice.

How Well Is the System Engineered?

Scalability involves adding more variables to the problem or increasing the range of values that variables can take. For example, scalability is a major issue when you're interested in going from a prototype system involving 10 variables to one with 30 variables.

In early AI projects, it was not uncommon to find systems that worked well for solving small problems (for example, do the patient's symptoms indicate meningitis or hepatitis?) but broke down when the problem size increased (given the *full range of human ailments,* what is wrong with the patient?) Scalability can be a real problem when the *interactions* among variables increase rapidly in unpredictable ways with the introduction of additional variables (making the system brittle) or where the computational complexity increases rapidly.

Compactness refers to how small (literally, the number of bytes) the system can be made. Once a system has been developed and tested, it needs to be put into the hands of the decision makers within an organization. It must be taken out into the field, be that the shop floor, the trading floor, or the ocean floor.

Compactness deals with the ease with which the system can be encoded into a compact portable format, whether that be embedding in a spreadsheet, coding into a computer language, or engraving on a silicon chip. If a system is too "bulky" to be easily embedded in a format that makes it usable where and when it is needed, then the system itself may not be very useful.

Flexibility is the ease with which the relationships among the variables or their domains can be changed, or the goals of the system modified.

Most systems are not designed to be used once and then thrown away. Instead they must be robust enough to perform well as additional functionality is added over time. In addition, many of the business processes that you might model are not static (i.e., they change over time). As a result, the ability to update a system or to have the system adapt itself to new phenomena is important.

Embeddability refers to the ease with which a system can be coupled with or incorporated into the infrastructure of an organization. In some situations, systems will be components of larger systems or other databases. If this is the case, systems must be able to communicate well and mesh smoothly with the other components of the organizational infrastructure. A system that requires proprietary "software engines" or specific hardware will not necessarily be able to integrate itself into this infrastructure.

Ease of use describes how complicated the system is to use for the businesspeople who will be using it on a daily basis. Is it an application that requires a lot of expertise or training, or is it something a user can apply right out of the box?

Quality of Available Resources

Tolerance for noise in data is the degree to which the quality of a system, most notably its accuracy, is affected by noise in the electronic data.

Tolerance for data sparseness is the degree to which the quality of a system is affected by incompleteness or lack of data.

The availability and level of detail of data and the accuracy are central issues in choosing among different techniques. It is sometimes not possible for an organization to get hold of the data that it would ideally like to have in order to develop a system. The data that the organization *can* get may not have the level or types of information required, the data may not go back historically as far as necessary, or may not provide as many data points as would be ideal.

Tolerance for complexity is the degree to which the quality of a system is affected by interactions among the various components of the process being modeled or in the knowledge used to model a process. Complex processes involve many, often nonlinear, interactions between variables. A prototypical example of this is weather prediction. Weather systems involve thousands of factors such as temperature, topology, wind speed, and so on. These variables all interact in very complex ways, which is why long-term weather prediction is virtually impossible.

The availability of knowledge about how to deal with the complexity of the problem at hand makes the problem easier to model. Lower complexity problems are easier to model.

Learning curve requirements indicate the degree to which the organization needs to experiment in order to become sufficiently competent at solving a problem or using a technique.

Logistical Constraints

Independence from experts is the degree to which the system can be designed, built, and tested without experts. While expertise is valuable, *access* to experts within an organization can be a logistical nightmare and can be very expensive.

Computational ease is the degree to which a system can be implemented without requiring special-purpose hardware or software.

Development speed is the time that the organization can afford to develop a system or, conversely, the time a modeling technology would require to develop a system.

Data-Driven Decision Support

. . . [C]ompanies today are manipulating data in the terabyte (one trillion bytes) to pedabyte (one thousand terabytes) range. If bytes were raindrops, that would be enough to float the QEII.
—Edgar F. Codd, *et al.*

"Data! Data! Data!" he cried, "I cannot make bricks without clay!"
—Arthur Conan Doyle, spoken by Sherlock Holmes

If we are to have a really fast machine, then we must have our information, or at least part of it, in a more accessible form . . .
—Alan Turing

Managers need information retrieval that matches the speed of thought.
—Anonymous

The fundamental input to any intelligent system is some sort of data. Although computers were originally developed to perform complex mathematical calculations, researchers soon realized that they had tremendous potential for organizing data. But fluid access to large amounts of data remained a problem for most business users. Although businesses stored lots of data, especially about their transactions, they rarely made good use of them. With the maturing of network and database technology, this has changed. Timely and accurate management information is becoming more of a reality. This chapter describes a new way of thinking about data and a new genre of tools that are making this possible.

INTRODUCTION

Several years ago, it was estimated that the amount of electronic data in the world was doubling every 18 months. By current standards, that estimate is probably far too conservative. As a society, we're awash in data not only because the volume of what gets recorded electronically is exploding, but also because people's *access* to it is increasing at a tremendous rate. Businesses, researchers, and even casual home Internet users, are experiencing intense "data overload." That's why there's a dire need, particularly in business, for systems that can find, summarize, and interpret large amounts of data effectively.

Businesses are recognizing the value of data as a strategic asset. This is reflected by the high degree of interest in new technologies like "data warehousing," and "OLAP" systems that make use of these warehouses.

As the name implies, a data warehouse is a large-scale storage facility for data. Like a conventional industrial warehouse that stores products from many different sources, bringing the goods together in one place until they are needed, a data warehouse stores *data* from many different *databases* until they are needed for business decisions. And, like an industrial warehouse, a data warehouse makes it possible and convenient to combine items from different sources into an integrated package. OLAP systems are the tools that help decision makers actually package the various data products in the warehouse and deliver them as needed.

Why are these types of systems useful from a business standpoint?

The current reality is that managers need to get information a lot faster if they hope to run a business intelligently. Suppose that as a sales manager of a line of copying machines, you have a hunch that your largest customers are the least profitable. If your hunch is true, you'd like to alter your pricing and customer support strategies to try to increase the profitability of these large clients.

Managers constantly want answers to such seemingly simple questions but rarely get them in time to be useful. There is generally a *long* time lag between the point that a business manager has a hunch or a hypothesis that needs testing and the point where an answer is retrieved. For many businesses today, that just isn't good enough. Managers need "information retrieval that matches the speed of thought."

So what are the barriers to this information-rich world and why do you need special systems to overcome them?

Businesses have long made use of *transaction processing systems* to manage huge amounts of data relating to operations: billing, invoicing, and auditing. These systems, in the language of our industrial warehouse metaphor, are like the individual producers. These are mission-critical systems. They have to be accurate, fast, and reliable. Each is specialized for a particular problem and finely tuned to do what it does as efficiently as possible. Each has its own format and structure. As a result, the data recorded in most of these transaction processing systems are not easily *accessible* to other systems and it is also not easy to look at the data in any way but the prescribed structure. A great deal of effort is still required to get useful information out of such systems.

Another difficulty is that data access can be prohibitively expensive from a computation time standpoint. Most transaction processing systems run on huge multi-million dollar mainframe computers. These machines usually have large staffs and special data centers that exist just to keep them running. As a result, mainframe computer time is very expensive, and management is under pressure to keep its usage under control. From an operations standpoint, most managers consider data access to be simply a lower-order priority than billing customers.

But the expense is not just the salaries of the data center staff. It can be measured in terms of time and inconvenience as well. Because of the complexity involved in using most database systems, it is easy for a well-intentioned user to unwittingly issue a query on a business database that will bog down the host computer. Such queries could execute for days, weeks, or months! Imagine what would happen if your billing system server were hit with such a query while it is generating invoices for the day. Even if a user is experienced, some queries just take a long time, no matter what you do. If you want to ensure that your operations go smoothly, providing users with ad hoc data access can be a dangerous thing to do.

Furthermore, because many of the applications that businesses need call for a lot of computing power and storage space, it is not uncommon for a single company's data to be spread out across many databases and many computers, sometimes even across many states or countries. While this allows the firm to process data more quickly, it makes it almost impossible for a single user to bring together pieces of data from different operational areas of the business.

Finally, even simple queries on a single database often demand a level of programming skill that most businesspeople do not have. The result: Managers submit requests for reports to a department of programmers who then try to bend the transaction systems into shapes that will satisfy the businesspeople.

The bottom line is that transaction processing systems cannot be used very easily to do anything except process transactions. Any other applications will tax them. But users have a hard time accepting this.

Why?

At the same time that businesses have been developing powerful mainframe computing architectures, software on the average user's desktop has become increasingly user friendly. This gives the average businessperson powerful data analysis and modeling tools right on the desktop. Many of the decision models that users want to play with can be implemented using simple spreadsheet or database software on a PC.

As a result, it is common to find users with individual models that are completely independent of the organization's MIS department. What users are crying for is data to feed into their powerful user friendly analysis tools. The lack of fluid access to corporate data has limited the inroads of desktop computers in providing good business level information.

To be able to put decision data into the hands of more decision makers, businesses are turning to data storage facilities that allow users to manipulate data more easily. The generic name for these types of systems is a *data warehouse*. The idea behind a data warehouse is simple: Siphon off and integrate data from various transaction processing systems into a single separate place where the data can then be used to feed a range of decision support applications. Typically, data warehouses contain between 10 and 500 gigabytes or more of data from across an organization.

But once the data are collected, users still need an easy way of digging through them to get to the pieces they are interested in. OLAP systems let users do this.[1] OLAP, which stands for *on line analytical processing,* is supposed to make possible "retrieval at the speed of thought." These systems eliminate the pain of waiting months for an application programmer to code up something and praying that it'll be what you need.

---

[1]Some OLAP systems bypass a data warehouse altogether, accessing transaction databases directly.

THE ABCs OF DATA-DRIVEN DECISION SUPPORT

To appreciate what data warehousing and OLAP are all about, consider an ad hoc kind of question that a sales manager might want to answer:

"What is driving sales in the Northeast region?"

This sounds like a simple question. It turns out, though, that most current information systems would have a very hard time bringing the data together to answer this type of question on the fly. The data that the sales manager needs to see would usually be spread over several database systems: billing, inventory, and personnel, for example. These databases might be on different computers or even in different states. Figuring out how to bring the data together and reconcile the different databases with each other can be daunting.

But data problems are only part of the issue. The sales manager's question is also sufficiently open ended, sufficiently "human" one might argue, that it could mean different things depending on how you interpret it. Is the user looking for the revenues of each of the top 10 products? Or the profit per sale by salesperson in the Northeast? Or the breakdown of revenues by city across the Northeast? Maybe the sales manager can't even be more specific about what he or she would really like to see unless he or she sees an overall picture first!

The point is that the sales manager's requirements are interactive. If you show some data, the sales manager will look at it and tell you more about what is needed. There is a loop being created: The manager makes a request, gets the results, analyzes the results, uses this new information to formulate another request, and so on.

This loop is not very satisfactory to users since there is always a bottleneck in the loop: the request. A user needs to go through some arcane database system or programmer to get at the data. Data warehouses and OLAP systems try to unclog this bottleneck.

So why doesn't every company run out and build a data warehouse and OLAP system?

It's not that easy. For users, access is the whole issue with respect to data warehouses, but for an *organization,* it is only one part of the equation. Creating a data warehouse requires serious business thinking since the *content* of the warehouse depends on the kinds of questions users are going to want to answer with the data.

If the data warehouse is to feed a variety of applications, it must be defined from a business-level perspective. This takes time and planning. It often means coordinating different business units and inventorying the data assets that the entire firm possesses.

To put data warehouses and OLAP systems in perspective, let's look at the forces that have led us there.

The Old Way

Let's say that you are a large toy manufacturer. Every day, hundreds of orders for hundreds of different toys and games come in to your firm and need to be processed, tracked, and billed. Manually, this would require an army of clerical and administrative staff.

But in the 60s and 70s, this began to change. Mainframe computer technology made it possible for large businesses to organize their order processing and billing electronically. These *on line transaction processing* (OLTP) systems came about in part because of advances in computer hardware, and in part because of the development of database software that ran on these new computers.

To make the access and organization of data easier, computer scientists developed database management systems (DBMSs). These systems were designed specifically to store, organize, and retrieve data quickly.[2] The early DBMS approaches were based on the *indexed sequential access method* (ISAM). ISAM databases store all of the data in a large file. In addition to the main data file, ISAM systems also created separate files called *indexes.* Indexes sped data access tremendously.

Index files work the same way that the index of a book works. The pages of this book are arranged in a particular order: by the chapters, sub-chapters, and so forth. But, if you want to find information about a particular subject, and you don't know which chapter it is in, you can use the index in the back of the book.

For example, if you want to find the part of this book that deals with the RETE algorithm, you can either start at the beginning of the book and keep reading until you see the words "RETE algorithm," or you can look at the index and find out on which pages in the book we mention the RETE algorithm. In effect, an index helps map a "value" such as RETE to a "physical location" on a hardware device much like the page number of a book.

For our toy example, Figure 4.1 shows how the toy manufacturing database might store and index orders. In the figure, the index *key* for the first index is the name of the customer. The data are ordered by this key. To find where the records for Funland Toys are, just look up the key "Funland Toys" in the Index-by-Customer file. Funland Toys is in database rows 2, 11, and 15. Going back to the main data file, you can see that the record at row 2 is indeed an order from Funland Toys and it shows that the store ordered 10 Messy Paint Kits on 12/1/96.

You could also print out a list of *all* customers that *ordered 10 items or more* by using the Index-by-Quantity file. Just go down the list until the quantity key is greater than 10 and print out the record at each row indicated in the index after that. Indexes let you change the order of the data, without actually sorting all of the data each time. In effect, the data are *simultaneously* in the order of *each* of its indexes all the time. (By the way, the data in Figure 4.1 can answer the question about what is driving sales in the Northeast region. Unfortunately, ISAM systems are not very good at letting users discover the answers to questions like this. Can you see what's driving sales?)

---

[2]It turns out that sorting and searching data can be very complicated. In fact, developing efficient algorithms for doing these things was what most early computer scientists spent much of their time thinking about. Being able to search and sort quickly can mean the difference between an application that increases the efficiency of a process twenty-fold, and one that is impractical for business purposes.

For example, let's say that you had 1,000,000 orders from different toy and department stores in your toy database. Let's say that you had a really fast disk drive that could read or write 10,000 records per second. To find a particular order could take 0.0003 seconds, a second and a half, or a minute and a half, depending on the way that you set up the search. If that doesn't impress you, consider that to sort all 1,000,000 orders by date could take you 1½ minutes, 23 minutes, or a staggering *3 years and 2 months* depending, again, on how you set up your data!

Complete Data

DB_ROW	DATE	CUSTOMER	REGION	PRODUCT	QUANTITY
1	12/1/96	Toy Town	SE	Mr. Snowman	10
2	12/1/96	Fun Land Toys	NE	Messy Paint Kit	10
3	12/1/96	Toy Town	SE.	Messy Paint Kit	25
4	12/1/96	Joe's House of Toys	NE	Death Avenger Doll	5
5	12/2/96	Toy Mania	SE	Mr. Snowman	10
6	12/2/96	Nutcracker Toys	SE	Puppet Maker Kit	10
7	12/2/96	Joe's House of Toys	NE	Puppet Maker Kit	20
8	12/2/96	Toy Town	SE	Death Avenger Doll	20
9	12/2/96	Nutcracker Toys	SE	Mr. Snowman	10
10	12/2/96	Toy Mania	SE	Messy Paint Kit	5
11	12/3/96	Fun Land Toys	NE	Mr. Snowman	25
12	12/3/96	Nutcracker Toys	SE	Death Avenger Doll	20
13	12/3/96	Toy Town	SE	Puppet Maker Kit	10
14	12/3/96	Joe's House of Toys	NE	Mr. Snowman	25
15	12/3/96	Fun Land Toys	NE	Death Avenger Doll	5

Index by Customer

CUSTOMER	DB_ROW
Fun Land Toys	2
Fun Land Toys	11
Fun Land Toys	15
Joe's House of Toys	4
Joe's House of Toys	7
Joe's House of Toys	14
.	
.	
.	

Index by Quantity

QUANTITY	DB_ROW
5	4
5	10
5	12
5	15
10	1
10	2
.	
.	
.	

FIGURE 4.1   A Toy ISAM Database and Two Indexes

ISAM represented a great step forward in storing and retrieving data. Most early DBMSs used ISAM architectures. But ISAM was not without its problems. For one, each index in a database needed to be updated any time a record was added to the database.[3] This meant that if there were 10 indexes, then each time a new record was added to (or deleted from) the database, each of the 10 indexes also needed to be modified. This became more and more time consuming as the number of records in a database and the number of indexes increased.

Even more troubling, however, was that the designer of a database had to determine, before the database was ever built, *how* the users were going to need the data arranged. In order to create indexes, a designer needs to specify which keys each index will use. This is the same as the designer telling the user in which orders the data can be arranged and by which criteria the database can be searched. This made retrieval inflexible.

---

[3]This could be necessary sometimes even if only a single field in a record was changed.

A breakthrough came with the advent of *relational database management systems* (RDBMS). Instead of storing all of the data in a single large file, RDBMS broke up data into smaller files that made it easier to keep data consistent and to maintain it. This is called *data normalization.*

To provide a flavor of normalization, consider our toy database. Notice that every time a record for Nutcracker Toys shows up in Figure 4.1, the Region field is always "SE." This is a waste of space. Why? Because every Nutcracker Toys is *always* in the SE region. Even if that field weren't stored in the database with each record, you could find the region for all of the Nutcracker Toys records just by looking it up once and copying it onto all of the records.

In recognition of this, instead of storing the fact that Nutcracker Toys is in the SE region in every record, an RDBMS approach creates a separate database file or *table* that maps each company to its region. The orders table can then be smaller, containing just the item ordered, the quantity, the customer name, and date.[4]

When a user wanted to print out a complete listing like the one in Figure 4.1, he or she would *join* the two tables. What this means is that the user would tell the RDBMS to look up the region of the customer in every record in the orders table. Figure 4.2 shows how this works. Note how the orders table is more compact now.

Although this might sound more involved, RDBMS were a major advance in data management. For one thing, much larger databases could now be constructed. The region field was pretty small in our example, but imagine if you wanted to include addresses, phone numbers, contact information, and account numbers with each record. In an ISAM system, this might mean adding separate fields for each item and storing each of these long items with each record. If you had 5,000 orders from Nutcracker Toys, you would have 5,000 copies of the address in the database (and 5,000 copies of the phone number, etc.).

With an RDBMS approach, you could store the exact same amount of data with only one copy of the address. In addition, this made it easy to change the address of Nutcracker if the customer moved. Instead of searching through all 5,000 records and making 5,000 changes (and updating indexes if necessary), you could just make one change in the addresses table.

But more importantly, in addition to making data storage less redundant and more efficient, RDBMS allowed users to tailor data more to their specifications. Users could combine different tables to create *views* on the data that the designers of the database had never imagined. Any table could be joined with any other related table to bring together related information. (Of course, joins take time, but that wasn't an issue . . . at first.)

The powerful thing about such systems was that they provided a flexible "query language" called SQL (*structured query language*) that allowed a user to write database queries tailored to specific needs. Database queries could now be much more involved and they could do much more complex things.

But there is no free lunch. Now in order to get at the data, a user had to know SQL in addition to knowing the structure of the database. This was fine for program-

---

[4]An RDBMS approach to record orders would actually be implemented a little differently, but this example serves to illustrate conceptually how RDBMS work.

Orders Table

DB_ROW	DATE	CUSTOMER	PRODUCT	QUANT
1	12/1/96	Toy Town	Mr. Snowman	10
2	12/1/96	Fun Land Toys	Messy Paint Kit	10
3	12/1/96	Toy Town	Messy Paint Kit	25
4	12/1/96	Joe's House of Toys	Death Avenger Doll	5
5	12/2/96	Toy Mania	Mr. Snowman	5
6	12/2/96	Nutcracker Toys	Puppet Maker Kit	10
7	12/2/96	Joe's House of Toys	Puppet Maker Kit	20
8	12/2/96	Toy Town	Death Avenger Doll	20
9	12/2/96	Nutcracker Toys	Mr. Snowman	10
10	12/2/96	Toy Mania	Messy Paint Kit	25
11	12/3/96	Fun Land Toys	Mr. Snowman	25
12	12/3/96	Nutcracker Toys	Death Avenger Doll	20
13	12/3/96	Toy Town	Puppet Maker Kit	10
14	12/3/96	Joe's House of Toys	Mr. Snowman	25
15	12/3/96	Fun Land Toys	Death Avenger Doll	5

Region Table

CUSTOMER	REGION
Fun Land Toys	NE
Joe's House of Toys	NE
Nutcracker Toys	SE
Toy Mania	SE
Toy Town	SE

*Join tables on
customer name to get region*

FIGURE 4.2 A RDBMS Approach Which Eliminates Keeping Many Copies of the Region Around for Each Customer

mers, but most managers didn't know it and were unwilling to learn it. Even though it was written to be easy to use, to most nontechnical people SQL looks threatening. For example, here's an example of an SQL query that might show pending orders for a particular product:

```
select count (*) from pending_orders_queue q, orders_main m
   where q.sold_by_id=20010
   and q.s_id = m.s_id
   and m.s_type=152
   and q.status_id =2
```

To write this query, a user had to know not only the syntax of SQL, but also the structure of the database (which tables to join) and the details of each table (variable names, etc.). While this was fine for database specialists, most managers and business-people had a tough time with it.

But managers still needed information. To get businesspeople the data they needed many firms tried to understand and systematize senior managers' data needs. They then predefined the access paths data to the data the managers needed.

These systems, known as *executive information systems* (EIS), were essentially front-ends to traditional transaction oriented database systems.[5] They attempted to provide the right intelligence to the decision maker by predefining the types of information a manager would typically want to see and putting it into an intuitive visual format.

For example, instead of requiring the user to type the cryptic (to a non-programmer) SQL query in the example above, an EIS might let the user choose "Sales Status Update" from a menu, specify items of interest, and from there, *the system* would make the appropriate translations for the database query. Figure 4.3 shows how this might work conceptually.

The key thing to notice about EIS is that they represent a major step away from using data to track transactions and toward using data to support decisions. Rather than using the database to fill out invoices and track the status of a particular order, EIS allow the user to ask, "How is John Smith doing on sales of games?" This was a fundamentally new view of data. Now data were not only an audit trail but they were also an input to management tools.

EIS allow users to take transaction-level data that are far too detailed to be useful to managers and aggregate them into more meaningful units. Instead of presenting information such as, "On 12/1/96, John Smith sold 15 units of the game Mr. Snowman to Toy Town," EIS present summary information like, "John Smith has sold 25 units of games, and 60 units of arts and crafts kits." Managers could use this summary information to decide how well John Smith is doing, how well game sales are going, and so forth.

Even though EIS provided much better access to data for decision support, they have some serious drawbacks. Since all of the database queries and reports are predefined in the EIS, users are limited in the information they could derive from the data. If a user wanted to see data organized along a criterion that didn't fit into the programmed framework, new programming needed to be done. This took time and cost money. EIS were, in fact, inflexible *by design* since the access paths were predefined.

Furthermore, these systems did not address a major drawback of using transaction processing systems for decision support. Most EIS still required a lot of effort to bring together data from disparate databases throughout the firm. For example, it might be difficult (or impossible) to combine data about the product sales of one subsidiary with data from product sales of another since the two subsidiaries used different databases and computers. Nonetheless, a manager might want to do this to look for corporate synergies among shared clients.

Scrubbing, Transforming, Slicing and Dicing with Data Warehouses and OLAP Systems

In response to the limitations of traditional EIS, a new approach to data access has begun to emerge. This new approach involves data warehouses and OLAP systems.

---

[5]Technically most true EIS performed some type of rudimentary data aggregation and moved transactions data into an interim storage facility. However, a large class of DSS similar in spirit to formal EIS, did not do this. In the business environment these DSS were often known as EIS as well, thus blurring the line.

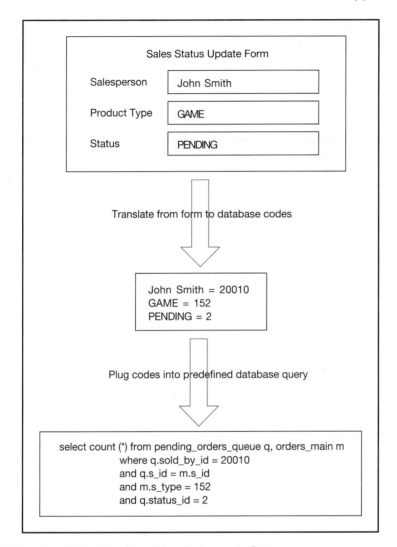

FIGURE 4.3 An EIS Provides User-Friendly Access to Data

These systems allow users to have flexibility *and* ease of use. Data warehousing applications and OLAP systems put more of the power of data retrieval and synthesis into the hands of business managers and decision makers.

A data warehouse is a database specifically designed to answer business questions. It serves as a repository for many types of business data from many sources. Data from these sources are transferred into the warehouse to make them easier to access. Once the data are in the warehouse, they are extensively indexed and combined for very fast access.

OLAP systems are high-powered software front-ends and data manipulation systems that sit on top of data. These systems are like very flexible EIS. Although we call them front-ends, they are usually a good deal more powerful than simple graphical user interfaces.

OLAP systems allow users to "slice and dice" data in almost any manner. Typically an OLAP system lets users select variables from a list, mix and match them, and perform business-related operations on them very quickly. For example, most OLAP systems allow a user to very simply convert individual records into regional totals, quarterly totals, percentages, or annual growth.

If OLAP system users need more detail about some piece of data, they can often *drill down* into the data as well. For instance, while looking at the sales of Messy Paint Kits by region, a manager may want to understand why the Southeast region is doing so much better than the rest of the sales zone. The manager might drill down into the region by customer and discover that a single large chain of department stores in the Southeast has made a series of large orders for Messy Paint Kits. Or maybe the manager drills down by salesperson and discovers that John Smith is selling larger volumes than other salespeople. By drilling down into John Smith's individual sales, the manager may discover that John Smith has offered a discount that makes the items more attractive to buyers without reducing profits very much. And wouldn't it be interesting if John Smith services that Southeastern chain of stores? And so on.

The key thing to note here is that the user has much more control than with traditional EIS. An EIS dictates beforehand what data a decision maker can or cannot use and in what sequence the user can see the data. OLAP systems allow the user to dive into the data and explore them at levels of detail more appropriate for his or her analysis. In most cases the user can get to the data, without resorting to special programming.

An easy way to think about the differences between OLAP systems and data warehouses is that data warehouses bring all of the data together from across the organization, and OLAP systems let you look at them and manipulate them interactively.

To understand how data warehousing and OLAP systems work, it is useful to consider the steps that data go through as they move from a collection of separate OLTP database into a single data warehouse and then through an OLAP system.

Figure 4.4 shows a rough schematic of how you can think about data warehouses and OLAP systems. Keep in mind when you look at the figure, though, that in many systems several components may be wrapped up in one. For example, some OLAP engines are also small data warehouses, and many data loaders incorporate data transformers as well.

The figure shows how data move through five steps on their way into the data warehouse. First the data are loaded from various remote data sources. As the data are loaded, they must be converted to a common format, scrubbed to get rid of errors, and transformed into things like aggregates that are useful for analysis. Finally, the data are put into the warehouse where they are indexed for fast access.

The data loader's job is to handle the operational side of moving data from a particular data source into the warehouse. It handles information like determining whether or not there have been changes to the original data source and how the new data should be added to the warehouse. It also determines how a particular set of data should be loaded. Does a specific request need to be made to a mainframe? Should a

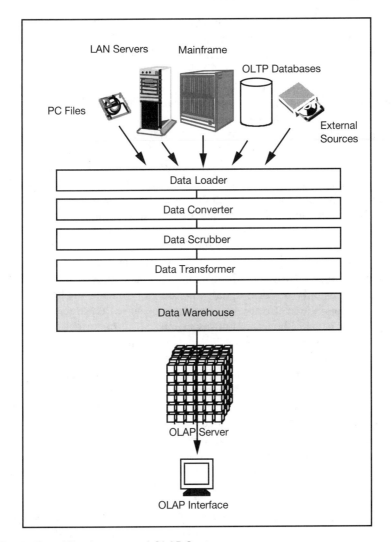

FIGURE 4.4 Data Warehouses and OLAP Systems

file be read from a local area network (LAN) server? Should a CD-ROM drive be read? And so forth. The loader is usually also responsible for scheduling when these activities will take place.

The data converter handles translating data to formats that are appropriate to the data warehouse. For example, the data warehouse might store text in ASCII format, but a mainframe computer might use EBCDIC to store its files. The converter would perform the conversion. Or a data vendor's CD-ROM might list industry codes as "FINANCE," "MANUFACTURING," "SERVICE," "UTILITIES," and "TRANS-PORTATION," but the data warehouse might use Standard Industrial Classification (SIC) codes. This type of conversion would also be done by the transformer. Or one database might call a variable "prft_marg," while another calls it "prof_mrg" and the data warehouse calls it "profit_margin." In order to be able to use the variable from these three different sources, the transformer would need to map them all to a standard variable name.

The scrubber cleanses the data. What this means is that it identifies and remedies errors or omissions in the data. Missing values, for example, might be replaced with a predefined code or a default value. If a character string is found in a field that is supposed to be an integer, the record may be flagged or discarded, or an error recovery procedure might be executed.

Finally, the transformer performs aggregation and summarization. For instance, all of the individual sales by John Smith might be summarized into a single variable to make the information more meaningful or easier to access. Depending on the business requirements, the detailed sale-by-sale information might also be included in the warehouse.

It is important to note that data warehouses don't generally need to be updated in real-time. OLTP databases are designed for fast writing and record keeping. They are constantly being updated with new information as it becomes available. In contrast, data warehouses usually perform updates periodically during off-hours. Most data warehouses cannot operate effectively in real-time because they are not set up for this.

On the other hand, data warehouses usually store historical information in a much more accessible manner than OLTP systems. Using OLTP systems, you have to do a lot of work to summarize information historically and you need to perform complicated operations to figure out when new records entered the database and for how long older records were valid. Since data warehouses are used for decision support, they usually do not flush out old data to make room for new data. Because of this, they are more easily able to capture historical trends in the data. And because the warehouse is designed with business objectives in mind instead of transactions, queries on them lead to more actionable answers.[6]

Once the data are in a warehouse, the OLAP server becomes important for answering these queries. But how?

OLAP systems let you explore data in ways that are decision oriented. For starters, an OLAP system lets you perform various types of "slicing and dicing" of data easily and without defining beforehand what you will need to do. In other words, you are able to view the data and get at them from many different perspectives along many different dimensions. But more importantly, the system gives you the entry points into the data *based on the characteristics of the data themselves.* The system would also allow you to drill down into data to get to higher and higher levels of detail if that's what you need. Finally, OLAP tools are usually fast and easy to use. You can plow through megabytes or gigabytes of data without having to wait hours for your results.

There are several different approaches to OLAP representation, but the most

---

[6]To be technically correct, data warehouses typically contain data spanning about a year's worth of history and they usually aggregate the data to facilitate analysis. A similar type of database called an *operational data store* is like a data warehouse but is typically used to store operational (not analytic) data for a period of only 30 days or so and wouldn't usually perform aggregation. The main purpose of the operational data store is to bring data together in one place for convenience in reporting, and so forth. In practice both are often referred to as *data warehouses.*

common is a *multidimensional* approach to data storage. Figure 4.5 shows this method of structuring the data. In OLAP terms this representation shows a *matrix* of customer *dimensioned on* product. The blocks or *cells* are like records in the toy database. A row of cells is called a *vector*.

To see why a multidimensional approach is so powerful, it is useful to consider how complicated data manipulation can get without it. Let's go back to our toy database. This database only contains 15 records, but you can imagine that it contains 15,000 or 15,000,000 if you like.

How would you answer the question,

"How many Mr. Snowman games were sold?"

Looking back at the database in Figure 4.1,[7] you can see that, in this case, since there is no index for product, you would have to run through all of the records in the database, totaling all quantities that corresponded to records with a product of "Mr. Snowman." This is not very efficient.

You might suggest adding an index for product. Let's say that you do that.
Now you ask,

"How many Mr. Snowman games were sold on 12/2/97?"

Well, again, since there is no index on product *and* date, you have to examine each record (or at least all of the Mr. Snowman records, assuming you made a product index in the last step).

But the problem here is that you don't know in advance how you will want to see the data. In the first case you looked at the dimension of product, in the second case you drilled down a little bit and looked at product by date. You could just as easily have wanted to see product by customer or customer by date, and so forth. It depends on what questions you need answered.

Our toy database has only a few columns, but most databases have many more. Each can potentially become a dimension of inquiry. It is impractical to try to anticipate every possible combination of dimensions and index your OLTP system on these dimensions. Even if this were possible, doing so would bring your system to its knees.

Now consider the *multidimensional* OLAP approach shown in Figure 4.5.

The white cells in the figure are *inputs* to the OLAP server. They represent the atomic level or simple data elements. The shaded cells represent *outputs*. These are the results of aggregating and transforming data.[8] Outputs are often formed by performing operations on the vectors. For example, in the figure, the outputs are various sub-totals and totals along different dimensions of the data. These were formed by simply summing along the vectors.

In this example, the gray cells are a "count" of items sold. However, the gray cells could result from applying other functions to the data such as average cost of sold items, total revenues, and so on.[9]

---

[7]We will be using Figure 4.2 in this discussion for simplicity. Although Figure 4.1 represents an ISAM database, similar reasoning to that which follows holds for RDBMS like the one represented in Figure 4.2.

[8]In some systems these cells might be computed by and stored in the data warehouse. In others they would be computed by the OLAP system.

[9]There could even be whole dimensions made up of measures (output cells) where one vector would represent averages, one vector would represent totals, one vector would represent maximums, and so on.

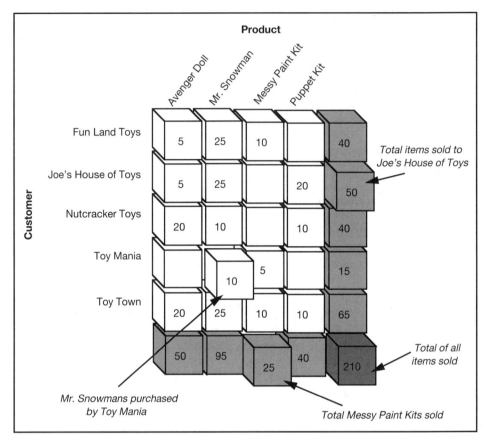

FIGURE 4.5 A Multidimensional OLAP Representation of Customer Dimensioned on Product

Notice that depending on the question you are interested in answering you can get the answer by simply going to the appropriate dimension and selecting the correct input or output cell. For example, to find the total number of Messy Paint Kits sold, you just need to find the cell at the intersection of the vector Messy Paint Kit and the total output vector.

Notice that for the customer dimension, the entry points into the data are "Fun Land Toys," "Joe's House of Toys," etc. In other words, every *value* of the customer attribute that appears in the database is an entry point into the data. Think about this. You can literally "see" every value of every attribute and dive into the data from any of these values. With data that are continuous, like revenues, the system might group it into various buckets or ranges.

The usefulness becomes even clearer when we add the dimension of time. Consider how many questions you can ask if you expand the matrix to a cube as in Figure 4.6. Answering even a handful of the questions shown in the figure would require a tremendous amount of programming in a traditional OLTP system. Furthermore, some queries would take hours or days to execute.

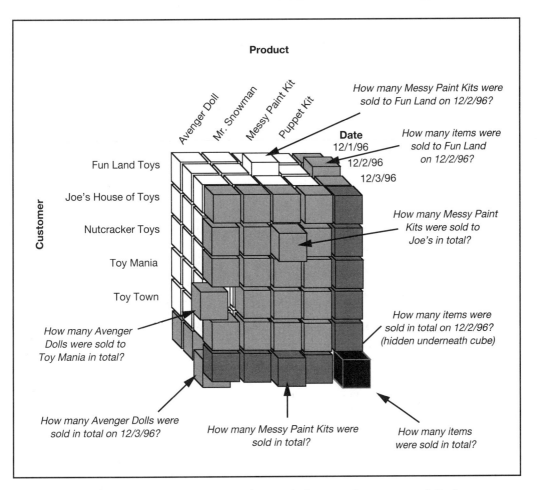

FIGURE 4.6 Hypercube data representations make it convenient to query data along any dimension.

Something else becomes clear when you examine Figure 4.6. Earlier we spoke of *drilling down* into the data. Looking at the cube, you can see how this might work.

You might start in the bottom right by asking simply, "How many items were sold?" Once you got this information, you might pop that cell out to reveal the next level of vectors. Let's say you had a hunch that overall sales were boosted by a large number of Messy Paint Kit sales. You might ask about the total number of units of Messy Paint Kits sold (the middle cell at the bottom). Now maybe you want to know why sales of Messy Paint Kits were so strong. Perhaps you suspect that sales to a particular client were particularly strong. You could check this by peeling away another layer of cells to determine how many Messy Paint Kits were sold to a particular client, say, Joe's House of Toys (the middle cell near the top). If you were still curious, you could peel away another layer to see if a particular day was a strong selling day to Joe's.

But this is only one possible path of analysis. You could easily have had a hunch that a certain date was a particularly strong sales date for all products. You would start by asking about the total sales on a particular day, say 12/2/97. From there you could branch off in a variety of directions by spinning the cube to the right place and drilling to the appropriate cell.

If you have more than three dimensions, the basic principle is the same, you just add another one to the representation. Vector and matrix operations work fine no matter how many dimensions you add. Unfortunately, as will often be the case with concepts we treat in this text, it is very difficult to imagine what a four- or five-dimensional *hypercube* looks like!

Most OLAP systems have graphical user interfaces that allow users to see data both numerically and in a variety of graphical representations. For example, the sales of a region might be shown in a table, as a series of bars on a bar graph, or as colored patches on a map of the United States. The user can drill down by pointing to the region of the screen for more detail.

Figure 4.7 shows one way a typical OLAP system might represent the toy data in our example on screen. Note how the data are shown in percentage terms. This simple step makes the data much more meaningful. (Most RDBMS would have to perform several queries and joins just to do that!)[10] For more detail on the sales of Messy Paint Kits in the Northeast region, the user might use the mouse to click on the Messy Paint Kits region of the pie chart on the left.

By the way, looking at the chart, you can probably figure out what is driving sales in the Northeast region. Fully 56% of the items sold are Mr. Snowmans. In fact 78% of the items sold are either Mr. Snowmans or Puppet Maker Kits. Death Avenger Dolls and Messy Paint Kits are not very popular in the Northeast.

Contrast this with the sales in the Southeast where Messy Paint Kits are the number one seller, with a 30% share of the quantity. In contrast, the Mr. Snowmans and Puppet Maker Kits that were so overwhelmingly popular in the Northeast only get about a third of the sales in the Southeast.

If you are a marketing executive for the toy manufacturer, you might try to figure out why Mr. Snowman and Puppet Maker Kits are so popular in the Northeast or, conversely, why Messy Paint Kits and Death Avenger Dolls don't seem to go over very well.

Maybe the demographics of the Northeast region are such that the age levels of the children tend to be lower than in the Southwest and also lower than the minimum suggested age for the Messy Paint Kit. Maybe the Northeast has more religious communities that frown on aggressive toys like the Death Avenger Doll. And so on. This could all have implications for how you market these and other products in the Northeast.

One thing is certain though. You now know what is driving sales in the Northeast.

---

[10]Even if you did that, you have no guarantee that would be how you needed to see the data. The strength of OLAP systems is that they let you try out many different hunches quickly to see which ones seem to pay off.

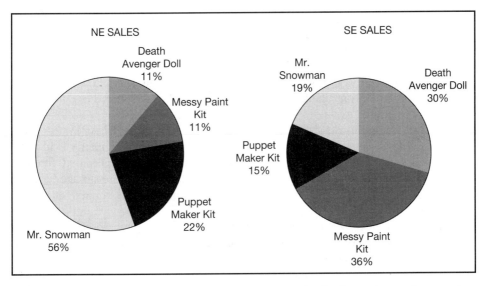

NE SALES

- Death Avenger Doll 11%
- Messy Paint Kit 11%
- Puppet Maker Kit 22%
- Mr. Snowman 56%

SE SALES

- Mr. Snowman 19%
- Death Avenger Doll 30%
- Puppet Maker Kit 15%
- Messy Paint Kit 36%

FIGURE 4.7   An OLAP Interface showing percentage of sales by region and answering the question, "What's driving sales in the NE?"

INTELLIGENCE DENSITY ISSUES

So when is it a good idea to think about an OLAP/data warehouse solution?

Clearly, if you want to be able to look at several different databases at once, combining their contents to make them more easily queried, a data warehouse might be a good idea. Similarly, if you want to give users the ability to quickly slice and dice data, OLAP solutions can be appealing.

Because data warehouses combine data from many different sources, aggregate and scrub the data, they make it much easier to get at the data. In fact, even for standard database queries, some data warehouses experience one to two orders of magnitude increases in performance for queries.

But, as always, there is no free lunch. What data warehousing applications usually give up to get that high performance is the ability to deliver real-time data. As a result, users need to realize that the data they are basing their decisions on may be several hours or days out of date. On the other hand, because the data have been scrubbed, the data may be of higher quality than those in the transaction databases that feed the warehouse. Missing values, nonsense characters, and incorrect data types will often be corrected. These two factors balance each other out to a certain extent, but the user must be aware of the limitations of the data nonetheless.

In general, data warehouses need to be run on special-purpose computers, usually their own mainframe or network server. While this seems like a big price to pay for ease of access in the short term, in the long term, this arrangement will save you a lot of traffic on the transaction processing systems. Recall that most EIS and database reports are run directly against an organization's OLTP systems. This can cause tremendous bottlenecks for those systems, so the cost may be worth it.

Because of the high demand for computing power, developers have put a premium on efficient storage of data. To understand why this is so important, look back to the first matrix we showed in Figure 4.5. Recall how not every cell in every row had a number in it. This made sense since not every customer ordered every item. Imagine if there were 400 products instead of just four. Think about how much space would be wasted storing blank cells if a customer had only ordered one item: The vector dimensioning customer by product would waste 399 cells.

To get around this inefficiency, many data warehousing and OLAP systems create a special kind of hypercube that uses *sparse matrices*. A sparse matrix is like the regular matrix shown in Figure 4.5, except that the empty cells are omitted. In other words, rather than storing blank values in the empty cells, the entire storage location is taken out of the matrix. These unused storage locations can then be used for storing other data.

Figure 4.8 shows what a sparsely populated hypercube might look like conceptually. Notice how the cube still holds its shape and how the vectors' output cells (darker shaded) still contain all of their values. This property allows the data to be used as if they were still stored in a complete hypercube, while at the same time saving a tremendous amount of space. For example, the cube of input cells shown in the figure only requires about 60% of the storage space that would be required for a fully populated matrix representation of the same data.

Conversely, data that are redundant can be eliminated from representations as well. For example, let's say that the price of the Messy Paint Kit was $19.95. Since the price does not change on a daily basis, every record for a Messy Paint Kit purchase during the time when the price is $19.95 will have the exact same entry for the price dimension. Again, imagine how many times $19.95 would occur over the course of a month if 200 toy orders a day come in. This is the converse of the problem above. Rather than records not having data, *every* record has the *same* data. Again this is wasteful. Most data warehouses and OLAP systems that have functionality for dealing with sparse matrices also can deal with this type of redundant data.

These types of innovations can greatly increase the amount of data that OLAP systems and data warehouses can manipulate. Nonetheless, most of these systems cannot approach the data storage and crunching power of OLTP systems specifically designed to work on massive amounts of data. As more dimensions are added and more data imported some systems begin to approach practical data limitations.[11]

It is interesting to note that when we discuss scalability in most places in this text, we are specifically *not* talking about hardware and storage issues, but instead about knowledge engineering issues. However, since data warehouses and OLAP systems are more similar to DBMS than to intelligent DSS systems, in this context scalability shares a comparable meaning with traditional database systems.

---

[11]Many OLAP systems use hierarchical representations for data to achieve sparse matrices. Say you had a dimension called *product line* containing each of your firm's ten product lines. If the company had 100 products total, you would need a 1000 cell hypercube ($10 \times 100 = 1000$). By collapsing the products into the product-line dimension you end up needing only 110 cells ($100 + 10 = 110$). The collapsing is usually done through aggregation. From a practical perspective many OLAP systems try to limit the number of dimensions to about seven or less.

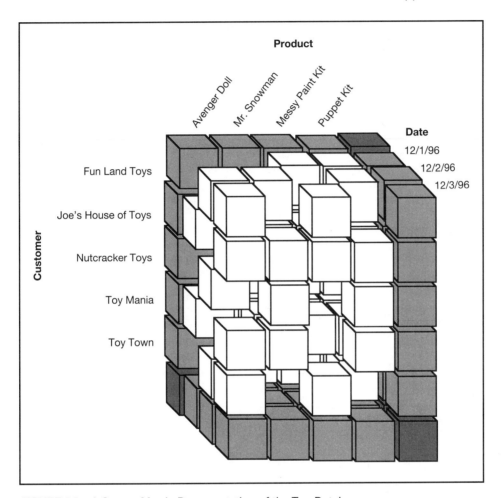

FIGURE 4.8 A Sparse Matrix Representation of the Toy Database

But, as we have discussed, OLAP systems are also quite different than traditional DBMS. Rather than just looking at a static query, users can bend and mold their data search to fit their exact needs. As the data or business changes, the user can respond by changing his line of inquiry or level of detail.

Because OLAP systems give the user this ability to dive into data and drill up or down for more detail, the user can understand the data much better. OLAP systems allow users to make the data speak for themselves. Rather than just getting a summary of the data, a decision maker can also explore why the summary came out the way it did.

Finally, you have to realize that the benefits of OLAP and data warehousing do not come for free. In order to understand which types of data to use and how to organize it, you need to spend time with the people who understand the business. These decision makers will tell you how they plan to use the data in the warehouse and what types of questions they will need answered. The organization itself will have to discover what types of data are available, where they are and what additional data elements might need to be collected to foster good decision making.

This can take some time. Add to this the need to set up an infrastructure to move their transactional systems to a warehouse and the need to configure new hardware and it could take even longer. And don't forget, you have to allocate time for the maintenance and training of support staff for the new systems. Nonetheless, you will still probably experience a great increase over the turnaround time you might expect if you were going to customize an EIS or create special reports for each user's needs.

In summary, OLAP and data warehousing systems stack up as follows:

Dimension	OLAP/Data Warehouse	But . . .
Accuracy	Moderate	Depends on how often data are updated and how well they are scrubbed.
Explainability	Moderate	User navigates through data to find explanation
Response speed	High	—
Scalability	Moderate	Depends on efficiency of data representation, use of sparse matrices, and redundancy reduction
Compactness	Low	—
Flexibility	High	—
Ease of use	High	Needs good OLAP interface
Independence from experts	Moderate	Needs to discuss uses to which data will be put; needs to inventory data
Development speed	Moderate	Depends on complexity of existing infrastructure and business uses of data
Computing resources	High	Tends to reduce traffic on other core business systems

Suggested Reading

Burkan, W. C., *Executive Information Systems from Proposal through Implementation,* Van Nostrand Reinhold, NY, 1991.

Codd, E. F., S. B. Codd, and T. S. Clynch, "Beyond Decision Support," *Computerworld,* July 26, 1993. (Note that there was an important correction to this article published in *Computerworld* on October 11, 1993.)

Date, C. J., *An Introduction to Database Systems,* Addison-Wesley, Reading, MA: 1975.

Date, C. J., *Relational Database Selected Writings,* Addison-Wesley, Reading, MA: 1989.

Inmon, William H., *Building the Data Warehouse,* QED, Wellesley, MA: 1992.

Inmon, William H., *Building the Operational Data Store,* QED, Wellesley, MA: 1996.

Poe, Vidette, *Building a Data Warehouse for Decision Support,* Prentice-Hall, Upper Saddle River, NJ: 1996.

Raden, Neil, "Data, Data, Everywhere," *Information Week,* October 30, 1995.

Ullman, Jeffrey D., *Principles of Database Systems,* Computer Science Press, MD: 1982.

CHAPTER

Evolving Solutions

Genetic Algorithms

I have called this principle, by which each slight variation, if useful,
is preserved, by the term Natural Selection.
—Charles Darwin

You can't always get what you want . . .
but if you try sometimes, you just might find . . .
you get what you need.
—Mick Jagger

The genetic algorithm does implicitly what is infeasible explicitly.
—John Holland

Optimization problems involve finding one or a series of very good (optimal) solutions from among a very large number of possible solutions. For certain problems, powerful algorithms exist for finding these solutions using mathematical techniques. However, in many cases, such as when there are trillions of potential combinations and "poorly behaved" functions involved, mathematical techniques can break down.

A genetic algorithm (GA) solves problems by borrowing a technique from nature. GAs use Darwin's basic principles of survival of the fittest, mutation, and crossbreeding to create solutions for problems. What is particularly appealing about the technique is that it is robust at finding good solutions for a large variety of problems. GAs can be especially attractive since they do not require that you be able to describe how to find a good solution. The approach only requires that you be able to recognize a good solution when you see it. When it does find a good solution, the GA percolates some of that solution's features into a population of competing solutions. Over time, the GA "breeds" good solutions.

We start this chapter with a general discussion of optimization problems and what makes some of these harder to solve than others. We then go on to discuss GAs and show how they can be used effectively to solve optimization problems.

■ **52** ■

INTRODUCTION

In daily conversation, you often talk about doing things "efficiently" or choosing the "best" option. For example, let's say that it's Saturday and you have to run some errands. You'd like to go to the bank to get money, have lunch with a friend, buy a Mother's Day gift for your mother, go to the travel agent to make reservations for your summer vacation, and drop the dog off at the pet groomer. Let's also assume that the different stops you have to make are not all near each other.

Before you set out in the morning, you would probably try to plan out mentally where you were going, and in what order. Your implicit objective would probably be to minimize the time that you spend running around between errands. Nonetheless, you would also have to consider certain realities in your planning.

For instance, no matter how efficient it might be to go first to the restaurant where you will meet your friend for lunch (it is closest), you cannot have lunch at 9:30 in the morning. Likewise, you cannot buy a gift for Mom until you go to the bank to get money. And while you might be *able* to run all of your other errands before dropping Spot at the groomer, do you really *want* to travel all over town with the dog?

The schedule that you choose reflects your assessment of the realities of the situation, your own personal preferences, the amount of time and energy you have to plan, and your opinions as to what is most efficient. Planning your daily schedule is an optimization problem in a microcosm: You know that there *is* an optimal, most efficient solution . . . if only you could find it.

OPTIMIZATION

The basic goal of optimization tasks is to figure out the best mix of components (combination of elements, permutation of activities, set of values, etc.) for solving some problem. "Optimal" is judged based on some pre-determined measure of goodness or fitness given some constraints.

Said another way, optimization is the process of reducing the space of potential problem solutions to one or a few of the best ones. The criterion for the *goodness* or *fitness* of a solution is also a part of the problem, defined by you, and acts as a uniform measure for judging the quality of solutions.

> *Examples:*
> - Provident Investments, a portfolio management firm, wishes to choose portfolios of financial instruments that will offer the highest yields, based on certain risk preferences and subject to various regulatory constraints.
> - Ultima Systems, a computer manufacturer, has many types of computers with many options and peripheral components. The firm wants to automatically generate computer component configuration recommendations based upon user needs and uses.
> - ACME Transport, Inc., a shipping firm, needs to plan a delivery route that will minimize the time and cost of the shipping, but at the same time, make deliveries to all 10 of its overseas clients.

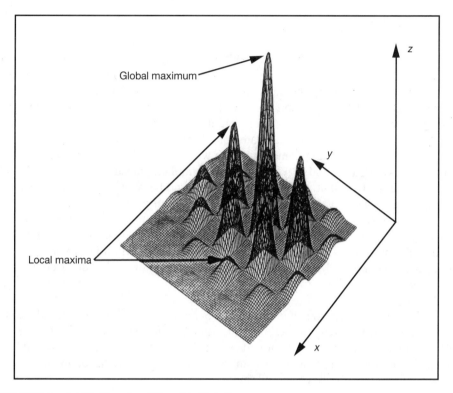

FIGURE 5.1 A Hilly Terrain of Possible Solutions

Optimization problems involve making decisions and formulating plans in situations where you have some sort of resource constraints: time, money, equipment, personnel, etc. The goal of optimization techniques is to try to make the best of such imperfect situations by taking the fullest advantage of what resources, time, etc. you have available.

Using a physical analogy, you can think of an optimization problem space as a hilly terrain like the one shown in Figure 5.1. The valleys of the terrain represent the worst solutions to a problem, and the peaks represent the best. An optimization method seeks to identify the highest peak and climb it in as little time as possible. Good methods need to avoid becoming stranded on top of a small hill or trapped in a deep valley since this would only make it harder to climb to the better peaks.[1]

To put it another way (and further extend our physical example), it might be impossible to explore every inch of every mountain in the Alps to find the highest.

---

[1]This is the general case in which we are trying to find an optimum value for some function or process. In some cases (Chapter 6, for example), it is more convenient to think of the terrain as an "error space" in which we want to minimize error and therefore seek out the valleys where the error is at a minimum rather than the peaks. In practice, it is trivial to convert a maximization problem into a minimization problem and vice versa.

But unless you had a lot of time, it probably wouldn't be a great idea to start in an arbitrary valley and try to explore neighboring peaks one at a time, on the off chance that you would find the highest! Instead, you would be far better off if you got into an airplane and flew over the whole region for a bit, surveying the area. You could then drop down to explore the most promising (highest) looking areas. This is essentially what optimization methods like genetic algorithms seek to do.

For example, consider again ACME Transport, the shipping firm. Let's say the firm had to make shipments to 10 different countries. Clearly, there are many routes that an ACME ship can take to make even a small number of deliveries[2] and some will be better than others in terms of minimizing time and costs. For instance, it makes more sense to go from San Francisco to London to Paris than it does to go from London to San Francisco to Paris since the first route would use much less fuel, time, etc. The better route would be on a higher place in the problem terrain than the second. The goal of the optimization process in this case is to find the route for a ship that best minimizes the time and cost: the optimal route.

You might be asking yourself why you couldn't just try *every* solution and pick the best one?

You might reason as follows, "ACME could just write a little computer program to try all of the routes possible, and just pick the best! They could write the program in a few hours and run it overnight."

Good news . . . you would be right! Such a technique, called an *exhaustive search,* would be guaranteed to find the right solution. (It generates and tests *every possible* solution.) In fact, we would not even have to wait overnight. A very fast computer could solve the problem described above in a few minutes.

The bad news is, if you were to increase the number of countries from 10 to 25, you would have to wait a little longer. Actually, you would have to wait *a lot* longer. Specifically, if you had a very, very fast computer that could construct and evaluate, say, a million routes per second, and you had started the computer computing just around the time that life began on Earth (about 4 billion years ago), then as of today you would have evaluated just under one quarter of 1% of all the possible solutions![3]

Clearly, ACME would not want to take the exhaustive search approach if the firm wanted to deliver any products on time.

The difficulty we have just illustrated is typical of what are known as *NP-complete* problems. *NP* is shorthand for *non-deterministic polynomial.* What the term means is that the time required to solve a problem increases very, very quickly as a

---

[2]If there were 10 customers and one ship, there would be $10! = 3,628,800$ different routes possible.

[3]Because there are $25! = 1.55 \times 10^{25}$ configurations and we can do one million (10^6) evaluations per second, it will take 1.55×10^{19} seconds ($25!/10^6$) to find the solution. Because there are 60 seconds in a minute, 60 minutes in an hour, 24 hours in a day, and 365.25 days in a year, there are $60 \times 60 \times 24 \times 365.25 = 31,557,600$ seconds in a year. In 4 billion years, there are $4 \times 10^9 \times 31,557,600 = 3.15576 \times 10^{16}$ seconds. Because we calculated that it will take 1.55×10^{19} seconds to completely solve the problem, we can calculate the percentage of the problem that we can complete in 4 billion years as $3.15576 \times 10^{16}/1.55 \times 10^{19}$, which is approximately equal to 0.0023 or 0.23%.

function of the number of elements in the problem.[4] In ACME's case this would imply that the time required to solve the problem exhaustively would grow very quickly with the number of deliveries.

What this means more practically is that while such problems are usually manageable for small numbers of elements, they quickly grow intractable if the number of elements gets even slightly large. This, in large part, is why more efficient optimization methods have been developed.

Optimization problems involve three components: a set of problem *variables*, a set of *constraints*, and a set of *objectives*. To explore what each of these means, consider how they apply to ACME.

To solve ACME's problem, you can start by defining a set of problem variables that describes various aspects of the problem. For the shipping firm, a variable might be something like where to send a ship next, which crew and ship would be best for a particular job, or the cost associated with sending a shipment to a particular location. Variables can be numbers, such as the number of products to be placed in the cargo bay of a ship or the time a customer must wait for a delivery. Variables can also be logical, such as the presence or absence of a particular type of storage facility on the ship.

Constraints restrict the allowable values that a variable can have. Each can be composed of expressions involving the variables you define as well as other constant values. For example, you might wish to constrain the number of ports visited by an ACME ship, or the number of tons of cargo it can carry. Here are three constraints that might apply to ACME:

- Shipping costs must be less than 70% of fees charged.
- Customer waiting time must be less than 90 days.
- If a customer does more than $ x of business with ACME then waiting time must be less than 60 days.

Finally, you need objective functions that are used to evaluate the fitness of solutions. Objective functions usually involve the minimization of some type of resource usage (like time, fuel, or money), and/or the minimization of some undesirable effect (risk of lateness, time wasted traveling with an empty cargo bay), and/or the maximization of some benefit, such as profit or efficiency.

The following are possible objective functions for ACME:

- Overall delivery time is minimized.
- Overall profit is maximized.

---

[4]When we talk about a particular problem being *polynomial* or *non-deterministic polynomial* what we mean is that the number of possible combinations to be considered in searching for solutions, and hence the *time* it takes to exhaustively search for a solution, is in *some way* a function of the number of elements that make up a combination in the solution.

The simplest form of such a relationship is a *linear* one. That means that if we doubled the number of elements (customers in our ACME example), we would expect the number of evaluations (and the time) required to find a solution to double as well.

On the other hand, sometimes a *polynomial* relationship exists. This means that the time would grow faster than the number of elements, perhaps growing at a rate proportional to the *square* of the number of elements. In this case, each time we doubled the number of elements, we would increase *by a factor of four* the amount of time it would take to find a solution. Finally, *non-deterministic polynomial* problems exist for which the time required to find solutions exhaustively grows even faster, as in the ACME example.

- Ship fleet wear is minimized.
- Number of repeated country visits is minimized.

The variables, constraints, and objective function used to describe an optimization problem define the basic "geography" of the search space, and determine which techniques might work. The objective function is the metric along which solutions are ranked, and it, in effect, creates the hills and valleys.

For example, in Figure 5.1, there are two variables, so the search space has three dimensions: the values of variable one (x), the values of variable two (y), and the objective function's value (z, the height) for every possible combination of x and y. If we had more than two or three variables, the search space would be harder to visualize, but the idea is the same.

The geography of the search space determines which optimization methods are suitable for solving the problem. If the variables and function that define the landscape are continuous (i.e., the z values in Figure 5.1 don't jump sharply with small changes in the x or y values), the solution space is continuous as in Figure 5.1.

Notice that there are no holes in the landscape and that the landscape is smooth: There are no plateaus, and there are no sharp points. As a result the high points in the landscape are all "continuously approachable." If you're standing at some point in the landscape, you can "see" the slope in every direction from that point, and move incrementally up a hill until the slope levels off and no further improvement is possible. This is what you do with calculus-based methods: Calculate the slope at *every* point in the terrain. Of all these points, the interesting ones are those where the slope is zero. These correspond to the peaks and troughs. The highest peak is the global maximum.[5]

But sometimes the terrain is not continuous. For example, the two-dimensional terrain in Figure 5.2 has "discontinuities." If X and Y represent two products that are being manufactured and sold, then a constraint such as "don't make more than 50 units of X," that is, $X < 50$, is a vertical line that imposes a sharp discontinuity in the space as shown in Figure 5.2: Every solution in the area to the left of the vertical line is legitimate, whereas the area to the right is not.

A constraint such as "don't make more than 75 units of Y" imposes a similar boundary as shown. Finally, if it costs \$A to make one unit of X and \$B to make one unit of Y, the constraint "ensure that the total manufacturing cost doesn't exceed \$5000," that is, $pX + qY < 5000$, represents a line (with slope $-p/q$) which slices off the search space at an angle (the slope) as shown in Figure 5.2.

The shaded region formed by the intersection of the various constraints is called the feasible region. That's where the best solution will be found. If you think about it a little, when X and Y have a positive sales price, the best solution will lie on one of the "extreme points" labeled B, C, D, and E. With more variables, the search space

---

[5]Using calculus, calculating slope requires differentiating the function. The derivative is then set to zero, which tells us where the peaks or troughs are in the landscape. For example, the function $x^3 - 4x^2 + 4x$, when differentiated, is $3x^2 - 8x + 4$. This function gives us the slope of the landscape (for every value of x) corresponding to the original function. Since we're interested in the peaks, we want those x values where the slopes are zero. Solving the equation $3x^2 - 8x + 4 = 0$ yields x=2 and x=2/3. Of these x=2/3 gives the higher value when substituted into the original function. It is the global optimum for this simple function.

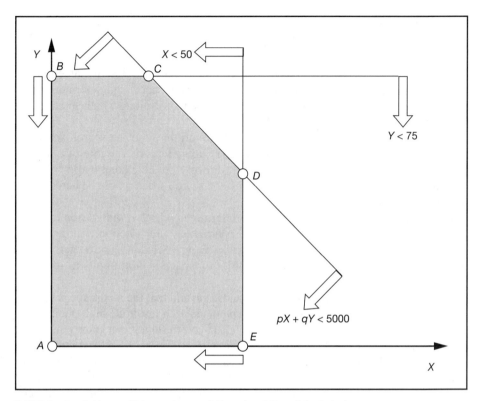

FIGURE 5.2 A Linear "Discontinuous" Terrain of Possible Solutions

becomes harder to visualize, but the idea is the same. The best solution will always lie at one of the extreme points.

Linear programming is the most common technique used for solving such problems. The linear programming algorithm typically begins at the origin (A) and hops from one extreme point to another while the solution keeps improving. As long as the surfaces are linear (that is, the constraints and objective function are linear), this procedure is guaranteed to improve with every hop and find the best extreme point. Linear programming is a very popular technique since many of the problems in the business or scientific world are linear or can be approximated as such.

But some terrains are not only discontinuous, they also have "holes" in them, or areas where solutions do not exist. For example, if there were certain combinations of routes that ACME could not use due to regulatory reasons, these might be discontinuities. Further, the constraints might be non-linear, involving ratios or products. It is hard to navigate such a domain, let alone find the best solution. You don't know the shape of the terrain to start, and once you do start, there's often little or no information about the terrain that helps you figure out in which direction to move once you start searching. These problems can be very tough.

This is where heuristic techniques such as genetic algorithms (GAs) excel. Unlike many mathematical techniques, solution times with GAs are usually highly predictable. Also, solution time is usually not radically affected as the problem gets larger, which is not always so with the more traditional techniques. The formulation of the problem and thus the shape of the terrain can be more flexible: The constraints and the objective function can be non-linear or discontinuous; GAs don't find these problems any more difficult than the linear or continuous problems!

But you don't get something for nothing.

Heuristic techniques *cannot guarantee* optimal solutions. Users must often settle for "near optimal" solutions. These solutions, while usually not perfect, can suffice for a broad range of problems. So, for example, using a heuristic optimization method, ACME might not get the "perfect" schedule (the absolute shortest route). Nonetheless, the schedules the firm *does* get will probably be very good and ACME will get them quickly.

Thus there is a constant tug-of-war going on between the degree of optimality achievable by using a particular technique (heuristic or numerical) and the operational advantages and disadvantages of that technique.

Genetic algorithms are simple yet powerful optimization programs. Like neural networks, genetic algorithms have their basis in biological theory. Whereas neural nets take their foundations from neuroscience, GAs adapt the evolutionary concept of survival of the fittest as their basis.

GAs were originally developed by computer scientist John Holland in the 1970s. Holland developed GAs as experiments to see if computer programs could evolve in a Darwinian sense. It turns out, though, that GAs are also very useful for solving classes of problems that were previously computationally prohibitive. GAs have had especially good success in the area of optimization. What is most surprising is that GAs achieve such power while using only a few simple operations.

To understand the fundamentals of GAs, we turn to the basis for the genetic algorithm: natural selection. In nature organisms have to solve a very simple problem: survival. Those organisms that solve the problem will flourish, and those that don't won't.

Imagine that there is a primitive evolving organism fighting for survival. We'll call this beast a *krome*. The krome is constantly competing with many other kromes for the same feeding grounds and to evade the same predators. There are two types of kromes, black kromes and white kromes, which have varying degrees of intelligence and physical prowess. Lastly, kromes, like their predators, feed only at night.

Different kromes will survive based on the compatibility of their attributes with their environment. Since kromes are hunted by their predators at night, we would expect the dark-colored ones to have an advantage. The same is true of kromes that are smart and can run fast. In fact, we can create a table of possible krome attributes, and rank each combination of attributes (Figure 5.3). Each type of krome represents one solution to the "survival" problem.

Genetic algorithms also use a ranking process. GAs start by creating an initial, usually random set of guesses about how to solve a particular optimization problem. The GA then ranks each of these solutions by how well it solves the problem. The GA removes solutions that do not seem to solve the problem well ("bad" solutions) from the population. In their place, the GA creates new solutions, made by combining bits and pieces of the "good" solutions. Occasionally, a GA will make a random change to one of the solutions, trying out something totally new to see if the solution can be improved upon. This process is repeated many times until a very good solution has been found.

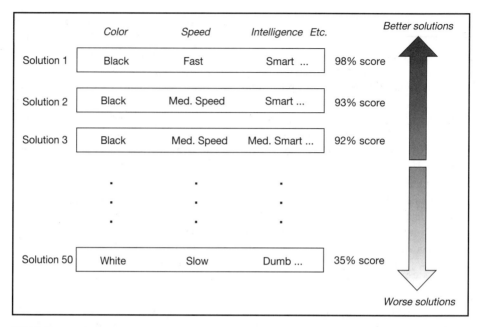

FIGURE 5.3   A Range of Nature's Solutions to the Kromes' Survival Problem

For example, if you were trying to balance a portfolio of stocks, like Provident, you might create a whole set of random portfolios, and then let each portfolio evolve. At the end of the process, you could select the best (the "king of the jungle" in Portfolio Land) and base your actual portfolio selection on it. On the other hand, to solve a problem like ACME Transport's, you could create a whole set of random shipping routes and let them evolve, choosing the best route when the GA finished.

A genetic algorithm experiments with new solutions while preserving potentially valuable interim results. If an experimental solution is not successful, it will be ranked poorly and, in all likelihood, it will be discarded. On the other hand, if the experimental solution is good, it will be ranked more highly, and its attributes will be carried into the next "generation" for further refinement. Thus the GA keeps the "best" parts of solutions, and discards the less useful parts. Genetic algorithms are able to search potentially huge and even discontinuous problem spaces efficiently by using this approach.

THE ABCs OF GENETIC ALGORITHMS

So how do GAs work?

The smallest unit of a GA is called a *gene*. A gene represents a unit of information in your problem domain. For example, if you were trying to balance a portfolio of stocks for Provident Investments, the unit might be the percentage of the portfolio given over to a particular stock; for ACME, the basic unit might be the name of a city in its delivery list.

A series of these genes, or a *chromosome,* represents one possible complete solution to the problem.

Examples

For the portfolio problem, a chromosome might look like

```
3% 5% 7% 2% 15% . . . 0% 3%.
```

Interpretation/decoding: "Buy 3% of Stock A, 5% of Stock B, . . . etc."
For a routing problem a chromosome might look like:

```
New York - London - Paris . . . - LA.
```

Interpretation/decoding: "Start in New York, proceed to London, then to Paris . . . etc."

The key to GA's power is that the chromosome itself does not do much of the work in *guiding* a GA to a good solution. It can't. The chromosome itself doesn't even *understand* the problem! Not specifically, anyway. The chromosome does not "understand" the problem in the sense that *it doesn't know the meaning it carries.*

In order to make use of a chromosome, the GA, therefore, needs to *decode* it and determine how good a chromosome's solution is for a particular problem. The GA makes use of a special program module that does understand what a good solution to the problem looks like. This module is called a *decoder.* The decoder converts the chromosome into a solution to the problem. The decoder for ACME's problem, for instance, knows how to convert a chromosome into a shipping route.

Once decoded, another module called the *fitness function* determines which chromosome solutions are good and which are not very good. (Remember the objective function from our discussion of optimization? The fitness function does the same thing.) These two components, decoder and fitness function, are the only parts of the GA that actually understand the problem domain.

What this means is that you can change how you rank different solutions to the same problem by keeping the same decoder, but changing how the fitness function evaluates the solutions. Even more impressive is that you can use the same GA to solve many different problems just by changing the decoder and fitness function. Figure 5.4 shows the different modules of the GA.

There are many ways to represent and code chromosomes, but to make things easier to understand in this chapter, we will use a very simple coding for most of our discussions. The simplest (and most commonly used) chromosome coding uses single bits (1s or 0s) to represent each gene. For the bulk of our discussions, we will use chromosomes that take the form of

```
1 1 0 1 0 1
```

in order to describe solutions.

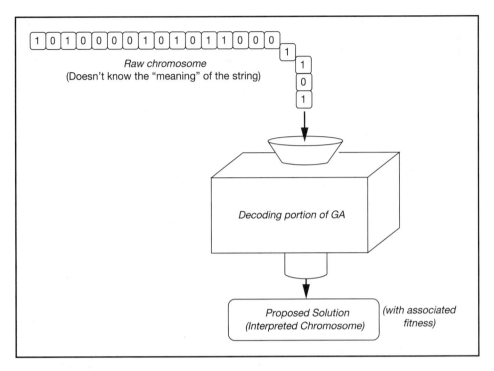

FIGURE 5.4 Decoding a Chromosome

We do this for two reasons. First, these codings are simple to analyze, explain, and understand. Second, and equally important, this simple coding format is robust enough to solve a wide variety of very different problems.

Just to get familiar with the idea of encoding and decoding, consider how the krome problem might be coded in a string of ones and zeros like the one on the previous page.

In our example, shown in Figure 5.5, a krome's color is encoded with one gene and can take on one of two values, *black* or *white*. Speed is encoded with two genes and can take on one of the four values of speed. Finally, intelligence can be coded with three genes. Using this scheme, the chromosome on the right of Figure 5.5, 1 1 0 1 0 1, would represent a white, slow, and dumb krome.

Now consider a couple of *very* different business problems shown in the following box.[6] We can solve both using our simple genetic algorithm. Note how we don't need to change the GA, we only change the way in which we interpret the *meaning* of each chromosome and how we evaluate its fitness. In this example, we consider a chromosome consisting of 20 genes, each coded as a single bit (0 or 1).

---

[6]We present two very simple examples for illustrative purposes. In actual practice, the usefulness of GAs over other methods of optimization for solving these problems would depend greatly on the problem's specific details.

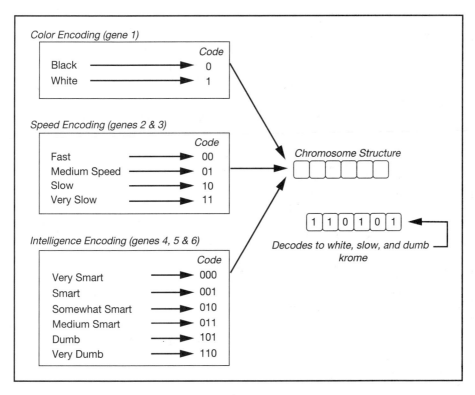

FIGURE 5.5   Coding and Decoding Binary Chromosomes

In the simplified example in the accompanying box on the next page, only the *interpretation* of the chromosome's representation changes. As Figure 5.6 shows, the same chromosome is decoded differently by the GA, but only the interpretational mechanism varies. In the first case, the chromosome represents a rule for predicting the S&P 500. In the second, it represents the percentage of employees on the night shift for a chemical manufacturer.

But remember that GAs do not only use a single chromosome. A GA creates an initial *population* of chromosomes (Figure 5.7). Each chromosome is different. By creating a diverse population instead of a single solution, the GA is trying many solutions at once. After an initial random population is set up, the GA begins an iterative process of *refining* the initial solutions so that the better ones (those with higher fitness) are more likely to become the top solution.

The GA experiments with new solutions by combining and refining the information in the chromosomes using three operations: *selection, crossover,* and *mutation.* These operations produce in new chromosomes which form a new population. Each new population is called a *generation.*

During *selection,* the GA chooses "fitter" solutions to remain and multiply in the population, but eliminates the poorer ones. During *crossover* the GA takes useful information about good solutions and *shares* it among other chromosomes. During *mutation* the GA tweaks solutions slightly in an attempt to improve them.

PROBLEM 1: Variable Selection

Find the best subset of 20 variables to predict the stock market. That is, we want to know which variables we should use as inputs to a neural network model for example, in order to predict the S&P 500 a week into the future.

PROBLEM 2: Production Levels

Find the optimal percentage of employees a chemical manufacturer should have on the night shift of a particular factory in order to maximize profit given a variety of other factors such as overtime, electrical costs, demand, and so forth.

The profit of a given level of production at day or night is hard to optimize since it increases and decreases many times as the number of night workers moves from zero to 100% of the total workers, and as different combinations of employees are used on each shift. This profit behavior is described by a very complex and poorly behaved (nonlinear, discontinuous) equation, $f(x)$ where x is the number of employees on the night shift.

PROBLEM 1: Solution

Decode/Interpret

1. Interpret each bit position as the presence (1) or absence (0) of one of the 20 variables. (Example: If bit 3 were 1, we would interpret that as meaning "include variable 3.")

2. Construct a neural network that uses as input the variables indicated as present in the chromosome.

3. Train the neural network for some prescribed period. Neural networks are discussed in Chapter 6.

Evaluate

4. Evaluate the performance of the neural network based on predetermined performance measures of prediction accuracy against the S&P 500.

5. The fitness of the chromosome is proportional to performance.

PROBLEM 2: Solution

Decode/Interpret

1. Convert the chromosome into an integer x by interpreting it as a 20-bit-long binary number (i.e., a number between 0 and $2^{20} - 1$).

2. Divide x by the largest possible x value, $2^{20} - 1$, to get a number between 0 and 1.0. Call this number *percentOnShift*.

Evaluate

3. Evaluate the value of *f(percentOnShift)*.

4. The fitness of the chromosome is proportional to the value of *f(percentOnShift)*.

As the GA progresses into later generations, you expect to see the average fitness of the population grow. The fitness increases as each new generation combines the traits of the chromosomes in the previous generation, eliminating those chromosomes that do poorly. That is, you expect that the solutions will get better toward the end of the GA's run.

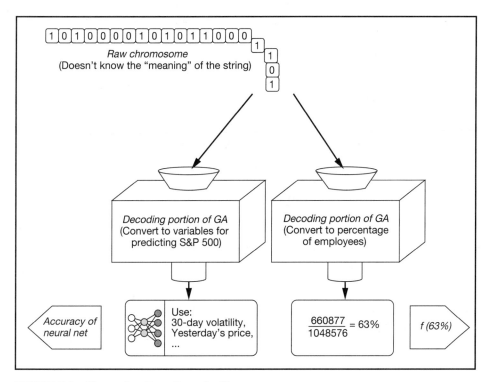

FIGURE 5.6   Alternative Decoding of a Chromosome

								Color	Speed	Intelligence	Fitness
1	0	1	1	0	1		1	White	Medium	Dumb	40
0	1	0	1	0	1		2	Black	Slow	Dumb	43
1	1	0	1	1	0		3	White	Slow	Very Dumb	22
0	0	0	1	0	1		4	Black	Fast	Dumb	71
1	0	1	0	0	0		5	White	Medium	Very Smart	53

A population of
chromosomes   **Decoding of**   **Evaluation of**
                              chromosomes   **chromosomes**

FIGURE 5.7   The Components of a GA

If you envision the problem domain as a vast search-space with many hills and valleys representing areas of good and bad solutions as in Figure 5.1, a GA allows you to search many of these areas at once. Figure 5.8 shows the three-dimensional landscape with a population of solutions. If this landscape were a graph of the survival space for kromes, each point on the *x* and *y* axes would represent one combination of two possible krome characteristics. On the other hand, if this were a graph of the solution space of the portfolio balancing problem, each point on the *x* and *y* axes would represent a different series of weights for the stocks in the portfolio.

The hills represent better solutions, and the valleys represent poorer ones. It would be impossible to *visualize* the complete problem space for the kromes since there are many more dimensions involved than we can show visually. But the idea is the same.

The graph in Figure 5.8a shows the solutions in generation 0. Each dot represents a chromosome or solution to the problem. In this first generation, the GA basically generates some random solutions as a starting point. This is the initial population. At generation 20 (Figure 5.8b), however, we see that more of the solutions are hovering around the peaks. There has been a clustering around some of the local maxima. This is because the GA has discovered that these areas of the search space hold more promise, and the chromosomes are concentrating on the peaks. Finally, in generation 50 (Figure 5.8c), we see that the population has, for the most part, converged around the global maximum (the biggest peak). Nonetheless, note that there are still instances of low-fitness chromosomes in the population. This is because the GA is still experimenting with new solutions.

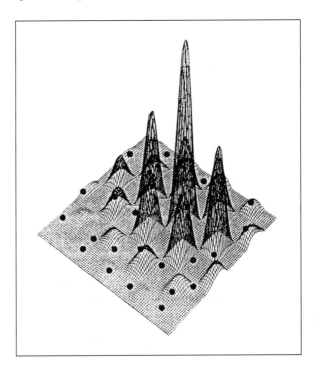

FIGURE 5.8a Population at Generation 0

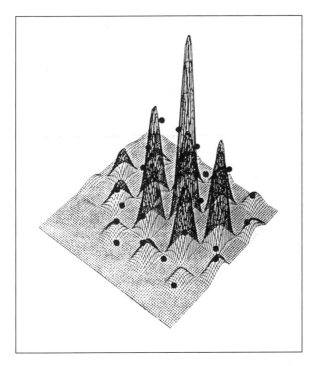

FIGURE 5.8b   Population at Generation 20

FIGURE 5.8c   Population at Generation 50

How do the poorer solutions get weeded out and how do better solutions get refined and improved?

The operation of *selection* determines which chromosomes will be carried on to later generations. Selection is the process in which chromosomes are chosen to survive. A chromosome that is not chosen "dies" and is not able to pass on its traits to the next generation.

A common form of selection is one where each chromosome's likelihood of being picked is proportional to its fitness. This type of selection is called *fitness proportional* selection. Thus, if chromosome A is twice as fit as chromosome B, it should have twice the chance of reproducing.

One way to think about this is to imagine that when the GA selects a chromosome to reproduce, it selects it by spinning a roulette wheel on which each chromosome has a slot. The size of the slot is proportional to its fitness. Figure 5.9 shows the five kromes (from Figure 5.5), each with a slot on the roulette wheel. Chromosomes with high fitness take up more space on the wheel, and therefore have a higher likelihood of being chosen on each spin.

In Figure 5.8a we pointed out that there were a good number of solutions in the "valleys" of the solution space. These represent low-fitness solutions. In ACME's routing case, these might have been routes like:

```
New York - London - Boston - Paris - LA . . .
```

Not very efficient: a zigzag transoceanic route.

When these chromosomes were evaluated, they had low-fitness values, and thus got small slots on the roulette wheel. They didn't get picked to reproduce too often. By generation 5, most of them have gone the way of slow dumb white kromes: They've been dropped from the population.

Selection explains how bad solutions are weeded out, but it doesn't explain how good solutions are improved. The refining process takes place as a result of two additional operators. The first of these, *crossover,* involves the exchange of information between two selected chromosomes.

During crossover, two chromosomes basically swap some of their information gene for gene. In the example shown in Figure 5.10, the two chromosomes exchange genes (crossover) after gene 2. Crossover allows the combination of the elements within one solution with those of another. This allows the GA to "share the wealth"

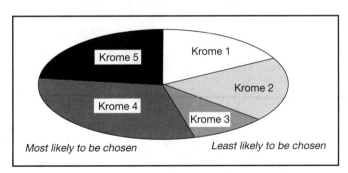

FIGURE 5.9   Roulette Selection of Chromosomes from a Population

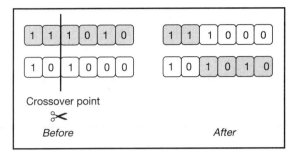

FIGURE 5.10 How Crossover Works

(or "spread the misery," depending on whether a solution swaps components that are good or bad). In our krome example, a "good" crossover might be one in which a smart krome crosses over with a fast krome. Their "offspring" is likely to be a smart fast krome who is fitter than either parent.

An important point to consider, though, is that crossover can only rearrange information that is already in the population. For instance, if our initial krome population did not contain any black kromes, then no matter how many genes we swapped, we would still never get a black krome! (Each pair of chromosomes would just be trading the value "white" over and over again.)

To get around this problem, we need a way to inject new traits into a GA population. The other refining operator, *mutation,* does just this. The mutation operator changes the value of a gene from its current setting to a different one. In the example below (Figure 5.11), the fifth gene from the left has been mutated. A GA can use mutation to experiment with components of new solutions that may not have existed in the current population by introducing new traits into the population. As in the biological case, most mutations are more destructive than helpful. As a result, in GAs, as in nature, mutation occurs very infrequently and randomly. However, occasionally a highly beneficial change will occur. The effect of mutation is that it provides opportunities for members of the GA population to jump from one area of the solution space to another, thus exploring new areas in search of better solutions.

These three operators, selection, crossover, and mutation, act to refine solutions to problems very quickly. When combined with the decoding/evaluation module, GAs can solve a very wide variety of problems.

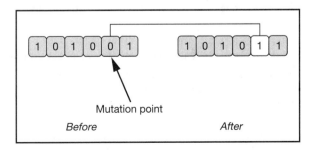

FIGURE 5.11 How Mutation Works

To solve a typical problem, a GA creates chromosome population of a particular size randomly. The GA then evaluates each chromosome in this population and assigns a fitness to it. Selection, mutation, and crossover then take over, weeding out and refining solutions. The whole process is then repeated over and over until a satisfactory solution is found. It is often surprising to some people that this simple decode, evaluate, select, crossover, mutate cycle, repeated over and over, is such a powerful optimization technique.

But this general approach is not new. It has been around for about 4 billion years.

INTELLIGENCE DENSITY ISSUES

So when is it a good idea to use a GA?

In general, if you are working on a problem that lends itself well to standard optimization techniques (the problem is well behaved) it is best to use them. On the other hand, when you find yourself in a situation where these mathematical methods break down or are painfully difficult to use, a GA is often a good heuristic method.

The applicability of a GA versus another heuristic method, such as a rule-based system or other heuristic methods, will depend on the nature of the problem, and which of the intelligence density determinants are important. Very often a GA can simplify the work required to solve a problem. In addition, you may wish to use a GA even when there are mathematical methods available or even where you discover special tricks that work well for a particular problem. A GA can sometimes provide a more flexible or more stable solution, even though it may take longer on average to solve problems. Because GAs scour the problem terrain very efficiently, their response time, even for complicated problems, is usually fairly quick and stable.

GAs form populations of solutions. Just the fact that the GA does this gives a hint as to why GAs stack up well in terms of response time. By creating an array of solutions, the GA is metaphorically stretching itself across the solution space in many different directions at once. GAs try lots of solutions *at the same time.*

But if this were all a GA did, it would be similar to a random search and not much more powerful. In fact, the response time of the random search approach can be very unreliable. Haphazardly wandering through the solution space, a random search might stumble on a good solution quickly in some cases, but drift about aimlessly for a much longer time in others. To get such high marks on response time, the GA's multi pronged search effort needs to be augmented by something else.

It is.

Enter selection, crossover, and mutation. What these operations mean to a GA is that it can quickly "distill" out the essential elements of a problem and its solution, concentrating on the areas that have the biggest payoff. Recall what is going on here: A GA is able to (1) try many solutions at once; (2) evaluate each of the solutions; and (3) refine the better ones. To accomplish this refinement, GAs *share* information between the different solutions (crossover) and experiment with new solutions (mutation). By experimenting with a range of solutions, the GA, early on, can determine the areas of the entire solution space that seem most promising and explore them in more detail. The GA accomplishes this distillation through the interplay of the three operators.

To understand why zeroing in on a solution tends to be efficient and take a predictable amount of time, consider the following. Since a GA always follows the same steps, the amount of time it will take to find a solution will depend only on the number of chromosomes in the population and the number of generations you run. If you know about how long it takes to evaluate the fitness of a single chromosome,[7] then you know that it will take that time, multiplied by the number of chromosomes in a single generation, multiplied by the number of generations. It will take approximately this amount of time *any time you run the GA* for that number of chromosomes and generations since it will always involve evaluating exactly the same number of chromosomes.

It gets even better. Since every population is full of *possible* solutions, you are usually guaranteed to find at least *some* kind of solution when the GA terminates. In fact the solution will often be a very good one.

But how do GAs manage to *consistently* find such good solutions?

In an attempt to explain how GAs search, Holland developed *schema theory.* The crux of schema theory is that each chromosome in a GA, while only representing a single possible solution, actually gives the GA information about *many* areas of the search space at once. What this means is that a GA only needs to evaluate a small number of chromosomes to get information about large areas of the search space.

Consider the chromosome representing the white, medium fast, very smart krome:

```
1 0 1 0 0 0
```

While this chromosome only represents a single solution, there is bonus information in the evaluation of the chromosome. In addition to its own fitness, the chromosome is also giving the GA information about *many other* possible chromosomes. How?

Holland proposed a concept called a *schema* which works as follows. A schema has the same length as a chromosome. However, each gene in the schema can take on the value of (in the case of a binary representation) 0, 1, or a special value, *, where * means "don't care." Consider the example below:

ACTUAL CHROMOSOME:
white, medium fast, very smart krome: 1 0 1 0 0 0

SAMPLE SCHEMA:
All white kromes: 1 * * * * *
All medium fast kromes: * 0 1 * * *
All very smart kromes: * * * 0 0 0
All white very smart kromes: 1 * * 0 0 0

All medium fast or very fast kromes   * 0 * * * *

---

[7]As we will discuss later, this can be where most of a GA's time is spent.

The 1 in position 1 of the first schema means "white chrome"; it represents *all* white kromes—slow, fast, dumb, smart, or otherwise. Likewise, the second schema represents all medium fast kromes, and the third schema represents all very smart kromes without regard to their other attributes.

The five schemata above are represented by our chromosome because in each of the above schema the values in the non- "don't care" (*) positions in the template match the value in the chromosome. In fact, since for any chromosome, each of the six positions on a template can take on one of two values (either the corresponding value in the chromosome or *) there are $2^6 = 64$ different schema being sampled by each chromosome. In a sense, like the GA itself, each *chromosome* in a GA also spreads its tentacles across many dimensions of the search space.

Looking at it the other way, a single schema can also be matched not only by the current chromosome, but by many other possible chromosomes in the population. Since all of this matching goes on simultaneously, we say that it takes place in parallel. This property of the GA is sometimes referred to as *implicit parallelism*. It is implicit because we get it without even trying!

There's another thing about schema theory that illustrates why GAs explore the solution space quickly and efficiently.

Note that the third template has "don't care" symbols for all positions except 4, 5, and 6 (for which the values are all 0). What this says is: "This schema votes that the gene positions 4, 5, and 6 should be 0s in the optimal solution." If bits 4, 5, and 6 in the actual optimal solution are, in fact, set to zero, then we would expect that, all things being equal, chromosomes that match this schema (very smart kromes) would, on average, be ranked higher (their votes would count for more) than those that do not since their fitness will be higher than solutions that don't match that pattern. If on the other hand this pattern did not represent part of a good solution, we would expect matching chromosomes to be ranked lower.[8]

But keep in mind that in addition to testing the validity of the one schema that we just discussed, the GA is also using this chromosome to test the validity of each of the other 63 schemata represented by the chromosome in exactly the same manner. The GA, without any special overhead, keeps track of how well different schemata perform simply by selecting the chromosomes that perform best. (What this really means is that high-fitness chromosomes match the high-fitness schema). Over many generations, chromosomes sharing the traits of high-fitness schemata should proliferate.

But there is no free lunch. Part of the price we pay for the quick convergence and stable response time is lower levels of optimality in our results.

Looking back to Figure 5.8c, notice that the solutions are scattered about the peaks. In most cases, *none* of the solutions will hit the top of the peak exactly. This is because the GA is only good at finding high-fitness *regions*. In other words, the GA is

---

[8]Actually, this would depend on the "deceptiveness" of the problem. Deceptiveness describes to what degree high-fitness interim solutions will lead to the ultimate optimal solution. If the good interim solutions resemble the final solution, then the problem is considered to have low levels of deception. However, if the optimum solution is very far away from the high-fitness interim solutions, then a problem is considered to be highly deceptive.

Note that in the case of finding the correct combination for a lock, for example, there is only one solution that will satisfy the problem. Every other solution, even those that have all but one digit correct, are wrong. Furthermore, there is no information in the "wrong" solution to tell a GA how far away the wrong guess is from the right one, or how much better one wrong guess is than another.

very good at identifying schema that result in high-fitness solutions. However, you need to realize also that while a GA can identify the schema that perform well, out of all of the millions, billions, or trillions of chromosomes that can relate to each schema *there is only one[9] chromosome* that is the best solution to a problem. It is exceedingly difficult to happen on that one optimal chromosome during a GA's execution.

To think of it another way, humans have evolved to higher and higher levels of physical and mental ability. Despite this fact, it is almost unimaginable to hope that any population of humans would yield a member with the raw intellect of an Einstein, the humanity of a Mother Teresa, *and* the agility of a Michael Jordan. Since GAs essentially mimic the evolutionary process, we must accept the fact that the solutions we get, like the humans in the world, will also generally be sub-optimal. (Most humans still have weak lower backs, a sign of sub-optimal engineering, and, unless it's been removed, most of us have an organ in our bodies called an appendix that seems to serve no purpose, a sign of wasted resources.)

A good sub-optimal solution does not mean that the model is a failure. Quite the contrary. For many problems, near optimal solutions are good enough. This is as true in natural evolution as it is in a GA.

In addition, a common observation of GA users is that GAs produce very novel solutions. Since at the end of a GA run, you have an entire population of alternative solutions, users can often look at an array of good options. There are frequently one or two, "Wow! I never would have thought of that one!" solutions in each population.

This is partly due to an attractive feature of the interplay between fitness functions and GAs. You never tell the GA *how* to solve a problem. For example, in our portfolio example above, we do not provide the GA with a theoretical framework or rules for selecting good combinations of stocks. We only give it a decoder and a fitness function that provide feedback as to how good a particular portfolio is and how well the GA is doing at finding a solution. As a result the GA will try almost anything, sometimes with surprising results.

What this means is that *you can use a GA to solve problems that you don't even know how to solve!* All you need to be able to do is describe a good solution and provide a fitness function that can rate a given chromosome. In essence you can say to the GA, "I don't know how to build it, but I'll know it when I see it!"

Since you only need to be able to describe a good solution, not define how to get there, GAs require low levels of access to experts. In cases where you can describe easily the process of optimization, an expert system might be a good choice. But GAs can be useful when you can only describe the quality of the *result*. For this reason, GAs can be attractive when compared to expert systems in that they often do not require as much explicit knowledge about *how* to find an answer to a problem. GAs only need to know how to *measure* the goodness of a solution (through a fitness function).

Even when you can describe the rules and steps that you would use to solve an optimization problem, there are cases where it still could make sense to think about using a GA. For example, while the rules describing a certain optimization process might be common sense, there might be *hundreds* of them to encode. Or the rules might be very dynamic, changing depending on the particular situation. There might be lots of exceptions to the rules that make it difficult to determine how to optimize

---

[9]Or in some cases, this may be a relatively small number.

some process. In all of these situations, a GA can offer an alternative approach to solving the problem.

By concentrating on the definition of a solution (defining the fitness function) rather than on the process of formulating a solution, you can limit the drain on an organization's expert staff considerably.

All this can also be a drawback, however, because GAs are themselves blind to the optimization process, it is difficult to determine why a GA produces a particular solution. In fact, the level of explainability associated with genetic algorithms is almost nil because the GA uses only the fitness function to guide it toward a better solution. Selection only looks at the fitness value for each chromosome without knowing what the fitness means. Crossover and mutation work blindly on chromosomes, and they work the same way regardless of what the 1s and 0s mean to the decoder and fitness function.

Since the only thing that ties a GA to a particular problem is the manner in which the GA's chromosomes are decoded and their fitness evaluated, to change what the GA tries to optimize, you only need to change the way in which the GA decodes and evaluates chromosomes. This is true not only when switching between different problems, but it is also true when modifying the conditions of a single problem. A GA has high levels of flexibility.

For example, let's say that in the night-shift problem earlier we hypothetically determined that we needed to ensure that the night-shift levels were always above 30% due to capacity issues. To accommodate this new constraint, we would need only to adjust the scaling of our decoder so that it produced values between 0.3 and 1.0 instead of 0 and 1.0.

Since so much of the GA's activity centers around the fitness function, many things such as accuracy, scalability, and response time will depend on how the fitness function works and therefore be problem specific.

For example, GAs tend to be moderately scalable. By adjusting the length of the chromosome to 30 instead of 20, we can easily expand the variable selection problem to one in which we examine 30 variables at a time. In fact, we are often able to scale up quite nicely in this manner. However, this scalability is not without its limits. It becomes more difficult for a GA to explore search spaces with very large chromosomes for a variety of reasons. The longer the chromosome, the larger the population needs to be since there are more potential combinations of genes.

This is only part of the story however. For many problems, the evaluation of the fitness function takes much longer than the other generic GA operations of crossover, mutation, and selection. This means that as you increase the size of the population or length of the chromosomes to be decoded and evaluated, the time required to execute a GA will be dominated by the large number of decodings and fitness evaluations, and *not* by the GA operations.

In addition, the computer power required to evaluate the longer chromosomes will also increase as the chromosome gets longer, since the fitness function will have more decoding to do. In fact, the amount of computer time and memory required to execute a GA will depend almost entirely on the complexity of the fitness function. This has obvious consequences with respect to the speed of response time as well. Fitness functions that require a large number of calculations or that run other programs or access databases can be computationally intensive and as a result, higher speed or parallel computers are often called for. On the other hand, many complex but not computationally involved problems can be solved on a good, high powered desk top PC.

On a PC?

That's right. GAs don't do very complicated things from an algorithmic perspective. Rather, their power comes from their relative simplicity. In fact, if programmed from scratch, GAs are usually reasonably sized programs that are self-contained. This is very convenient. It makes a GA a very compact optimizer relative to, say, an expert system.

In addition, GAs tend to be embeddable. Depending on the problem being solved, the elegance of a GA can vary greatly, but because of its relative simplicity, it is usually possible to easily include a GA program as a module in other systems. This all depends on what the fitness function is doing in terms of accessing other programs or databases.

Matters get more complicated when you try to assess the data requirements of a genetic algorithm. In general GAs are convenient since they do not require extensive databases to run. However, for certain GA applications, the fitness function may need to access and process an organization's data. For these types of applications, data quality and quantity are important.

What about the people in your organization who might be involved if you were going to develop a GA-based solution? Well, from a development standpoint, you would be concerned about time commitments. Good news! The algorithms themselves are straightforward. A good programmer can develop an experimental GA in a couple of days. Most of the work is in understanding the problem and formulating appropriately, and determining a good fitness function.

But what makes GAs so attractive to lay people is how easy it is to understand the basic workings of the method. Everyone has had high school biology. Everyone knows who Darwin was. "Survival of the fittest" is a phrase used over and over in fields from finance to football. The method works. It makes sense. People tend to like that.

In summary, the profile of a GA looks like this:

Dimension	Genetic Algorithm	But . . .
Accuracy	Low to high	—
Explainability	Low to moderate	—
Response speed	Moderate to high	Varies with respect to complexity of problem
		Performance may be poorer than other methods on "easy" problems
Scalability	Moderate	Bounded by length of chromosome and computing resources available
Compactness	Moderate	—
Flexibility	High	Depends largely on how the fitness function is designed
Embeddability	High	Highly problem and software dependent
Ease of use	Moderate	—
Development speed	Moderate to high	—

Suggested Reading

Belew, R. and L. Booker, ed., *Genetic Algorithms: Proceedings of the Fourth International Conference,* Morgan Kaufmann, San Diego, CA: 1991.

Davis, L., ed., *Handbook of Genetic Algorithms,* Van Nostrand Reinhold, NY: 1991.

Goldberg, D. E., *Genetic Algorithms in Search, Optimization, and Machine Learning,* Addison-Wesley, NY: 1989.

Holland, J. H., "Genetic Algorithms," *Scientific American,* July 1992, pp 66–72.

Holland, J. H., *Adaptation in Natural and Artificial Systems,* MIT Press, Cambridge, MA: 1992.

Simulating the Brain to Solve Problems

Neural Networks

Put the problems before him and let him solve them himself. Let him know nothing because you have told him, but because he has learned it for himself. Let him not be taught science, let him discover it.
—Rousseau

Learning preserves the errors of the past, as well as its wisdom.
—Alfred North Whitehead

The idea of parallel distributed processing. . . [is that] intelligence emerges from the interactions of large numbers of simple processing units.
—David Rumelhart, *et al.*

An artificial neural network (ANN) builds models by using a simple computer emulation of biological neural systems. Neural networks attempt to "learn" patterns from data directly, by sifting the data repeatedly, searching for relationships, automatically building models, and correcting over and over again the model's own mistakes. The technique can derive good models even when the data are incomplete or noisy.

In this chapter, we discuss how neural networks do this, and the factors that can determine whether a neural network approach will be an effective solution for a particular problem.

INTRODUCTION

Suppose you're running a software development group. One of the things you need to do is estimate how long a certain project is going to take to complete. But software development is tricky since projects are very sensitive to things like the complexity of the logic involved, the user interface, hardware, programmer quality, and so on.

You're an expert, though. You understand the process and know pretty well how various factors affect the quality of your product.

But that wasn't always the case. There were plenty of earlier less than satisfactory attempts when your firm first started developing new software. Over time, you "homed in" on the right staff, and learned to adjust your deliverables depending on the time allotted. And now, your expertise even allows you to do a pretty good job with new types of projects that you have never tried before.

What happened during your "learning" phase? Essentially, you learned about the different things that can affect the quality of a project. You tried to deliver software under different sets of conditions. What you learned was not only that certain combinations of inputs give you a certain result, but more importantly, how the various inputs *interact*. In understanding these interactions, what you developed was essentially a mental model for producing good projects. In other words, you *generalized* the data into a model that you can now use to deal with inputs you've never dealt with before.

What do *data, generalization,* and *model* have to do with learning how to estimate software deadlines and quality?

Let's make the example more concrete. Let's say that you only consider the size of the project[1] and the time that you try to develop it in. Over the years, you tried various values of each of these and observed the quality of your result. Quality would be based on cost and time. Each attempt provides a data point.

But a data point only tells you about what happened with a particular single project. This is only useful if you need to repeat the exact same project under the exact same conditions again. One or two data points are not enough to really understand how the process works.

When you have enough data points, though, you can begin to see the more general "shape" of the space. Figure 6.1 shows what this shape might start to look like after experimenting with about a hundred different projects of different sizes and with various deadlines. The height of the bar indicates the quality of the finished product in each case.

If you were to take a sheet of rubber and drape it over Figure 6.1, you would get a *continuous* surface as shown in Figure 6.2.

This rubber surface is, in effect, a model. It is a generalization. Most parts of the rubber don't touch any of the data points. But the surface can now be used to handle inputs that were not part of the original data. The model has been "learned" from the data. The surface in Figure 6.2 would allow you to predict the quality of the product, even without knowing the details of the 100 individual data points that you collected.

Now imagine including another changing variable, the number of programmers, as part of the data. And cost. Certainly these would help you make better forecasts of the final product quality. Although it's hard to visualize more than three dimensions, the model becomes a complex multidimensional surface.

---

[1] This could be measured in terms of something like "function points," which is a crude measure of the number of input/output and logic functions that need to be implemented.

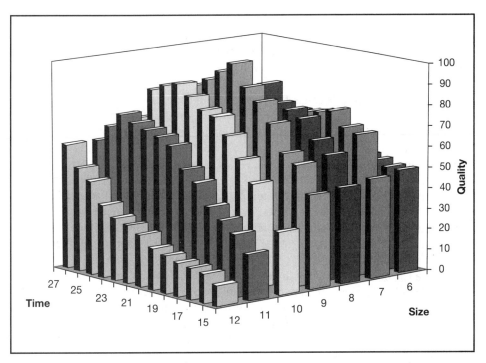

FIGURE 6.1 Quality as a Function of Time and Size

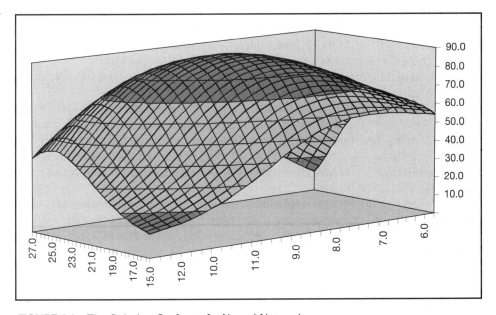

FIGURE 6.2 The Solution Surface of a Neural Network

The larger the set of input variables, the more complex the resulting surface or model. In fact, these surfaces can become very complex as the variables interact with each other. Nonetheless, an expert is able to build such mental models and often understand these complex processes intuitively.

Neural networks can also build such models from data. They have been dubbed *universal approximators,* because they can often uncover and approximate relationships in many types of data. Even though an underlying process may be complex, a neural net can approximate it closely if it has enough data points from which to construct the type of multidimensional surface that we've been talking about. Neural nets help computers "learn from experience."

Neural networks were first theorized as early as the 1940s by two scientists at the University of Chicago (McColloch and Pitts). Work was done in the mid-1950s as well (McCarthy, 1956; Rosenblatt, 1957) when researchers developed simple neural nets in attempts to simulate the brain's cognitive learning processes. Since then neural nets have been, at various times, the subject of both great interest and skepticism in the research community.

In the last decade or so, neural nets have been reexamined and are again attracting considerable attention, this time not only in academia, but in business and finance as well. Neural networks have been found to be very good at modeling complex poorly understood problems for which sufficient data can be collected. They can sometimes find better solutions to problems than might be achieved using traditional statistical, numerical, or other types of methods.

Artificial neural nets (ANNs) are simple computer programs that build models from data by trial and error. The concept is pretty straightforward: You show a piece of data to a neural network. The net predicts an output, in this example, quality. The net then compares its guess with the actual correct value, which you also present to the network.

If the ANN's guess is right, the net does nothing. If it is wrong, however, the network analyzes itself to try to figure out how to adjust some internal parameters so that it can make a better prediction if it sees similar data again in the future. The second piece of data is then presented to the network, and it goes through the same predict–compare–adjust process again. And so on.

Getting the parameters right, though, can be tricky. For example, when the neural net sees the second piece of data and makes its adjustments, it might "undo" some of the adjustments that it made when it saw the first piece of data! Because of this, the net must make many passes over the data set, trying to reconcile what it learns about the data in each pass. Over time, if everything goes well, the net should converge on a good model of the process.

For example, Figure 6.2 is the actual output surface produced by a neural network that was trained many times on the data from Figure 6.1. Note how there are estimates for every point along the data surface even though the data only cover about 100 of those points.

Examples:
- Asian Business Trading (ABT) is an exporting firm that deals primarily with Japan and Hong Kong. ABT would like to develop a model to help it predict the direction of

exchange rates so that the firm can better hedge its contracts. The firm will use historical data about the direction of the currency rates to drive its system. It is the firm's hope that the system will be able to discover patterns of movement in the data that are predictive of directions of the market.

- Virtual Realty is a real estate firm that wishes to develop a model to assess property values based on features of the properties. The firm has a good database of past properties that it has sold and of the characteristics of each property. The firm hopes to build a model and use it to get quick estimates of new properties.
- Herigel Target Marketing (HTM) has a database full of direct marketing information about products and the demographics of the target groups that consume these products. HTM would like to find a way to leverage these data to pinpoint the most likely prospects for future campaigns.

THE ABCs OF NEURAL NETWORKS

The principles that underlie neural network technology are based loosely in biology.

In biological terms, our nervous systems (including our brains) consist of a network of individual but interconnected nerve cells called *neurons*. Neurons can receive information from the outside world at various points in the network. For example, when you walk into a bright room, the neurons in your eyes register the levels of light in the room; when the doctor taps your knee with a rubber mallet, the neurons in your knee register the sudden impact of the mallet.

These pieces of information (the bright light, the mallet hit) are called *stimuli*. The stimuli are processed by your brain and nervous system. The information travels through the network by generating new internal signals that are passed from neuron to neuron. These new signals ultimately produce a response.

For example, after the nerves in your eye receive the "bright light" stimulus, the raw input is processed by your brain and then new signals are passed back to the nerves in your eye. These new signals make your pupils smaller. Or, after the doctor hits your knee with the rubber mallet, information from the nerve cells in your knee is processed and the result is (if you are healthy) a "knee-jerk" response.

A neuron passes information on to neighboring neurons by *firing* or releasing chemicals called *neurotransmitters*. A simple way to think about neurotransmitters is that they act like little bursts of electricity that go from one neuron to the next in order to transmit information. The connections between neurons at which these transfers occur are called *synapses*.[2] Conceptually, the more important a particular stimulus is, the larger the burst will be at the synapse.

There is an important biological fact that is also useful for understanding how ANNs work. It turns out that when information is received by a nerve cell at one of the synapses, the information can either *excite* the cell, or it can *inhibit* the cell. If the receiving cell is excited, it will fire when it gets the input and pass the information on to other neurons in the area. On the other hand, if the receiving cell is inhibited, it will

---

[2]Neurotransmitters are, in fact, chemicals that are released at the synapse. Once released, neurotransmitters encourage or inhibit *electrochemical* reactions in surrounding neurons.

not fire, in effect damping the impact of the information. What each nerve cell is doing is processing the raw input but passing it on only if it is important.

This makes sense. When you walk into a bright room, it is useful for the neurons that close your pupils to be excited and pass on the information, but it would not be very useful for the neurons that cause a knee-jerk response to also fire. (Imagine what would happen when you walked into a bright room if the "bright light" information, in fact, made its way to both your pupils and your knee!)

Synaptic connections can be strengthened (learning) or weakened (forgetting) over time and with experience. Through this process you can establish new responses to stimuli, modify old ones, or remove unused ones all together. In fact, with constant practice, many actions requiring thought initially can be relegated to the level of reflexes. Think about what happens when the car in front of you suddenly stops short. You slam on the brakes of your own car without thinking. This reflex occurs even though, at one time, you had to learn how to drive.

To bring all of these concepts together concretely, consider another example. What happens when a child learns how to throw a ball into a basket? At first, her performance might be very poor. The neural connections needed to throw the ball accurately are relatively weak. However, each time the child throws the ball, she observes the result and tries to adjust for errors. This time she used too much strength. That time she aimed too far beyond the basket. Another time she let go of the ball too late. Each time she notices one of these mistakes and feeds this information back. She makes slight adjustments, some conscious, some unconscious, to the way she throws the ball. This adjustment process is similar to the adjustment in the strength of connections between neurons.

In fact, if she practices long enough, she will be able to hit the basket from angles and locations that she has never even practiced before. This means that her learning was robust enough to allow her to *generalize* her experiences.

It's useful to note that although the child was able to develop good ball throwing skills, she would probably *not* be able to explain the physics, partial differential equations, or dynamics of air turbulence associated with the skill. She has, in essence, developed a reflexive command of the skill. Her ball-throwing methodology is a "black box" that approximates the laws of physics associated with throwing the ball without any knowledge about the actual physics.

How does all this biology tie back into allowing computers to learn? What is a neural network in *computer* terms?

Like its biological counterpart, an artificial neural network simply involves a system of *neurodes* (or *nodes*) and *weighted connections* (the equivalent of synapses) inside the memory of a computer. Nodes are data storage locations, like variables in a program, or cells in a spreadsheet. A node is analogous to a biological neuron, but much simpler.

In artificial neural networks, nodes are typically arranged in layers, with the connections running between layers. Figure 6.3 shows what a simple neural network might look like conceptually. The balls represent nodes and the lines represent the connection weights.

In principle, the artificial neural network operates in the same way as the biological model on which it is based. Data are fed into the net, the data are processed in-

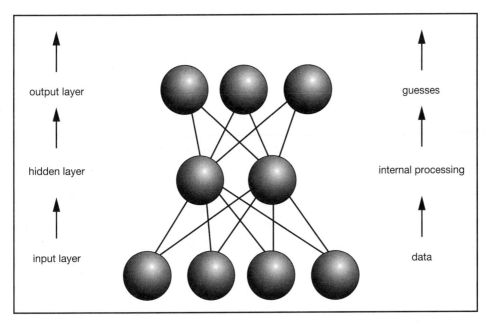

FIGURE 6.3 A Simple Neural Network

ternally based on the strength of inter-neurode connections or weights, and a result is output.

You will notice Figure 6.3 shows how the neural network is divided into layers. By convention the layer that receives the data is called the *input* layer, and the layer that relays the results of the neural network out of the net is called the *output* layer.

The internal layer, where intermediate internal processing takes place, is traditionally called a *hidden* layer. You might think of the hidden layer as being hidden from the outside world, unlike either the input layer (which takes information *from* the outside), or the output layer (which passes information on *to* the outside). Although Figure 6.3 only shows one hidden layer, there can be, and often are, more than one.[3]

How does this architecture help neural networks solve problems?

To understand how an artificial neural network learns how to guess accurately, you have to understand how the weights in the network affect its output. Learning, for neural networks, involves adjusting these weights.

But before we get to how an ANN adjusts its weights, it is first useful to understand what happens when data are input into a network that has *already learned* about a problem. So for now, we will start by ignoring the issue of how the network actually *learns* about a problem and concentrate instead here on how it *applies* what it has learned, once its weights have been adjusted properly.

---

[3]It is also possible to construct a primitive neural net containing *no* hidden layers. The early neural networks were configured in just this fashion.

To do this, we need to look a little more closely at the individual neurodes within a neural net to understand how they pass information among themselves. Figure 6.4 shows a more detailed schematic of an individual neurode.

Neurodes can only do a few simple things. Each neuron essentially collects a bunch of data (inputs), then takes stock of what it has collected, and processes the information. The neurode then passes the result of this collection and analysis process on to the next layer. If there are no additional layers, the neurode's output information becomes the output of the neural network—its answer.

In the figure, each of the lines feeding into the neurode is a connection from the lower layer. The "body" of the neurode is divided into two functional sections. The lower section *combines* all of the inputs that feed into the neurode. The upper portion takes this sum and calculates *the degree to which the sum of the input is important.* The output produced then forms the *input* to the next layer.

To follow how the data get transformed from raw input into the node's output, start at the bottom of Figure 6.4. The neurode first multiplies each input by the connection weight leading into it. The weights are shown as lines feeding into the neurode in Figure 6.4. The thickness of a line is proportional to its weight. The hollow line signifies a negative weight. A weight determines how important a given input will be in contributing to the output of the neurode. More important inputs will have bigger weights and less important ones will have smaller weights. All of the weighted inputs are added together in the neurode.

Next comes the "taking stock" phase. This taking stock occurs when the weighted

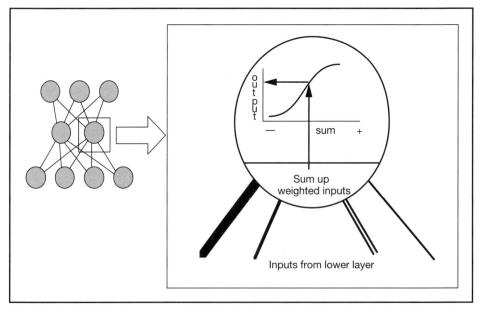

FIGURE 6.4 The Inside of a Neurode. The thickness of each input is proportional to its weight. A solid denotes a positive weight and an unfilled one a negative weight.

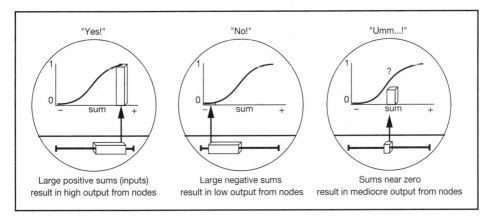

"Yes!"

"No!"

"Umm...!"

Large positive sums (inputs) result in high output from nodes

Large negative sums result in low output from nodes

Sums near zero result in mediocre output from nodes

FIGURE 6.5 How the Sum of Inputs Affects the Output of a Neurode. Notice how the rate of change of the output is non-linear across the input range.

sum is processed by the second half of the neurode. The sum is converted into an output value using a function referred to as a *transfer function.*[4]

What's the purpose of the transfer function? Why not just pass the summed information on? The transfer function serves as a kind of "dimmer" switch for turning the neuron on and off, depending on the input to the neuron. The transfer function determines to what degree a given sum will cause a neurode to fire.

You can see from looking at Figure 6.5 that the transfer function's value will be high (excited) when the sum of the inputs is large and positive (a lot of important positive signals are passed into the neurode from the lower nodes), and the value is low (inhibited) when the sum is large and negative.

Because the function is usually S-shaped (*sigmoidal*), it adds non-linearity to the neural network. What this means is that the output of a node will increase or decrease at different rates in different parts of the input range. As a result, the rate of change of a neurode's output depends on the "region" in which the node is operating. The behavior of the node, its output, is therefore non-linear.

So how do you build up more complicated functions?

That's where the hidden layers come in. By combining several layers of simple sigmoidal functions, the neural network essentially builds up more complicated curves. By combining these curves a neural net can approximate more complex shapes.

Figure 6.6 shows an example of this. In each case, the transfer function is the same, but the number of hidden nodes and the values of the weights leading into each node are different. Notice how very different curves can be constructed using these simple units. In this case, we used only one input. In most problems, though, there would be several inputs which would create even more complex surfaces.

---

[4]In the preceding example, we have chosen the logistic function as our transfer function. This function is defined for all values of the sum and the functional value ranges from 0 to 1. Note that the function is approximately zero when the sum of inputs is large and negative, approximately one when the sum is large and positive, and exactly 0.5 (the midpoint) when the sum is zero. Another popular function is a *radial basis function,* which is shaped like a bell curve.

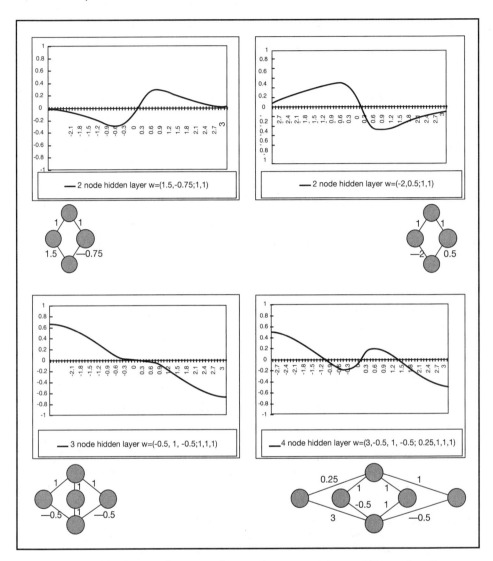

FIGURE 6.6 Hidden layers allow neural networks to approximate different functions.

The remarkable thing is that a collection of these very simple non-linear neurodes connected together can bend and twist in response to input data to *approximate very complex non-linear functions*. It turns out that many practical problems as diverse as credit card fraud prediction and financial market behavior are inherently non-linear. Neural nets can be suitable for such problems.

At this point you might be thinking, "So far, so good, but we still haven't learned how the neural network adjusts itself! How does it actually learn from the data?"

To illustrate this part of the process, called *training* the neural network, let's reconsider Asian Business Trading (ABT), the import-export firm, that is interested

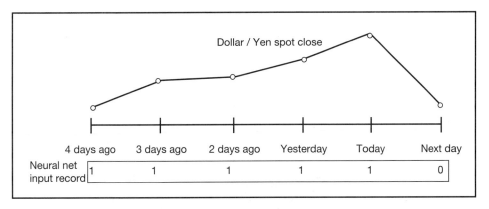

FIGURE 6.7   Coding Exchange Rate Movements as 1s and 0s

in predicting the dollar/yen exchange rate based on historical data. Figure 6.7 shows how the yen/dollar movement might be coded using zeros and ones.[5]

A 1 in the leftmost position indicates that, four days ago, the dollar closed higher than it opened against the yen. A 0 in that position would indicate that the dollar closed lower on that day. Likewise a desired *output* of 1, in the rightmost position, would be a prediction that the dollar will move higher, and an output of 0 would be a prediction that the market will move lower. The lower part of the figure shows the input record to the neural net. In this case, the input record says that four successive days of an increase resulted in a drop the following day.

Suppose we want to make a prediction based on four previous days' worth of data. In the example in Figure 6.7, the input would be {1,1,1,1} and the output would be 0.

Let's use the very simple neural network shown in Figure 6.8 to see what happens inside the net when a data record is presented. To keep things simple, there is no hidden layer in this net.

Now, let's say that you have just presented the above data to the net: The values of this input are all 1s, and that actual desired output is 0. That is, ABT's data record indicates that the network should guess the value 0 when presented with four 1s as input. How can the neural network do this?

Think about what has to happen inside the neural network in order for the output to be 0. Working backwards from the output node, you can see from Figure 6.9 that in order for the output of the node to be low, the transfer function (the top half of the node) must be low. This will only happen when the weighted sum into it, its input, is small.

In order for the weighted sum to be small, the weights into the neurode must act to *decrease* the sum, on average. For the net to produce the correct output, we could expect to see relatively large negative weight values between each of the input nodes and the top node (Figure 6.9, top), since this configuration will achieve an output of 0. Thus, in order to "learn" the

---

[5]We do not recommend that you use this very simple model to forecast exchange rates!

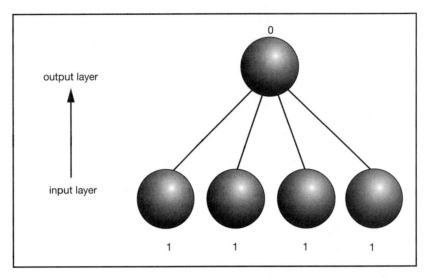

FIGURE 6.8 A Very Simple Neural Network with No Hidden Layer. The numbers state that if the inputs to each neurode are 1 the output should be 0.

```
1 1 1 1 → 0
```

record, the net must adjust each of its weights so that they are large and negative.

If instead you wanted the network to learn the pattern

```
1 1 1 1 → 1
```

where the network output were 1 when presented with the 1 1 1 1 input, the weights should be relatively large and positive, and thus *increasing*, on average, the weighted sum (Figure 6.9, bottom).

A more interesting case occurs if you have to determine the weights to model a problem involving the two patterns

```
0 0 1 1 → 0 (Pattern 1)
```

and

```
1 1 0 0 → 1 (Pattern 2).
```

Here, just setting all of the weights to large positive or large negative values won't work since each pattern is made up of mixed signals.

In this case, the net must adjust its weights so that, on average, they cause the weighted sum to be increased when Pattern 1 is presented, but they cause the weighted sum to decrease when Pattern 2 is presented. A little thought shows that you can do this easily enough by setting the weights on the first two inputs to large *negative* values, and the weights of the other two inputs to large *positive* values. This is shown in Figure 6.10.

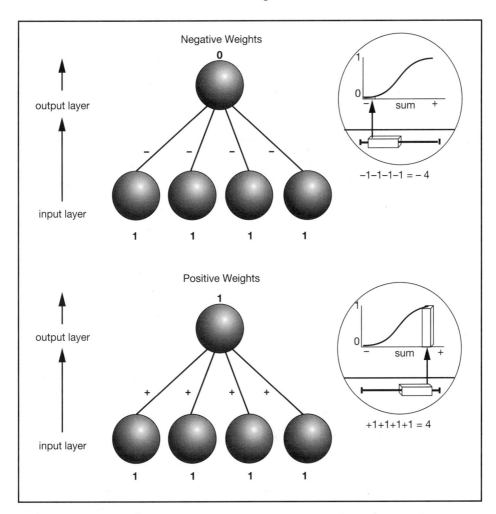

FIGURE 6.9 Changing the weights of a neural network changes the output.

Note that if we had set *all* weights to either very *small* positive or very small negative values (representing very weak connections) the result would be to produce a weighted sum of approximately 0 *no matter what the inputs were*. This is because all of the input would be weighted by very small values and, as a result, all of the information would be whittled away.

When the input sum is around 0, the output of the neural net would be about 0.5. Since the value 0.5 is located equally between 0 and 1, this output gives us very little new information. It is the electronic equivalent of shrugging shoulders. The small values of the weights have, in effect, caused *all* of the information to be suppressed or ignored by the net.[6]

---

[6]This is why, incidentally, neural network weights are often initialized with very small random values before they are trained.

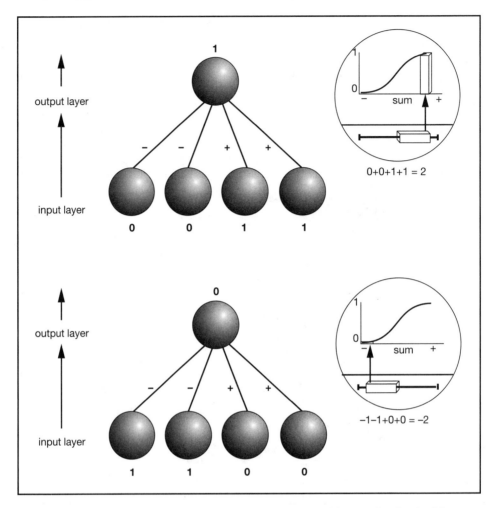

FIGURE 6.10 A More Involved Example of Setting Weight Values to Get Desired Output

In order to get the weights set up the way you want, so that the net produces accurate output, you train the network by presenting it with sample data. To train the net, you would first set all of the connection weights to small random values, essentially creating a "blank slate." You would next give the neural net a single record or *observation* of data, which the net processes, and then uses to guess at an answer, as we just described.

Since the network has not been trained yet and the weights aren't set correctly, you would expect the first guess to be pretty bad, and it usually is. But this is still useful. Remember that the child was able to use the information about her misses to help her throw better next time. The neural network can also learn from its mistakes. In fact, the first thing that a neural network in training mode does when it finishes processing a data record is to compare the result of its calculations with the desired, correct output.

If the network result matches the desired output, the network does nothing. If, however, the result does not match, the neural network needs to find out where it went wrong. You know from the previous discussion that the values of the weights, in large part, determine the output of a given neural network. So it makes sense that the neural network should attempt to train itself by adjusting its weights, and it must adjust the weights so that, on average, it brings its own output more in line with the desired results. Said another way, the neural network must adjust its weights in such a way that the error of its output is minimized.

To do this, neural networks train themselves in a series of steps:

Step 1: The network makes a guess based on its current weights and the input data.

Step 2: The net calculates the error associated with the output (at the output node). For example, if the desired output were 1, but the network output were 0, the error would be +1, based on the difference between 1 and 0.

Step 3: The net determines by *how much* and *in what direction* each of the weights leading in to this node needs to be adjusted.

How?

This is accomplished by calculating how much each of the individual weighted inputs to the node contributed to the error, given the particular input value. So, for example, if a node's output were too small, the net might need to concentrate on (that is, increase) small or negative weights that lead up to that node. In essence the network *feeds back* the information about how well it's doing to the neurodes in the net, and where possible problems might be.

Step 4: The net adjusts the weights of each node in the layer according to the analysis in the previous step. For example, in the case where the output was too small, the neural network will try to increase the values of the *positive* weights since that would make the weighted sum larger. This would bring the output closer to 1, which is what you want in this case. Similarly, the neural net should also try to decrease the size of the *negative* weights (or even make them positive).

Step 5: The net repeats the process by performing a similar set of calculations (*Step 1–Step 3*) for each node in the hidden layer below it. But since you cannot tell the net what the desired output of each of the hidden nodes should be (they are internal and hidden), the neural network does a kind of sensitivity analysis to determine how large the error of each of these nodes is and by how much to adjust the weights that feed into them. (For more details on this process, see the Appendix at the end of this chapter.) This pattern of checking errors and adjusting weights is continued for each hidden layer in the network.

The net repeats the above guess–feedback–adjust process using each of the cases in the data, (often many times) until the network is done training. At this point the network can be tested to determine how accurate its output is.

Earlier in this text, we discussed how optimization problems can be viewed as landscapes in which the peaks are the best solutions, and the valleys are the worst ones. The job of an optimization method is to search across the landscape and try to find the high peaks where the good solutions are.

You can picture a neural network's error as a similar type of landscape, where the dimensions of the space would be represented by the neural network's weights. The peaks and valleys are the errors corresponding to those weights, peaks being high errors and valleys low errors. But the optimization problem in the neural network's case is to adjust the internal weights to *minimize the amount of error* in the output. Since the neural net is trying to minimize the error, it is trying to settle in a valley representing a low-error solution.

The neural network therefore seeks out the *valleys* in this space. You can visualize this adjustment process as one in which the weight settings of the neural network are bouncing around, trying to find optimal values. Figure 6.11 shows a graphical representation of an error space. Note how the weight value "bounces" down toward a minimum as the neural network adjusts its weights.

The manner in which the neural network actually finds weight settings is called its *learning method*. Learning methods or *learning paradigms* can be classified broadly into those involving *supervised* learning and those involving *unsupervised* learning.

The particular paradigm we have been discussing up until now is called *back propagation (backprop)*, because the errors between the desired output and the network output are passed back or *propagated* back through the network in order to adjust the weights.

However, this approach to training and using neural networks is only one of many learning paradigms. *Supervised* learning paradigms (such as backprop) work by presenting the neural network with input data and, along with these input data, the desired correct output results. The network makes an estimate and then compares its output with the desired results. This information is used to help guide the network to a good solution. In essence, the network is being "supervised" by an unseen mentor who shows the net how the answer should look and where the net might be making mistakes. While backprop is the most common supervised learning paradigm, there are numerous others as well.

On the other hand, neural networks being trained using an unsupervised learning paradigm are only presented with the input data but *not the desired output results*. The network *clusters* the training records based on similarities that it picks up from the data.

One way to think about how this clustering works is to imagine that you presented some strangers with a stack of photographs of different scenes and asked each person to classify them. Without any foreknowledge of what was in the stack of photographs, one person might group things based on the types of photographs (color, black and white), another might group the photos based on the various types of scenes (outdoor scenery, indoor scenes, portraits, etc.), and a third person might group the photos based on the types of activities (sports, business, entertainment, etc.). Each grouping would make sense from a certain perspective, and we might discover interesting relationships among the photos by seeing how each person arranged them.

A neural network trained in unsupervised learning mode is similar to the stranger. In such a case, the network is not being supervised with respect to what it is "supposed" to find. Instead, it is being left to its own devices to discover possible relationships. In unsupervised learning, the network seeks to find similarities among the different data records. With this type of learning, certain portions of the network tend to specialize or respond to different dimensions of the data.

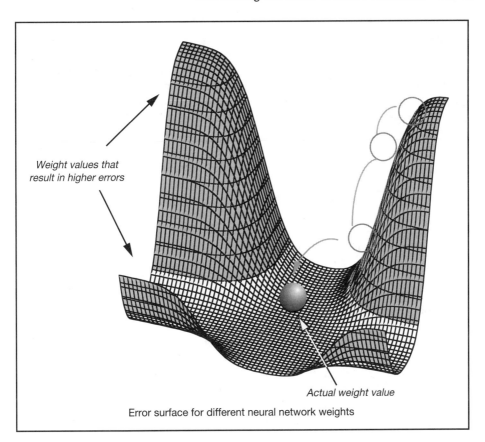

Weight values that result in higher errors

Actual weight value

Error surface for different neural network weights

FIGURE 6.11 How a Neural Network Finds Good Weight Settings

An application in which unsupervised learning is often used is that of direct marketing. Herigel Target Marketing, the company mentioned earlier might use a neural net to develop such an application. HTM would start by feeding large amounts of demographic data into a neural network and then allowing it to train unsupervised. A portion of the network might find patterns in income levels, while another might find patterns in education levels of target clients, still a third might look at ages. That is, the network seeks to combine these in such a way so as to form clusters of records that are similar along these dimensions.[7]

By combining these different features, a neural network can come up with clustering that highlight similarities among various data records. While many of the clusters will be easily identified (middle-aged college graduates or single parents, for example), others might represent sets of relationships that were unknown and thereby show new ways of looking at the data.

---

[7]The relationships that unsupervised learning neural nets find are very often much more complicated than these. In fact, one of the challenges in using unsupervised approaches is in trying to interpret the dimensions along which members of a cluster are similar.

The clustering will vary depending on the contents and distribution of the data. By examining how clusters are formed, the staff of HTM might try to identify clusters of cases where a marketing campaign was or was not successful to try to determine which factors and relationships are significant in this respect. Alternatively, they might try to use the trained neural network to classify new target clients for an upcoming campaign, possibly eliminating those who fall into clusters that had low hit rates in the past. By using this information, HTM would then save the expense of approaching low-likelihood clients.

INTELLIGENCE DENSITY ISSUES

So, when is it a good idea to use a neural network?

One of the main advantages to using a neural network approach to a problem over some other knowledge-based approaches such as rule-based systems or fuzzy systems is that you don't need as much direct input from domain experts. This can be good for several reasons. The most basic reason is that in some fields it just may not be possible to speak with an expert since no one really *understands* in detail the process that you are trying to model.

But, even when you *have experts*, it may be very expensive to get access to their time. A top bond trader who spends 2 hours a day talking to a knowledge engineer could be costing his company millions of dollars. Even if you *can* get the access you need, experts can sometimes have a very difficult time articulating and formalizing their expertise. It's instinctive. The benefit of using a neural network is that as long as you have appropriate data, a neural net can often find useful patterns in them without requiring an expert's judgment.

In fact, neural networks *excel* at mapping relationships onto data that are noisy and incomplete. This is a huge plus since when you try to model real-world problems, high-quality data are a luxury that is rare. More often than not, the data that are available are noisy, poorly distributed, and spotty. Neural networks can often deal with this kind of data better than many statistical and AI methods.

How?

Each of the various computing units (neurodes) attacks a small portion of the problem. Since each node looks at the data from different angles, a neural network can often reconstruct what missing or corrupt data "should" look like and fill in the blanks based on the data available. The neurodes interact in such a way as to provide many checks of the data from many different perspectives.

This also makes neural networks very flexible. In fact, for processes that do not undergo drastic fundamental changes, updating a neural network can be as simple as just retraining the net with newer data or with the addition of a few new variables.

On the other hand, this doesn't mean you can just *dump* data into a neural net and hope for the best. Before neural network technology got wide exposure in business, proponents and software vendors often claimed that users of neural networks did not have to be concerned at all with data quality and content. However, experience has borne out the fact that the approach of just gathering any old sample data into an informational "paper bag," shaking it, and then dumping the data into a neural network and hoping for the best tends not to produce good results.

While neural nets are *theoretically* capable of approximating a wide range of mathematical and logical functions, the reality is that you usually need to spend a good deal of time inspecting and pre-processing your data prior to training a neural network. While you cannot usually control the amount of noise in the data you get, you *can* help the neural net "understand" the data better. In fact this is where many users of neural networks spend most of their time.

Steps as simple as developing ratios and differences can improve tremendously the ability of a neural network to learn. For example, giving a neural network the ratio of sales and profits rather than giving the net the individual variables sales and profits will save the network the time and trouble of having to figure out the relationship itself.

But ratios and differences are just the tip of the iceberg. By putting some work into understanding, massaging, and manipulating the data, you help ensure that the bulk of the neural network's training time will be devoted to finding the more interesting relationships in the data that you *don't* know about, rather than mapping simple relationships that you already do.

In addition to filling in the blanks in missing data, the multiple node architecture of neural nets buys you other benefits. Recall that each node is also equipped with a non-linear transfer function. The neurodes are grouped into layers, and information is passed between neurodes and layers via connections. This architecture allows neural nets to model complex, highly non-linear relationships, by modeling many local dimensions simultaneously.

Since each node acts as an internal processor that models a small piece of the problem, it makes sense, then, that more complicated problems can be solved with more hidden nodes. By the same token, when you increase the number of hidden *layers* in a neural network, you increase the ability of the network to use the results of neurodes in the lower layers, and for those neurodes to interact. Some complex problems that are not solvable with a small set of nodes are easily solved if the number of nodes and hidden layers is increased to facilitate this interaction.

As a result of these features, in general, neural networks are usually very good at interpolation and classification of types of problems and are often able to mimic exceptionally well the subtleties of a process.

The fact that you can easily add layers and nodes to a neural network also means that neural network models can often be expanded to deal with more complex or larger problems, providing there are sufficient data and time to train the neural net. It is usually fairly easy to add new variables to a neural network, or to present another 1000 or 2000 training examples, without going to a lot of additional trouble.

But all of these benefits do not come free.

There are drawbacks to having *too many* hidden nodes. The larger the number of hidden nodes, the more *time* will be required for training. (Each node has a set of weights associated with it. Each set of weights must be adjusted during each training pass.) And, the larger the number of nodes, the more data will be required to prevent overfitting, or "memorizing" the data (we'll get to that in a second . . .).

In addition, the more complicated the network becomes, the less likely it is to find good solutions. This is due to the fact that when you increase the number of neurodes, you increase the number of interactions between neurodes in each layer. This can make it difficult for the network to "settle down" to find a good set of weights since an adjustment to one weight might have unforeseen effects on other weight settings in the network. When you increase the number of weights, you also increase the size and dimension of the search space.

The search space?

Remember we talked about the weight adjustment process of a neural net being like a ball bouncing down a hill. The different combinations of weight values form a very hilly terrain or search space (each weight being one axis of the space). The more the weights, the larger the dimensions of the terrain. The degree to which the neural network is able to scour this terrain to find good combinations will determine in large part how accurate it is. This comes down to how efficiently the network sets its weights.

If the network adjusts the weights too gradually (tiny bounces), training it can take a long time since in each iteration the paradigm covers only little pieces of the terrain. The neural network is also less likely to explore fully all of the geography in the terrain. Consider that if the network is in a valley, but that valley is *not* optimal, the network would need to effectively *climb out*, little by little, from the current valley before it could move into a different area of the weight space where better solutions are found. However, in order to move up, the network would need to worsen its performance by moving away from the current valley. In essence it would need temporarily to *increase* the overall network error. Since the network generally tries to adjust weights so as to move in the direction that *decreases* the error, the end result is that the network will tend not to leave whatever valleys it starts settling in, even if there are better ones around.

On the other hand, if you make the learning rate large, the neural network will tend to train too quickly. It will tend to bounce around the weight space, exploring many possible weightings, possibly jumping over peaks in the process and landing in valleys other than the one in which it started. However, because the steps it takes are actually "leaps" it may not be able to settle down to an optimal set of values. Figure 6.12 shows this phenomenon.

Fortunately, there are some very good methods for helping neural networks train well and avoid these pitfalls. Unfortunately, in addition to this adjustment process, other factors, such as the number of nodes and layers, the quality of the data, and the complexity of the problem can all impact performance in a problem-specific sense.

There are many choices to make when you design a neural network: the number of hidden layers, the number of nodes in each layer, the various data and variables to use, and the settings of network training parameters (such as learning rates). As a result, it's usually necessary to develop several networks and experiment with different topologies and parameters (like the size of the bounces). This experimentation time can add up. Compounding this is the fact that, as we discussed, the collection, analysis, and pre-processing of data can also consume a lot of time. Since data must often be prepared differently for each of the various runs in a neutral network development cycle, the combination of pre-processing and training can take significant time. All of this takes experience and patience.

Yet much of this depends on the nature of the problem, the data available, and the type of computers being used. Depending on the complexity of the network, volume of data, the power of the computer hardware available, and the type of neural

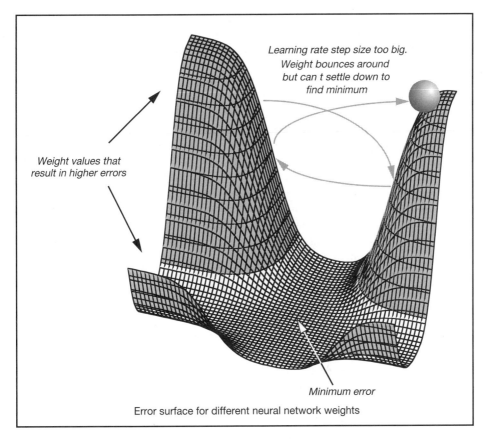

Learning rate step size too big.
Weight bounces around
but can t settle down to
find minimum

Weight values that
result in higher errors

Minimum error

Error surface for different neural network weights

FIGURE 6.12 Too big a step in the learning rate parameter can prevent a neural network from finding good weight settings.

network, training times can range from several minutes to several hours to several days *per network*. This has implications as to the type of computer hardware you might need. While a large number of problems can be solved easily on a PC, others might require high-powered workstations, parallel processing computers, or special purpose neuro-computing hardware.

Paradoxically, the fact that neural networks are excellent at finding subtle relationships in observational data can also be a drawback. Since the neural network scours the data, looking for any possible relationship to exploit, it can find patterns in the data that are not even relevant to the problem. Because of this, neural networks sometimes learn the patterns in the *noise*, not the patterns in the *data*.

There is a somewhat notorious example of this phenomenon from the field of military research. A research team was trying to develop a neural network model to distinguish between photographs in which there were combat tanks and those photographs in which there were none. The team took two sets of photographs of various scenery: One set of scenes had tanks in the pictures, and one set did not. The team converted these images into machine-readable format, fed these data into a neural network, and let the net train. To everyone's delight, after the network was trained, it did a surprisingly good job at discriminating between the two sets of pictures. However, when a new set of photographs was used, the results were horrible. At first the team was puzzled. But after careful inspection of the first two sets of photographs, they discovered a very simple explanation. The photos with tanks in them were all taken on sunny days, and those without the tanks were taken on overcast days. The network had *not* learned to identify tank like images; instead, it had learned to identify photographs of sunny days and overcast days.

This little story highlights a major drawback. The results of processing inputs are opaque. This stems in part from the fact that the original knowledge is not coded in an explicit form. Rather, ANNs are highly non-linear functional equations and mappings. The result is that it is difficult to understand which variables caused what behavior in a neural network. While mathematical and operational methods do exist for the analysis of neural networks, the methods are fairly involved and can be less than satisfying. In addition, unlike most statistical modeling methods, it can be difficult to say, even generally, which variables are significant in what respect.

While the tank spotting case above is extreme, it is not uncommon for neural network users to get very good results on training data, but get poorer results in real practice. In the tank example, the results were skewed partially due to the way that the data for the problem were gathered. However, in some cases, even if the data are quite accurate, a network can be "over trained." This can occur when the network spends too much time training on a specific set of data that is not large or representative enough of the process. As a result, the network identifies idiosyncratic patterns in the data. In essence, it picks up on and starts to model little clues that are particular to specific records in the training data, but are *not* particular to the underlying process itself. Nonetheless, these little clues aid the network in getting the right answers *with the training data*, and, as a result, the network's error decreases and the performance seems to be getting better. In essence, the net comes up with a surface that exactly fits the training data, even the noise in it. This *overtraining* often occurs when a net is allowed to train for too long on a particular set of training data, or when there are not enough training data to support the size of the network.

The same problem occurs if the data do not adequately sample the range of inputs that the net will have to deal with in practice. That is, not only do neural networks need lots of data to train well,[8] but the data must be distributed in such a way that most of the interesting features of the process being modeled are reflected in the sample data. Remember, neural nets basically *interpolate*. If the points between which it must interpolate are missing, it will perform badly.

One way that people minimize the risk of overtraining is by monitoring closely the performance of the neural network as it trains. A second set of "test data", such as the set in Figure 6.13, is usually kept separate and used for periodically checking how well the network guesses on the test set versus how well it does on the training set. By doing this, you can determine whether the network is learning the process or simply the

---

[8]One rule of thumb is that ANNs usually require that there be at least an order of magnitude of more training cases than there are connection weights, so the more variables, hidden nodes, and output nodes there are in a neural net the more data is required. Moreover, additional data are often required since it is usually desirable to partition the data so that models can be tested.

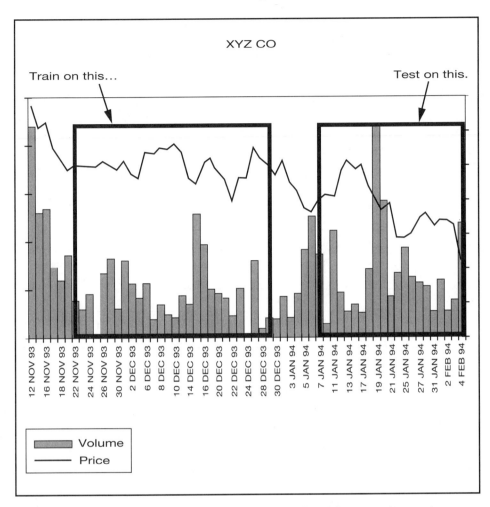

FIGURE 6.13 Out of sample testing on data is not used to train a neural network.

noise. Since the test data cannot be used by the network to adjust its weights, the network cannot learn the peculiarities of the test data. It can only use the information that it has learned from the training data. If the net has, in fact, learned about the *process,* then the accuracy on the test set should be comparable to the accuracy on the training set.

On a day-to-day basis, most applications that take advantage of neural network technology incorporate the neural net into some larger system, be that a trading system, process control system, or a database system.

This is easy to do. Neural networks typically evaluate to simple algebraic equations. If you wanted to, for example, you could write the equation for the schematic of the neural network in Figure 6.9 as follows:

$$sum = (weight_1 \times input_1) + (weight_2 \times input_2) +$$
$$(weight_3 \times input_3) + (weight_4 \times input_4,)$$
$$output = f(sum)$$

where f(sum) is the transfer function.[9] A more complex neural network would involve more equations, but they would take essentially the same form as the one above.

This makes the trained neural network both a small program and easily integrated into other systems. A trained neural network can be evaluated using the same relatively small number of basic mathematical steps. For example, the equation above can always be evaluated using exactly four additions, four multiplications, and one evaluation of f. While larger nets require many more evaluations, the number for a particular neural net does not change. As a result, neural networks tend to have response times that are fast and reliable.

To summarize, neural nets stack up as follows on the various intelligence density dimensions:

Dimension	*Neural Network*	*But...*
Accuracy	High	Needs comprehensive training data
Explainability	Low	Some mathematical analytic methods exist for doing sensitivity analysis
Response Speed	High	—
Scalability	Moderate	Depends on complexity of problem, availability of data
Compactness	High	—
Flexibility	High	Needs representative training data
Embeddability	High	—
Ease of use	Moderate	—
Tolerance for complexity	High	—
Tolerance for noise in data	Moderate-High	Preprocessing is useful in dealing with noise
Tolerance for sparse data	Low	—
Independence from experts	High	—
Development speed	Moderate	Depends on understanding of process, on computer speed, and learning paradigm
Computing resources	Low to Moderate	Scale with respect to amount of data and size of network. Trained ANN needs little computing resource to execute

---

[9]Readers familiar with traditional statistical methods might notice that if we make the transfer function linear (output = f(sum) = sum + constant), the equation for an individual neurode now bears a close resemblance to the model produced by that of a technique called regression analysis (OLS regression):

$$y = \beta_0 + \beta_1 x_1 + \beta_2 x_2 + \beta_3 x_3 + \beta_4 x_4.$$

In fact, if we replace each *weight* with a β and each *input* with an x, we get an identical equation to within a constant. Furthermore, most neural networks employ an additional input node, called a bias, which takes no actual data, but acts only as a constant.

Suggested Reading

Dayhoff, J., *Neural Network Architectures: An Introduction,* Van Nostrand Reinhold, New York, NY: 1990.

Freeman, J. A., and D. M. Skapura, *Neural Networks: Algorithms, Applications, and Programming Techniques,* Addison Wesley, Reading, MA: 1992.

Haykin, S., *Neural Networks: A Comprehensive Foundation,* Macmillan College Publishing Company, New York, NY: 1994.

Hinton, G. E., "How Neural Networks Learn from Experience," *Scientific American,* September 1992.

Lippmann, R. P., "An Introduction to Computing with Neural Nets," *IEEE ASSP Magazine,* April 1987.

Rumelhart, D. E., and J. L. McClelland, *Parallel Distributed Processing: Explorations in the Microstructure of Cognition,* MIT Press, Cambridge, MA: 1984.

Stein, R. M., "Selecting Data for Neural Networks," and "Preprocessing Data for Neural Networks," *AI Expert,* February 1993 and March 1993.

Wasserman, P. D. and T. Schwartz, "Neural Networks: Part 1," and "Neural Networks: Part 2," *IEEE Expert Magazine,* Winter 1987 and Spring 1988.

APPENDIX TO CHAPTER 6:
The Back Propagation Algorithm

The back propagation algorithm seeks to minimize the error term between the actual output of a neural network and the desired or target output as presented in a training data record. Throughout the course of this discussion, we will assume that the transfer function of the neural network is the logistic function, defined in Eq. 6.3.

To adjust the weight, w_{ij}, from a given node, n_i, to the current node, n_j, we update w_{ij} as follows:

$$w_{ij,(t+1)} = w_{ij,t} + (\lambda)(\varepsilon w_{ij})(n_i), \qquad \textbf{(Eq. 6.1)}$$

where λ is the learning parameter, the subscript t refers to the number of times the network has been updated, and εw_{ij}, defined more fully below, is the sensitivity of node n_j to a change in the weight w_{ij}. The term εw_{ij} will be calculated differently depending on whether n_j is an output node or a hidden node.

Before we determine how to calculate the middle term (εw_{ij}) of Eq. 6.1, we should review how a neural network arrives at its output values.

Recall that the total input to a neurode can be described as:

$$s_j = \sum_i n_i w_{ij}, \qquad \textbf{(Eq. 6.2)}$$

where s_j is the sum of all inputs to the neurode, n_i is the output from the ith node of the previous layer, and w_{ij} is the weight of the connection between the ith node of the previous layer and the current node.

This output is then transformed using a non-linear squashing function (such as the logistic function shown in Eq. 6.3, below) to yield the total output, n_j, of node j:

$$n_j = \frac{1}{1 + e^{-s_j}} \, .$$

(Eq. 6.3)

To determine the overall error for a single pass of the neural network:
1. We calculate the (RMS) error, E, for the output layer as follows:

$$E = \frac{1}{2} \sum_{\text{output}} (n_j - d_j)^2,$$

(Eq. 6.4)

where d_j is the desired output for output node j.

Once we have the error term for the entire network, we can begin to adjust the weights. Some higher-level mathematics are required for adjusting the connection weights. However, if we are clever enough in how we choose our transfer function (Eq. 6.3), we can ensure that it is easily differentiable, and that the mathematics will therefore simplify nicely.

For the remainder of this appendix, we will present the mathematics such that those interested in the full details of the derivations can follow them. However, those less familiar with partial differential equations can still follow the discussion by looking to the last line (numbered) in every set of equations, which represents the simplified equations. In practice, the simplified equations are most commonly used for implementing neural networks.

2. We next calculate the error term εo for each output node. What we are trying to determine is how much the error term changes with respect to a change in each output node. In other words, we are trying to see how much each node's error contributes to the overall error of the network:

$$\varepsilon o_j = \frac{\partial E}{\partial n_j},$$

$$\varepsilon o_j = (n_j - d_j).$$

(Eq. 6.5)

3. We now need to determine how much the error changes as we vary the *input* to a given *output* node. To do this we need to see how the result of Eq. 6.4 would change if the total input to the node (the sum in Eq. 6.2) were changed:

$$\varepsilon s_j = \frac{\partial E}{\partial s_j},$$

$$\varepsilon s_j = \frac{\partial E}{\partial n_j} \frac{dn_j}{ds_j},$$

$$\varepsilon s_j = \varepsilon o_j n_j (1 - n_j).$$

(Eq. 6.6)

4. We next calculate how much to adjust the weight, w_{ij}, from a given node on the layer below the current layer, n_i, to the current node, n_j:

$$\varepsilon w_{ij} = \frac{\partial E}{\partial w_{ij}},$$

$$\varepsilon w_{ij} = \frac{\partial E}{\partial s_j} \frac{ds_j}{dw_{ij}},$$

$$\varepsilon w_{ij} = \varepsilon s_j n_i. \qquad \text{(Eq. 6.7)}$$

5. Now we can continue this operation on nodes in the lower layers by allowing the nodes on the lower hidden layers to play the role of the output nodes in Eq. 6.6 and Eq. 6.7. We must sum all of the contributions of inputs to the errors of the hidden nodes in the lower layers, however. In addition, we will calculate the error of the hidden node by examining how the error of nodes above the node change with respect to changes in the node. Thus, in the following equation, note that the variables subscripted with a j are variables from the layer *above* the current layer. As a result, they will have been calculated already. The variable εh will take the place of variable εo in Eq. 6.6. Now, εh may be calculated as follows:

$$\varepsilon h_i = \frac{\partial E}{\partial n_i},$$

$$\varepsilon h_i = \sum_j \frac{\partial E}{\partial s_i} \frac{\partial s_j}{\partial n_i},$$

$$\varepsilon h_i = \sum_j \varepsilon s_j w_{ij}. \qquad \text{(Eq. 6.8)}$$

In this manner the error is propagated backward recursively through the entire network and all of the weights are adjusted so as to minimize the overall network error.

Putting Expert Reasoning in a Box
Rule-Based Systems

Like all Holmes's reasoning, the thing seemed simplicity itself
when it was once explained.
—Arthur Conan Doyle, *The Memoirs of Sherlock Holmes*

Learn to reason forward and backward on both sides of a question.
—Thomas Blandi

In place of brute-force search we have now substituted a combined
system of search and "reason."
—Herbert Simon

Rule-based systems (RBS) are programs that use preprogrammed knowledge to solve problems. RBS grew out of the field of logical theorem proving as a way of establishing the truth or falsity of particular assertions. Typically, an RBS stores heuristic problem solving facts in a special database called a rule base. *The facts are generally stored in the form of "IF-THEN" rules. The RBS can use these rules as they are needed to solve problems when presented with data. In this chapter we discuss RBS and the ways in which they can be used to solve a variety of business problems.*

INTRODUCTION

You can view much of problem solving as consisting of rules, from the common sense "If it's too warm, lower the temperature," to the technical "If the patient appears to have pallor, then he must have an excess of bilirubin in his blood or be in shock; and, if there's an excess of bilirubin in the blood, then administer drugs to lower it."

Of all the situations you can think of, whether they involve planning, diagnosis, data interpretation, optimization, or social behavior, many can be expressed in terms of rules. It is not surprising, then, that for several decades rules have served as a fundamental knowledge representation scheme in Artificial Intelligence.

A rule-based system (RBS) is a model that expresses all of its knowledge in terms of explicit rules. It is appealing to have *all* of a system's knowledge described in terms of a uniform structure, a rule. Uniformity of the building blocks is appealing. It makes it easier to understand, implement, and maintain a large system.

Rule-based systems have been built in a variety of problem domains. Much early work was done in medicine. MYCIN, an early expert system developed in the mid-70s that diagnosed blood infections, expressed all its problem-solving knowledge with rules. INTERNIST, a more comprehensive project encompassing all of internal medicine, also represented a lot of its knowledge about associations among symptoms and diseases as rules.

Researchers also built rule-based systems in the engineering arena. The most famous of these, XCON, developed in 1979, was and is still used by Digital Equipment Corporation to configure VAX computers. XCON's knowledge consists of thousands of rules gleaned from engineers that specify how the various computer components needed to satisfy a customer's computing needs should be configured.

Following the successes in medicine and engineering, rule-based systems saw a fair amount of action in the 80s. DuPont adopted a strategy of encouraging end users to develop their own small applications, typically consisting of a few dozen rules. Other organizations developed more complex applications that supported a core business process. Cooper and Lybrand, one of the "Big 6" accounting firms, devoted a considerable amount of effort to developing Expertax, an expert system aimed at providing large clients with tax advice. Peat Marwick, another Big 6 firm, used an expert system to help auditors with audit planning; it used client and industry data to flag client accounts that might have a high degree of risk associated with them.

What kinds of problems lend themselves to an RBS approach? In business, administration is often rule based. Accounting and tax practices are also inherently rule oriented. More generally, in business and engineering, systems that raise alarms or enforce quality control tend to involve rules. On the other hand, design problems tend to be harder to express as rules, particularly when a significant amount of creativity is required.

Examples:

- AutoCare, a chain of auto service centers, would like to develop a system that would allow its mechanics to more quickly diagnose mechanical problems in customers' cars. While there are specialists in repairing various types of cars, very few know how to repair *all* types of cars. AutoCare hopes to collect the knowledge that these experts have and make it available to their entire staff.
- HPC Consulting has a very complex billing structure that has resulted from a long series of contracts with clients. The structure is different for each type of contract, depending on which primary services were previously offered, which additional services are currently being offered, whether the client is part of a larger organization that also has a contract with HPC, etc. The consulting firm wants to develop a system that will

help it make its billing practices more consistent, understandable, and accurate, but also allow the firm to make changes as new services are offered.

- CreditBank is a retail bank that does a fair amount of lending to individuals. The firm would like to do a better job of screening loan applicants. The bank hopes to develop a system to flag potentially risky applicants for closer analysis by bank officers. The bank needs the system to indicate which areas of the applicant's profile may be cause for concern.

THE ABCs OF RULE-BASED SYSTEMS

The basic units of rule-based systems are rules. Rules take the form "If *X*, then *Y*." In such a rule, *X* is typically a description of some situation and *Y* is some action or conclusion.[1] The idea is that by using enough of these rules, you cover the scope of the reasoning that an expert uses in a particular problem area.

What do we mean by "cover the scope of reasoning"? Let's elaborate a little on CreditBank's loan application example.

Suppose CreditBank has data on the credit history of its customers. It also obtains customer employment history. CreditBank's objective is to assess each customer's degree of credit risk.

To keep things simple, assume that a loan officer describes two variables: *credit history* and *employment stability*. The officer describes them as being *very high, high, medium, low,* or *very low*. He also describes riskiness using the same five categories.

Figure 7.1 shows the relationship between these variables and risk. The heights of the bars in the figure indicate the levels of risk corresponding to different combinations of credit history and employment stability. With risk also broken down into five categories, Figure 7.1 would contain 125 cubes. This region is called the *problem space*. Each cube is essentially a rule. In other words, a rule "samples" a region of the problem space. For example, we can think of the bar in the leftmost square as the rule:

> **IF** employment stability is very low
> **AND** credit history is very low
> **THEN** credit risk is very high.

The rules that describe a particular domain are called a *rule base* or a *knowledge base*.

What did we do in this figure? Essentially, we *categorized* credit history, employment history, and risk into buckets between very low and very high and expressed relationships between these buckets.

Experts do this kind of abstraction all the time as a way of reducing the complexity of the problem space. For example, to a physician, high fever might mean temperatures between 102 and 108 degrees Fahrenheit. The doctor would also ex-

---

[1]This is a rough interpretation. *X* could also be a conclusion and *Y* could be facts that need to exist for the conclusion to be justified. In general, the meaning of the rule can vary, depending on the application.

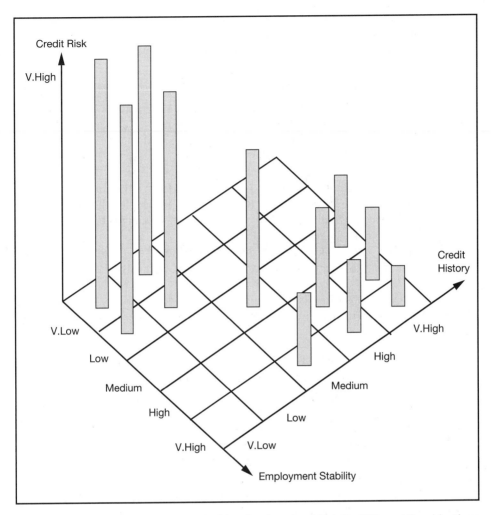

FIGURE 7.1   A Discontinuous Terrain Showing Levels of Risk for Different Combinations of Liquidity and Income Levels. Blank cells indicate undefined regions.

press knowledge in terms of high or low fever, swollen glands, heavy discoloration, and so on, which are essentially qualitative abstractions. Similarly, for a loan officer, high income might mean between $80,000 and $200,000 per year, and so on. Again, the officer's reasoning would be described in terms of these abstractions.

Abstraction simplifies thinking about the relationships among variables by reducing the combinations you have to worry about. Of course, the categories must be natural and enable the right distinctions to be made. If the categories are too coarse, you're likely to miss important distinctions. If they're too fine, you end up having to consider a large number of combinations, many of which don't make useful distinctions.

In general, knowledge is expressable as rules under the following conditions:

1. The problem variables are naturally expressible in terms of categories or intervals ("buckets") that are used in expert reasoning.

2. A rule covers a combination of inputs that will be encountered in practice—it actually "samples" a significant part of the problem space.[2]

3. The rules tend to be non-overlapping and sample the problem space comprehensively.

For example, consider the CreditBank example in more detail. CreditBank is a community lending institution. CreditBank has been making consumer loans for many years. Over the years, CreditBank has collected a significant amount of demographic and financial data on people who have had accounts, applied for loans, etc. The bank collected much of these data on paper and later converted them into electronic form. The data are not complete and some records have items missing.

The basic objective of the bank is to make loans to people who are likely to repay them. How would CreditBank develop a rule-based system to classify potential loan applicants into risk categories?

For starters, CreditBank would need to round up some of its experienced loan officers and ask them to identify the variables that are important in the lending decision.

After a few rounds of brainstorming, let's say, CreditBank's experts come up with the following variables they considered important in order to make a lending decision:

- number of years of credit (a number)
- goodness of credit history (a category, like *very low, low, medium, good,* and *very good*)
- number of years of unemployment (a number)
- profession (a category, like *engineer, lawyer, doctor,* etc.)

Next, they would begin to identify the rules. Here's an example of one that relates the number of years of credit to degree of credit history:

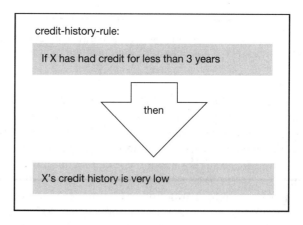

credit-history-rule:

If X has had credit for less than 3 years

then

X's credit history is very low

---

[2]Mathematically, one can say that a rule expresses a *mapping* between domains of variables.

The part before the "then" is referred to as the *condition* part of the rule or the left-hand side (LHS), and the part after the "then" as the *action* part, or the right-hand side (RHS).

How can this rule be used?

CreditBank's rule-based system can use the rule in two ways. First, suppose the system is processing a client named Mr. Cash. If the data indicate only 1 year of credit history, the system would draw the conclusion that Cash's credit history is very low. In this case, the data about Cash's credit history triggered the LHS of the rule, causing the action in the RHS to be executed. When a series of rules is executed in this way, it is referred to as *forward chaining*.

On the other hand, suppose the system moves onto another potential customer, Mr. Bumm, for whom there happens to be *no* data on years of credit. As a default strategy, in the absence of information, the system might *hypothesize* that Mr. Bumm's credit history is very low.

Now the RBS would try to *support or refute* its above hypothesis. To do this, it must first support or refute another hypothesis, that Bumm has had credit for less than 3 years. When a series of rules is involved in this way, it is referred to as *backward chaining*. In this mode the RBS must use other rules and the data that are available to check the validity of the hypothesis. In essence, the RHS of the rule becomes the hypothesis that is to be proved by finding evidence to satisfy the LHS of the rule.

To see how chaining works, consider the following additional rule:

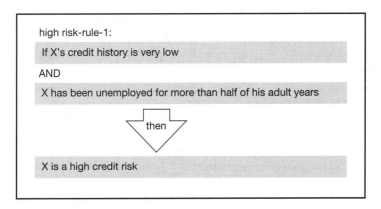

high risk-rule-1:

If X's credit history is very low

AND

X has been unemployed for more than half of his adult years

then

X is a high credit risk

In this case, if the system were to try and show that Bumm is a high credit risk, it would have to first show that the credit history is very low *and* that Bumm has been unemployed for at least half of his adult years. In order to prove the very low credit history, the system would need to use the first rule (the credit-history rule). In effect, the system needs to chain backward through the rules until it gets enough facts to verify its original goal, that Bumm is a high-credit risk. In contrast, using forward chaining, an RBS would match the LHS of the rule and work toward a conclusion, making whatever inferences it could until it had enough facts to reach a conclusion.

The point above is that one can reason forward or backward *with the same set of rules*. The rules just represent pieces of knowledge. *How* the rules are used is flexible and is also referred to as the *control strategy*.

The control strategy adopted depends on the "shape" of the problem space. If you need to acquire information about a situation very selectively[3] it makes sense to backward chain, asking very focused questions with a goal in mind. On the other hand, if lots of data are readily available, it might make more sense to work forward from the data, making whatever inferences are possible and seeing "what the data tell you."

Sometimes it makes sense to employ *both* types of reasoning alternatively: Make whatever inferences are possible based on available data, select a plausible goal based on whatever data were available, and gather additional data to prove it.

The simplest kind of rule-based system consists of three components as shown in Figure 7.2:

- a *rule base*
- *working memory*
- a *rule interpreter*

The *rule base* contains all the system's rules. For instance, the two rules Credit-Bank's experts identified would go into the rule base.

Working memory stores initial facts (data) and intermediate conclusions or hypotheses. The role of working memory is similar to that of a person's short-term memory.

The last component of an RBS is the *interpreter*. The interpreter consists of a kind of pattern matcher that recognizes which rules apply, given the current contents of working memory. Once the system identifies these rules, a selector determines which of the rules to *actually* invoke or *fire*. By fire, we mean that the rule is processed. The actual execution of the rules for Cash's and Bumm's cases was done by the interpreter.

A match occurs when there exists a piece of data in working memory that is an instance of the pattern expressed in the rule.

For example, "*Cash* has been unemployed for *three-fifths* of his adult years" is an instance of the pattern "*X* has been unemployed for *more than half* of his adult years": The variable *X* in the pattern matches the individual *Cash* in the data, and *more than half* in the pattern matches the *three-fifths* in the data. The match is shown in Figure 7.2.

Figure 7.3 shows how the interpreter works. The steps are as follows:

1. *Rules are matched against the data.*
   This is referred to as the *recognize* part of the cycle. When a rule is matched by the data, it is *instantiated*, meaning that an instance of the pattern expressed in the rule has been found.[4] During the match phase of the cycle, the interpreter collects all the instantiated rules. It puts these into a "bag," referred to as the *conflict set* (don't forget this term, it's important). If no matches occur at all, the system is done and it halts.

---

[3]For instance, there are 3000 possible questions that you could ask, but it is feasible to ask, perhaps 50 at most in order to arrive at a conclusion.

[4]A rule could be instantiated several times in one cycle if it matches many data items. For example, risk-category-rule could match the data for Joe as well as others in the database who have been unemployed for more than half their adult years. In this case, there would be multiple instantiations of the rule that would result from doing the pattern matching.

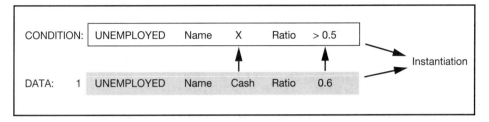

FIGURE 7.2   An Example of Pattern Matching

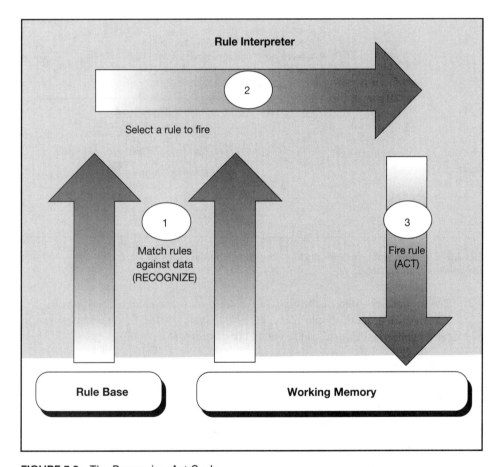

FIGURE 7.3   The Recognize–Act Cycle

2. *The interpreter selects one instantiated rule.*
   In effect, it looks into its bag and picks out the rule that should be fired next.

3. *The selected rule is fired.*
   The actual firing of the selected rule is known as the *act* part of the cycle. By firing the selected rule, the interpreter is allowed to "do its thing," which usually results in working memory being modified, or in input/output. If the selected rule happens to tell the system to stop, the system grinds to a halt. Otherwise, it goes back to step 1 and starts all over.

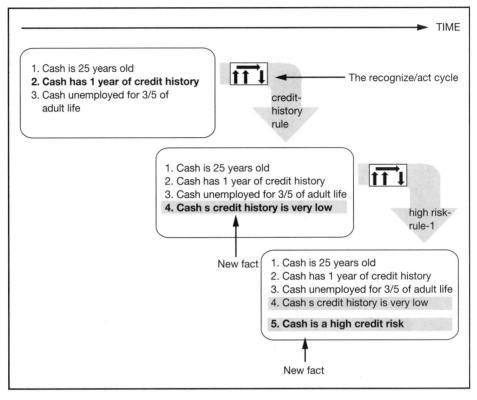

FIGURE 7.4 Contents of Working Memory over 2 Cycles for Mr. Cash. The data that fire the rules are in boldface.

The sequence of steps 1 through 3 is referred to as the *recognize–act cycle*.

Figure 7.4 shows a couple of cycles of the system (rule firing and changes in working memory) with Cash's data, which are as follows:

1. Cash is 25 years old.
2. Cash has 1 year of credit history.
3. Cash has been unemployed for three-fifths of his adult life.

The labels 1, 2, 3, 4, and 5 associated with the facts are time stamps indicating when the data item was created (so, "Cash is 25 years old" was created first, etc.). Each downward arrow indicates a rule firing.

Figure 7.4 shows the contents of working memory over the two iterations. The system has inferred two *new facts*. At each step the system holds on to its new conclusions, which can be useful in further inference.[5] In this example the system comes to a halt with five facts in working memory.

One of the advantages of rules is that they make it possible to "see" the relationships between facts and conclusions. To show how, let's make the above example a little more realistic by introducing the following four rules about risk assessment:

---

[5]In this example, working memory grew. It can also shrink if data are removed from working memory.

profession-rating-rule:	If X is an engineer, doctor, or lawyer	THEN	X belongs to a high paying profession
high-earnings-rule-2:	If X is a successful business owner	THEN	X has high earnings
high-earnings-rule-1:	If X belongs to a high paying profession	THEN	X has high earnings
low risk-rule-1:	If X has high earnings	THEN	X is a low credit risk

The six rules are shown in Figure 7.5. The network, also known as an *inference net,* shows the relationships among observations, intermediate inferences, and conclusions. The top part of the network shows the two rules we walked through earlier, and the bottom part shows four new rules that deal with low risk cases. These four rules are listed in the box above.

What is the difference between an inference net such as the one above and a decision tree? Why not specify the logic in an application using a decision tree instead of bothering with rules?

One difference has to do with how well you understand the problem at the time you start codifying the expert's knowledge. If an expert can articulate clearly and without much trial and error the sequence of steps involved in reaching a conclusion, and if these will not need modification, then a decision tree might in fact be an appropriate representation.

However, if parts of the expert's knowledge are *tacit,* they may not emerge for some time. In such cases, the decision process cannot be articulated completely and accurately up front. For such problems, especially if a significant number of variables and conditions (more than a dozen or so levels in the tree) are involved, a decision tree can be a bad idea.

Why?

As a decision tree gets large, it becomes difficult to make changes to it. This is because to understand why a certain point is reached in a decision tree, it is necessary to consider *how* one gets there. You end up examining a large part of the tree to understand the consequences of making modifications to the logic. As long as the number of variables and levels in the tree is small, the task of making modifications to it is manageable. However, the complexity of updating a decision tree rises exponentially as the levels in the tree increase.

Another difference is that a decision tree incorporates two kinds of information about the problem—decisions and events—and information on *how* to arrive at them. In essence, the *control knowledge,* which is what tells you how (the order in which) to do things, is part of the decision tree.

In contrast, the inference network in Figure 7.5 specifies the relationships among facts and conclusions but says nothing about *how* it should be traversed. Thus, there's no *control* information in the inference network, "just the facts." You can traverse the net in any direction, beginning anywhere within it. Since it does not incorporate any control information, it tends to express knowledge in self-contained "chunks," separate from the information about *how* these chunks will be used. As a

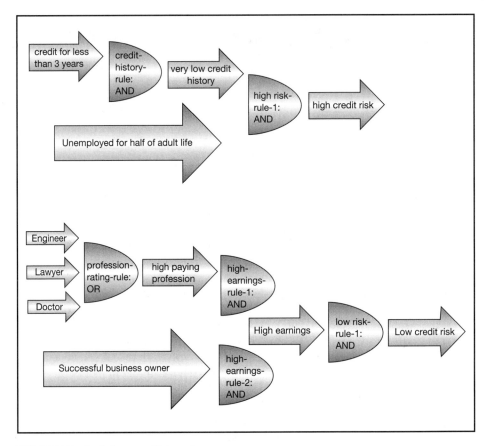

FIGURE 7.5 An Inference Network

consequence, this kind of representation is better suited for incremental specification of knowledge. When a new rule is specified, you don't need to be concerned with *where* in some predetermined sequence of steps it will be used. Rather, the rule interpreter figures this out during problem solving.[6]

---

[6]While decision trees are at least possible for some problems involving classification, such as credit risk determination, they are not even feasible for problems involving what is referred to as a large *search space*. Chess is typical of such a problem: It has been estimated that a tree of possible moves for chess would have about 10^{120} branches. It doesn't make sense to build a decision tree for such a problem because enumerating all possible moves is not feasible. (Remember that in the GA chapter, we analyzed how long it would take to evaluate 1.55×10^{25} items. We saw that we would easily run into problems.)

Yet, it is quite reasonable to specify a few dozen rules designed to recognize board configurations and make moves. Such a system wouldn't need to map out to all possible sequences of moves from the beginning for every possible chess game. Instead, it could have rules for opening moves, intermediate board configurations, endgame strategies, etc. It could then mix and match these rules depending on the context, without having to specify beforehand the exact sequence of play from the first move. This gives you tremendous flexibility over the branching logic approach. It allows you to use your expert knowledge dynamically as opposed to forcing you to structure it rigidly.

Intuitively, this separation of *what you know* and *how you use it* is appealing. After all, there are many things you know that turn out to be useful in unexpected ways, depending on the context. On the other hand, when you acquire a new piece of knowledge, you don't need to determine immediately the ways in which it will be used.

One of the implications of separating the *what* from the *how* is that a rule-based interpreter has a *choice* in every cycle as to which rule it should fire. An RBS makes the decision about which rule to fire at "run time" as opposed to being specified beforehand. This is a natural consequence of the separation of the what and the how: If you're not going to specify the decision process (the how), the system must figure it out. If several possible rules are matched by the data in working memory in each cycle, the system must select one to fire. To illustrate how selection works in a rule-based system, we will rerun the reasoning process for Cash, with the following initial facts:

1. Cash is 25 years old.
2. Cash has 1 year of credit history.
3. Cash has been unemployed for three-fifths of his adult years.
4. Cash is a doctor.

In this case, to begin with, either *credit-history-rule* or *profession-rating-rule* can fire. If *credit-history-rule* fires, Cash ends up with a very low credit history. Not a good sign. On the other hand, using the same pieces of data, if *profession-rating-rule* fires, Cash belongs to a high paying profession. Right away, you can see that you would come to very different conclusions about Cash depending on the order in which the system selects rules to fire. Figure 7.6 shows the two possible outcomes. You can see that by ordering rule firings differently, you can end up with very different behaviors from a system.

So, how *should* a rule-based system decide which instantiation to select? Interestingly, the choice of *which* rule to fire can itself be viewed as a rule-based problem: We can apply another type of rule, a *meta rule*, to decide which rule to fire.

One common meta rule is to favor rules that match the most *recent* data. In the example shown in Figure 7.6, the *profession-rating-rule* would win since it matches the most recent fact, number 4.

But *why* does it make sense to use recency of data as the meta rule? One rationale is that when a system has a choice between using inferences made recently versus those made earlier, the most recent ones focus on a more immediate goal that should be addressed instead of letting a system's attention bounce around between recent and older goals. By focusing on the most recent facts, reasoning does not get "distracted" by older facts, but is directed at the tasks or goals on top of the agenda. Inference is focused in this respect by *recency*.

But there could be other meta criteria. For example, why not give precedence to *more specific* rules, that is, ones with a larger number of conditions on the left-hand side? In our example, risk-category-rule-1 is the most specific since it has *two* conditions on the left-hand side whereas all others have only *one*.

A justification for this strategy could be that a highly restrictive left-hand side, if matched, indicates that a highly *specific* condition has been matched from which a

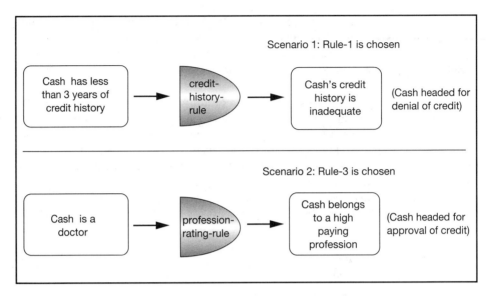

FIGURE 7.6 The order in which rules are processed affects the results.

valuable conclusion might be derivable. It should therefore be derived as soon as possible. In this case, reasoning is focused by *specificity*.

The two meta-rules above, recency and specificity, are *independent* of the problem area we're dealing with. That's good and bad. It is good because it is a *general* strategy. It is bad because it ignores problem-specific information.

An example of a problem-specific meta rule would be "give precedence to rules that deal with high credit risk." If the system used this risk-averse meta rule, it would indicate that when in doubt, the system should turn down people for credit! Another example, say for a medical consultation system, might be "ask the physician for lab test data before requiring him to provide his own judgmental data about the patient."

You might be wondering whether there's any reason to restrict ourselves to two levels of rules. There isn't! We can have meta meta rules and so on. Figure 7.7 shows that a rule-based system, in general, consists of *layers* of rules.

A two-layered system where one layer expresses domain knowledge and the other layer *how* to apply the knowledge is commonly used. In systems that use more than two layers, the basic idea is that as you go higher, the meta rules become simpler and more general, until at some level, the choice is trivial. For example, in a medical diagnostic system, a meta meta rule might be "ask for data that are routinely available before data that require invasive procedures." Similarly, for a credit risk scoring system a rule at this level could be something like "gather data about the client that are the least expensive to acquire first." At the *lowest* level, you would have rules like the six generated by CreditBank's experts.

In summary, a rule-based system consists of *layers* of rules—at least two layers. Each layer expresses a specific *type* of knowledge. This layering is appealing in that it partitions knowledge into modular chunks that can be maintained somewhat independently of each other.

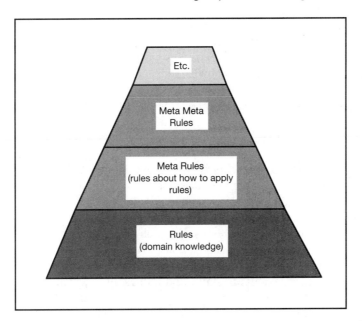

FIGURE 7.7 A rule-based system consists of layers of rules

INTELLIGENCE DENSITY ISSUES

So, when is it a good idea to consider using a rule-based system?

Let's reflect a little about how we answered this question for genetic algorithms. Recall that a GA is good for problems where you can specify *a global* criterion that helps us recognize good solutions, but where you're *not* able to specify any *knowledge about how to solve the problem.* A rule-based approach makes sense in exactly the opposite situation, when you *can* specify with confidence several small, selfcontained pieces of knowledge that indicate what conclusions to draw or actions to take in specific situations. At the same time, you are not required to specify a clear-cut global criterion to guide your search for solutions.

For example, you'd expect an experienced loan officer to be able to tell you about interpreting information regarding loan applicants and arriving at a conclusion about their creditworthiness. The loan officer might have several strategies for analyzing the data. While he might not be able to describe the process algorithmically, chances are that the loan officer would be able to articulate small pieces of the reasoning process.

On the other hand, it might be very difficult for the loan officer to give you a single measure of "goodness" to apply to all loans. To analyze a particular case, the loan officer would *invoke the right pieces depending on the data.* This is the essence of rule-based reasoning: It is *data driven,* meaning that the reasoning process is guided by the data instead of requiring the complete decision process to be laid out completely a priori.

A rule-based approach is worth considering when you have experts who are able to specify with a high degree of confidence what they do in specific situations. The trick for the model builder is to extract as much knowledge as possible in as short a period of time as possible. This knowledge is then turned into rules. These rules, in turn, must cover the problem area comprehensively so that there are no inappropriate "holes" in its knowledge base. Good coverage usually happens when experts have been solving a problem for a long time and retain heuristics that have proved useful in generating the best solutions. For such problems, we can be more confident about the quality of the solution.

If a problem is "decomposable," where the interactions among variables are limited and experts can articulate their decision process with confidence, a rule-based approach is a good candidate and a system may scale well. In contrast, if the problem is one with a large number of subtle interactions among numerically valued variables, the *complexity* of the problem increases. For such problems, it becomes increasingly impractical to conduct knowledge acquisition and extract meaningful rules. Such systems, like the weather or financial markets, are referred to as "complex systems." In trying to analyze them, experts begin to find it difficult to articulate confidently the large number of interactions among the variables. For such problems, a rule-based approach doesn't scale well, simply because knowledge engineering becomes the bottleneck.

In fact, scaling up rule-based systems from a dozen or so rules to hundreds of rules can be a very illuminating, if unpleasant, ordeal. In general, experience thus far suggests that about *60 to 70% of the time taken to develop rule-based systems is spent on knowledge acquisition!* Often, this is because of interactions among variables that only begin to emerge as a system scales up.

One way to cut down the knowledge engineering part of the process is to use whatever historical *data* are available on the problem. For example, CreditBank had data available on its customers. Could it glean these data to try to come up with something useful? The answer, surprisingly, is yes. In a later chapter, we will discuss techniques available called *machine-learning algorithms* that take a set of data and come up with rules that reflect the choices present in the data.

Perhaps the most important reason for considering an expert system approach to a problem is that an RBS approach seeks to *behave* like an expert. It exhibits the "feel" of an expert. What are the most valuable things about having access to a human expert for consultation?

Good decisions, of course. However, it's not just the accuracy of the decisions, but the ability to back them up. An expert usually provides a *justification* for a conclusion, a hypothesis, a test, and so on. In addition, an expert also questions the validity of existing facts or brings hypotheticals into the picture. The expert ponders alternative scenarios and so might say, "I think under the circumstances, X, the most likely conclusion is Y, but if an additional fact, say F, were present, hmm, the more likely conclusion might be P."

Explanation and hypothetical reasoning (or what-if analysis) are perhaps the two most compelling reasons for adopting a rule-based approach. That a system can apparently *reason* about how changes affect an existing solution and provide explanations for its decisions can add significant comfort value for the user.

But explanation and hypothetical reasoning come at a cost.

First, you have to understand the problem area much better than you can with a black box approach like a neural network; you have to extract all kinds of problem-solving knowledge. This takes time and effort. Second, from a computational standpoint, you incur a lot of overhead in terms of memory and reasoning machinery. To see why, let's see how explanation works.

The kind of explanation and hypothetical reasoning we describe is referred to, for obvious reasons, as "reason maintenance" (and sometimes as "truth maintenance"). A reason maintenance or truth maintenance system can be a separate module that "plugs into" a rule-based system.

The most primitive kind of explanation is an audit trail of a system's reasoning. What is an audit trail for a rule-based system?

Consider the inference network of Figure 7.5. Problem solving using such a network involves determining which parts of it have been "excited" for the case under consideration. For example, when we ran Cash's data through our rule base it told us that Cash is a low credit risk. If we wanted to know *why* Cash was classified as a low credit risk, we trace back through those parts of the network that were "excited" by the rule applications.

In Cash's case, he was a low risk *because*: we determined that he had high earnings; this *in turn* was justified by the fact that he belonged to a high paying profession. Figure 7.8 outlines the reasoning. The solid black circle stands for a *justification*. The system justifies the conclusion *"Cash is a low credit risk"* by the fact that *"Cash has high earnings"* is valid, and the fact that we believe low-risk-rule-1 to be a valid rule. Each justification is indicated by a solid black circle.

Now how about the truth maintenance and hypothetical reasoning? What would happen if we retracted *either* low risk-rule-1 *or* the fact that Cash has high earnings? Clearly, Cash would cease to be a low credit risk. Unless, of course, there were *other* reasons to believe that Cash is a low credit risk.

One of the interesting things to note about Figure 7.8 is that the *validity* of the rule itself is questionable. That is, you can question facts *as well as rules* in doing a what-if analysis. Experts do this all the time. That is, not only do they question facts, but also the general applicability of the rule. After all, rules are usually heuristics, not axioms. Questioning the validity of rules "broadens" the set of possibilities in the analysis.

We should point out that facts can be justified in many ways. Figure 7.9 shows such a scenario where we used another rule, which states that if someone has assets that exceed five times their loan amount, then he or she is a low credit risk (we've called this low risk-rule-2). And Cash is assumed to have cash and securities that add up to over five times the loan amount. Notice that the conclusion has *two* justifications, indicated by the two solid black circles feeding into it.

You can imagine that if a system maintains the kinds of dependency networks sketched out above, it can do fairly sophisticated kinds of what-if reasoning with ease. For example, what happens if we find out that Cash is only an intern and not a doctor? Easy. We just "gray out" that fact. What happens as a consequence? Well, the fact that "Cash belongs to a high paying profession" goes out of the window. When that happens, the fact "Cash has high earnings" isn't valid anymore either.

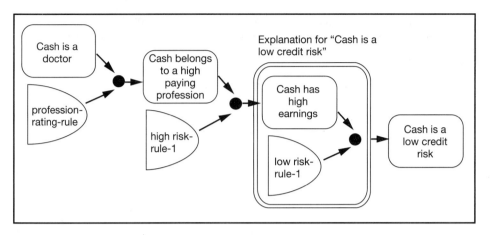

FIGURE 7.8 A Dependency Network to Explain Why Cash is a Low Credit Risk

The net result, shown in Figure 7.10, is that the conclusion "Cash is a low credit risk" loses one of its justifications. But it's still valid since it still has one justification intact.

Networks such as the above can also be extended to handle contradictions. In such cases, the status of some facts or rules must be adjusted to get rid of the contradiction. Some truth maintenance systems let you work with multiple contradictory situations at the same time, which is handy for exploring multiple perspectives simultaneously.

As we mentioned earlier, all of this comes at a cost. Other than the knowledge engineering cost, such systems tend to be space and time intensive. Keeping around justifications requires lots of memory. Even more importantly, computing the status of all facts every time a new inference is made is a computationally intensive process. With more than a few hundred facts in working memory, the status assignments algorithms can grind for a long time in order to check for contradictions and find ways of resolving them.

Another operational issue to consider is that rule-based systems are usually *not* compact, especially when you compare them to neural nets or GAs. Furthermore, each rule in an RBS expresses a small piece of knowledge *explicitly*. Each rule typically encodes knowledge about one small step of the problem-solving process. To cover a reasonably complex problem domain, you usually need a fair number of rules. In addition, you need the rule-interpreter and working memory sections as part of your system for doing the pattern matching at run time. This makes rule-based systems somewhat harder to embed into other systems.

Flexibility is a tricky issue in rule-based systems. Consider what makes traditional systems *inflexible*. For the most part, it is the large number of complex interactions between the various pieces of software. Because of this, making small changes can force you into doing a lot of analysis to ensure that you're not introducing unwanted side effects.

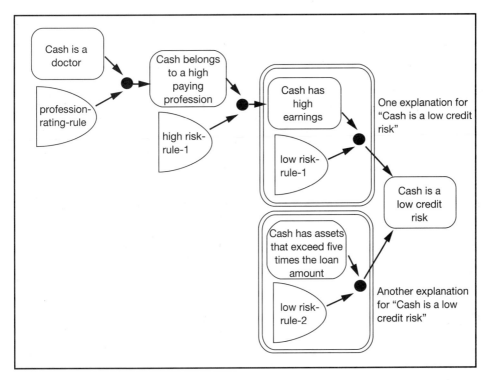

FIGURE 7.9 A Dependency Network Showing Two Supports for a Conclusion

In contrast, think about how an RBS's rules "interact" in solving problems: through working memory. That is, no rule "calls" another. Rather, rules are "invoked" by the interpreter depending on what shows up in working memory. This makes a rule-based system flexible in the sense that when you add a rule you don't need to consider whether it will "call" other rules or be called by them. Rather, a rule is stated without regard to *how* it will be used. Remember, there's a separation between the *what* and the *how*.

Having said that, however, the reality is that the rules are often specified with the conflict resolution strategy in mind (the *how*). As long as a rule set is not very large (i.e., fewer than a hundred rules or so), this isn't a serious problem. However, as a rule base becomes larger, getting the system to exhibit the behavior it is supposed to becomes harder to do by simply tweaking the rules. After a few rounds of tweaking, the content of rules begins to diverge from what the expert might have stated. In fact, the real danger can often begin when a modeler starts resorting to "tricks" to *make the right rules fire at the right time*. Over time, this can become increasingly difficult to orchestrate, and the modularity of the system can be compromised.

These difficulties can be lessened if the rule base is kept as small as possible. Furthermore, if a problem is decomposable, the rule base can also be decomposed into independent rule sets, which reduces the danger of unforeseen interactions. Experienced developers also tend to develop the rules themselves without considering unnecessarily

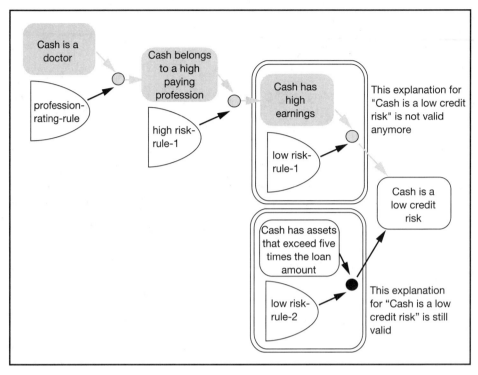

FIGURE 7.10 The Dependency Network of Figure 7.9 but With the Fact "Cash is a Doctor" Retracted. Notice how "Cash is a low credit risk" loses one support but is still valid.

the conflict resolution strategy. This reduces the danger that tricks will come back to haunt a developer.

The following table summarizes the intelligence density issues for rule-based systems:

Dimension	*RBS*	*But...*
Explainability	High	—
Response speed	Low to Moderate	Slows if data are rule-based or if data are too large; tends to get a lot slower with sophisticated explanation capabilities
Scalability	Moderate	Good for decomposable problems but poor for complex problems with a large number of variable interactions
Compactness	Low	—
Flexibility	Moderate	High for smaller rule bases, but decreases as rule base gets larger

Dimension	RBS	But...
Embeddability	Low	—
Tolerance for complexity	Low	—
Independence from experts	Low	—
Speed of development	Moderate to High	The speed is high for prototypes and small rule bases, but tends to get lower for large rule bases

Suggested Reading

Brownston, L., et al., *Programming Production Systems in OPS5*, Lawrence Erlbaum, Hillsdale, NJ: 1985.

Dhar, V., and N. Ranganathan, Integer Programming Versus Expert Systems: An Experimental Comparison, *Communications of the ACM*, Volume 33, number 3, March 1990.

Forgy, L., RETE: A Fast Algorithm for the Many Pattern/Many Object Pattern Match Problem, *Artificial Intelligence*, 1981.

Pople, H., Imposing Structure on Ill-Structured Problems: The Structuring of Medical Diagnostics, in *Artificial Intelligence in Medicine*, P. Szolovits, ed., Westview, Boulder, CO: 1982.

Quinlan, J.R., Induction of Decision Trees, *Machine Learning*, 1, pp. 81-106, 1986.

Shortliffe, E., *MYCIN: Computer Based Medical Consultation*, Elsevier, North-Holland, NY: 1976.

Simon, H., *Human Problem Solving*, Prentice-Hall, Englewood Cliffs, NJ: 1972.

APPENDIX TO CHAPTER 7:
How Rete Works

Rule-based systems typically handle pattern matching involving about a thousand working memory elements and rules without difficulty. This is because there's a clever way of doing pattern matching that does not require iterating over working memory in each cycle. The algorithm, well known as the *Rete* algorithm, makes use of the fact that the *contents of working memory change only a little after each rule application.*

Because of this, it makes more sense to think about what *change* has occurred in working memory (and hence the conflict set) after each cycle, instead of computing the entire contents of working memory from scratch each time. Specifically, the Rete algorithm figures out which instantiations from the previous cycle *will not* fire in the next cycle, and which new instantiations that *did not* fire previously will fire in the current cycle.

The Rete algorithm avoids doing the pattern matching from scratch in each cycle by maintaining an internal representation that tells it the *state* of each rule in a cycle. It does this by recording which working memory elements have matched each of the conditions of each rule. Specifically, it stores with each condition a list of working memory elements that match it as shown in Figure 7.11. The lists are updated whenever working memory changes. For example, when a new datum enters working memory, the interpreter finds all patterns that match it and adds the datum to their lists; when a datum is deleted, it deletes it from their lists. When *all* the conditions of a rule have data that match them, the rule is instantiated. Likewise, when a previously instantiated rule *ceases* to be matched by the current data, it is removed from the conflict set.

To figure out whether a rule is now instantiated or ceases to be instantiated, the Rete algorithm keeps a counter for each rule corresponding to the number of conditions in the rule. Each time a condition is instantiated, that is, a working memory

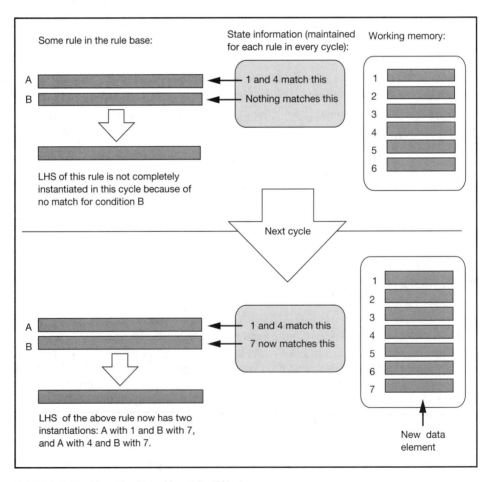

FIGURE 7.11 How the Rete Algorithm Works

element matches it, the counter is decremented. When the counter reaches zero, the rule is instantiated. Likewise, when a zero value becomes positive, it means a rule that was instantiated in the previous cycle is no longer instantiated. This is how the Rete algorithm is able to compute *changes to* the conflict set rather than computing it from scratch each time. In effect, by saving information about the *state* of each rule (i.e., whether it is completely or partly matched) in each cycle and figuring out what changed from the previous cycle, the interpreter can avoid figuring out the conflict set from scratch after each cycle.

Dealing with
Linguistic Ambiguity

Fuzzy Logic

We think in generalities, we live in detail.
—Alfred North Whitehead

*True genius resides in the capacity for evaluation of uncertain,
conflicting and hazardous information.*
—Winston Churchill

*As complexity rises, precise statements lose meaning and
meaningful statements lose precision.*
—Lotfi Zadeh

*Fuzzy logic is a method of reasoning that allows for partial or "fuzzy" descriptions of
rules. The power of fuzzy logic comes from the ability to describe a particular phenomena or process linguistically and then to represent that description in a small number of very flexible rules. The knowledge in a fuzzy system is carried both in its rules
and in* fuzzy sets, *which hold general descriptions of the properties of phenomena.*

*In this chapter, we introduce fuzzy logic and show how it can be used to build
fuzzy systems. We then discuss how and when these systems make sense for solving
business problems.*

INTRODUCTION

Sometimes rules are clear-cut. If your income is above a certain amount, you fall into
a specific tax bracket. If you've committed more than two moving violations in a year,
then your license is revoked. If you have an M.D., you can practice medicine. If a

payable account has been outstanding for more than 120 days, then send the case to a collection agency. Bureaucratic and accounting systems are full of exceedingly clear-cut rules (no matter how inappropriately they might sometimes be applied).

But more often than not, it's difficult to describe things in terms of hard, black-and-white distinctions. Language, our primary means of communication, is anything but precise. We talk about *strong* people, *intelligent* people, *green* vegetables, *highly leveraged* companies, *medium-sized* companies: All of these adjectives are approximations we use to categorize things.

Categorization provides a simple means of expression. It lets us state things in general terms and interpret these generalizations depending on context. For example, we might believe implicitly that "highly paid" is upwards of $100,000 per year. This is a generalization. But even though a woman who made $102,000 and a woman who made $190,000 would both be considered highly paid, the latter is clearly so to a greater degree. And what of the person who makes $99,900 a year? Isn't that person also highly paid? Fuzzy logic supports reasoning about these kinds of situations. It is based on gradations instead of sharp distinctions.

It is not hard to think of dozens of examples where this kind of reasoning applies. If someone referred to Yamamoto, who could lift 215 lb., as *strong,* we would tend to agree completely[1]; if Yamamoto could lift 80, we might be willing to go along with the description but be somewhat less convinced; if Yamamoto were only able to lift 25 lb., we would probably disagree if someone called him strong.

The kinds of categorizations that we've been discussing do not have precise boundaries. Rather, these categories encompass a *range* or *sensitivity* of values; highly paid, for example, encompasses a range of values. And each of the values that we consider "highly paid" belong to the category of "highly paid" to a degree ranging from 0 to 100%. For instance, $500,000 a year is certainly more "in" that category than $80,000.

The "truth" of these statements *varies* like a dimmer switch, where completely off is 0% agreement, and completely on is 100% agreement, with an infinite number of gradations in between.

Thinking about the world in terms of "degrees of membership" in categories has a natural appeal to it since you can express many problems easily in fuzzy terms. For example, it is easy for a train operator to say "If the station is *near,* I begin to *slow* the train," where *near* and *slow* are inherently fuzzy notions. Similarly, a process control operator of a blast furnace might say something like "If the temperature is *declining rapidly,* then I let in a *quick blast* of oxygen." Again, *declining quickly* and *quick blast* are fuzzy concepts used to state generalizations. If we asked these operators to be more specific, we probably wouldn't get too far. Or we might end up with a very large set of very complex but exact rules that collapse like a house of cards when changes need to be made to them.

Interestingly, fuzzy logic has found an amazing degree of applicability in consumer electronics and engineering applications. Vacuum cleaners, washing machines, and image stabilization in camcorders are a few such examples. In particular,

---

[1] A panel of Olympic class weight lifters, however, might not consider anything below 300 "very strong." We will talk about how to deal with these kinds of "relativistic" issues later in the chapter.

Japanese researchers have been instrumental in demonstrating the practical use of fuzzy logic in these areas. They have shown their appreciation of the technique and the profits it has generated by awarding the Honda prize, a most prestigious award in Japan, to Lotfi Zadeh, the inventor of fuzzy logic.

Until recently, however, fuzzy logic had probably led to many more intelligent *machines* than to intelligent software systems. Lately, this gap is beginning to narrow. Given the impressive array of applications to machines, it is natural to ask what it is about the technique (or these problems) that has led to these successful applications. And equally important, for what kinds of *business problems* is fuzzy logic a good candidate?

> *Examples:*
> - The Global Bank, a large international bank, would like to create a system to monitor potential investment opportunities. Because the bank deals in many emerging markets, however, there are often little data on the assets and markets in which the bank invests. These markets are sometimes quite complex and a model would be useful. The bank has several economists and traders who have a good deal of global trading experience.
> - Data Quick is a data vendor. The firm supplies market data on a wide variety of commercial products and services to its clients. The firm would like to develop a database that would allow its customers to perform more natural queries. For example, Data Quick would like to allow customers to do things like search for all cosmetic products that have sales volumes *about the same* as MoisturePlus in the areas *near* Chicago.
> - William Tell Direct Marketing has a large database of client market information about a large number of consumer products. The firm would like to know whether the amount of money their clients are allocating to promoting each of their products in each market is appropriate. The firm hopes to rely on its marketing team's experience in developing a model.

THE ABCs OF FUZZY LOGIC

We should begin with a clarification: Fuzzy logic does not mean vague answers.

As you might imagine, controlling the stability of a video camera is anything but vague: A vaguely stabilized image wouldn't do a camcorder much good. The same is true of controlling a steel plant: Temperatures, pressures, and flow rates are all precise, quantitative things. Control requires precise answers, such as "introduce 2.3 cc of oxygen per second," not vague statements like "introduce some oxygen slowly!" And imagine a foreign exchange prediction system that said to sell *some* dollars *pretty soon*!

Fuzzy logic only implies that the *reasoning process* is stated in terms of approximations. However, this approximate reasoning is applied to precisely stated (numerical) inputs, and produces precise numerical outputs.

The term *fuzzy logic* originated in the early 1960s when Lotfi Zadeh introduced the concept of a "fuzzy set." Zadeh reasoned that most things in life do not fall cleanly into one "crisp" category or another (hot-cold, high-low, fast-slow, etc.). In fact, Zadeh contended, many phenomena belong to *several* categories at the same time, and the categories can even appear to be mutually exclusive on the surface.

To understand what fuzzy rules are, it makes sense to begin with "regular," "crisp" rules. Take the example of CreditBank from the previous chapter, which dealt with years of unemployment and credit risk. Suppose the bank's experts articulated the two rules:

> **IF** years-of-employment is *LONG*
> **THEN** credit-risk is *LOW*

> **IF** years-of-employment is **NOT** *LONG*
> **THEN** credit-risk is *HIGH*

To make use of these rules, you need to determine what *LONG* means. Let's say that you decide that *LONG* means 15 years.

Suppose you have a database of clients and you wish to separate them into low and high risk categories for car loans. You come across Bill Borrower's data. Bill has been employed for 14 years, 11 months, 3 weeks and 6 days (1 day shy of 15 years). You fire your rules...Bill fails and you send him on his way.

Don Debtor has also applied for a car loan. Don's employment history shows that he has been employed for 15 years and 1 day. Don walks out with a new car loan.

What happened here? Two applicants with essentially the same employment history have applied for loans. Because Don was employed for 2 days more than Bill, your rule indicated that Don was able to get a loan (he was of "LOW" credit risk), and that Bill was not (he was of "HIGH" credit risk). But you know that the employment histories of the two men are almost identical. Bill has suffered because in this case your rules were too brittle (*crisp*). According to the two rules above, reality must be broken up into only "black" and "white" or LONG and NOT LONG.

What is unnatural in the above example is that we are trying to deal with inherently fuzzy concepts in a *crisp* way.

Precisely what do we mean when we use the terms *crisp* and *fuzzy?* Figure 8.1 shows the concepts LONG and NOT LONG as crisp sets of values. The numbers 15 and 30 define the boundaries of the set LONG, which means that all values in the interval [15,30] belong to the set, whereas those outside this range do not. Similarly values in the set [0,15] belong to the set NOT LONG and those outside this range do not.

Figure 8.1b shows what is referred to as the *membership function* for the set LONG. What it shows is that numbers in the range 0 to 15 years have 0 membership (FALSE) in the set LONG whereas those between 15 and 30 have complete membership of 1 (TRUE). In crisp sets, membership of an object in a set is either 0 or 1.

Consider another example. Suppose Data Quick, the market data vendor, has a user who wants to find medium-sized companies in a large database. Say the user defines medium-sized companies crisply as companies having sales between $25 and $75 million. Is there a significant difference between a company with $24.5 and one with $25 million in sales? Not really, but the former would not show up if you

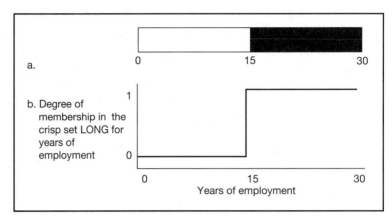

FIGURE 8.1a A Crisp Set Showing LONG for Years of Employment **b** Membership in the Crisp Set LONG

queried the database for medium-sized companies. If you make the boundary $24 million, the $23.5 million company gets excluded. And so on.

Fuzzy logic provides a methodology for dealing with "gray" areas that involve concepts such as LONG, MEDIUM, and others like them. By allowing sets to have "fuzzy boundaries" rather than sharp ones, rules tend to be more flexible, compact, and intuitive for modeling complicated processes whose components are not simply black and white.

How does this work?

Zadeh proposed that the degree to which a given object or phenomenon falls into different categories, as defined and quantified via the membership function, need not be an "all or nothing" step function as in Figure 8.1b. Rather, membership can range *continuously* between 0.0 and 1.0, where 0.0 indicates no membership, or FALSE, and 1.0 indicates total membership or TRUE, and all other values indicate some intermediate *degree* of membership.

Figure 8.2 shows a fuzzy set for MEDIUM-sized companies. It is fuzzy in the sense that there are no sharp boundaries where the set ends. The boundaries of the set fall off gradually. Instead of companies being MEDIUM or NOT MEDIUM, *any* company belongs to the set, with a value between 0 and 1 indicating the extent to which it belongs.

The degree of membership in Figure 8.2 is depicted by the shading: A company with sales of $50 million is a *prototypical* medium-sized company, with membership of 1. The degree to which a company belongs to this set begins to taper off on either side of $50 million. At $25 and $75 million, the membership drops to 0.

What this means, is that the concept of *medium* applies most strongly to companies that have sales of exactly $50 million, and the concept is less strongly applicable as you move away from that value. Figure 8.3 shows the membership function for medium-sized companies. In this case, membership increases linearly between $25 and $50 million and declines linearly after that.

Figure 8.4 summarizes some of the differences between crisp and fuzzy sets. Concepts such as small, medium, and large are described in terms of gradations in-

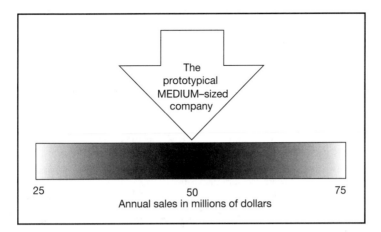

FIGURE 8.2   A Fuzzy Set Showing MEDIUM for Company Size

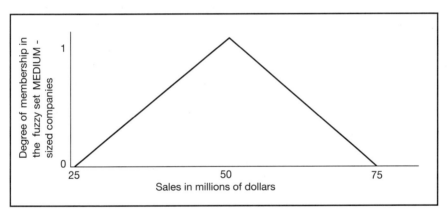

FIGURE 8.3   Membership in a fuzzy set: A company with 50 million in sales has complete membership (of 1); degree of membership declines on either side of $50 million.

stead of sharp boundaries. The boundaries between sets are gradual, not dramatic. It is equally simple to define sets such as SOMEWHAT SMALL, PRETTY LARGE, NOT VERY HIGH, SORT OF LOW, etc.

It's also worth noting that, unlike fuzzy sets, crisp sets provide you with no *sensitivity* to the closeness of a particular value to the prototypical value. Thus, in your crisp set *medium* company example, you had no real way of knowing that $25 million was at the very edge of the set while $50 million was right in the middle of it. As you can see in Figure 8.4, a fuzzy set provides this information naturally; even though $24.5 million has 0 membership in the set MEDIUM, $25 million is very close to 0 as well. Thus there's very little difference between them.

The fact that we think in terms of linguistic approximations (such as HIGH and LOW, LARGE and SMALL) and the fact that we have ideas about the *extent* to

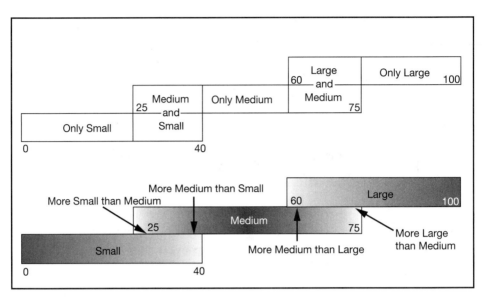

FIGURE 8.4 How Memberships Differ in Crisp and Fuzzy Sets

which these concepts apply to various object make it possible to create powerful rules using fuzzy sets. A single fuzzy rule is applicable in a large number of situations to different degrees, depending on the context.

The natural consequence of this in practice is that the right-hand side (RHS) or action part of a fuzzy rule gets applied or executed *only to the degree* that the left-hand side (LHS) or condition part is true.

This makes sense. Consider the following rule.

> **IF** years-of-employment is *LONG*
> **THEN** credit-risk is *LOW*.

When we were discussing crisp rules, we decided that LONG meant greater than 15 years (Figure 8.1). The action (RHS) part of the rule ("credit risk is LOW") was only established to the extent that the conditional (LHS) part was true. If the LHS were false, then the RHS was not established and did not apply. Since the rule was a crisp rule, the memberships were always 100% or 0%, so the rule was always "on" or "off." There were no gray areas.

In contrast, with fuzzy sets, if membership in the set LONG for years of employment is 0.8, then the associated credit risk would be LOW to degree 0.8 as well. In a few moments, we will see how this actually happens. At this point, the important thing to realize is that fuzzy rules apply to ambiguous categories in an intuitive manner. Just like in the case of Yamamoto the weight lifter, you are able to use a particular concept in your reasoning depending on how strongly a fact (object) agrees with (is a member of) your view of that concept (a fuzzy set).

If you believe strongly that the concept applies to a situation, then you rely more heavily on the concept in your reasoning. If you believe less strongly, you rely on the concept less. In effect, fuzzy sets and fuzzy rules allow you to reason about gray areas using a simple numerical scheme.

To understand how all of this comes together, we need to describe how *inferencing* works using fuzzy rules and how it differs from inferencing using crisp rules.

Consider William Tell's problem from the beginning of the chapter. The marketing firm is trying to develop a system to help it identify clients whose products may be overmarketed or undermarketed in various regions. Specifically, the firm would like to know whether their clients are allocating appropriate amounts of money to promotion.

Why is this a complex decision? First, William Tell needs to know how each product has been "behaving" in the market. By behaving, we mean a number of things. How well established is the product? Has its market share been going up or down lately? How have promotions impacted sales volume in the past? How have *others'* promotions impacted the sales volume? And so on. How can a system inform the decision maker about how many promotion dollars to allocate to each product?

Let's say that William Tell has consulted its marketing experts and they give the following high level reasoning for understanding market behavior and promotion decisions:

> *Well, if you've got a high margin, price sensitive product, promoting that product via ads, displays, etc. is likely to have a high impact on sales volume. If the volume impact is high, it's a good candidate for allocation of promotion dollars.*
>
> *But you also want to promote products more heavily when they're relatively new in order to increase market awareness and to establish market share . . .*

For simplicity, we'll restrict ourselves to the small subset of variables and relationships described by the expert above. Of course, in reality several other variables can also impact promotion decisions.

Let's define some rules and a few fuzzy sets based on the expert's reasoning.

The first rule: If a product is new, then a client should spend more money promoting it.

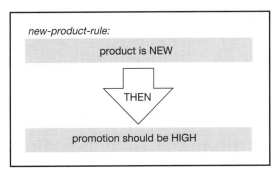

In order to use this rule, we need to define the fuzzy sets that it references. The expert might have described the concept of "new" as being less than 9 months old.

The fuzzy sets NEW for product and HIGH for promotion might be described as shown in Figures 8.5 and 8.6. In fact, since we will be referring to various levels of promotion we also define MEDIUM for promotion and LOW for promotion as shown in Figure 8.6.

The next three rules express the relationship between price sensitivity and promotion. Highly price sensitive products should be highly promoted, and so on:

low-price-sensitivity-rule:	medium-price-sensitivity-rule:	high-price-sensitivity-rule:
the *price sensitivity* of a product is LOW	the *price sensitivity* of a product is MEDIUM	the *price sensitivity* of a product is HIGH
THEN	THEN	THEN
promotion should be LOW	*promotion* should be MEDIUM	*promotion* should be HIGH

Price sensitivity could be measured using historical data, perhaps as the ratio of the percentage change in volume per percentage change in price lagged by an appropriate time period.

Figure 8.7 shows the meaning of the above rules graphically. As the figure shows, each rule defines a "fuzzy patch."

To keep things simple, we will focus on the middle patch, which corresponds to the **medium-price-sensitivity-rule**. You can see that depending on the value of the input, the rule applies with different intensity levels. For example, if price sensitivity is 2.5, the system applies the MEDIUM rule with maximum intensity. This happens since the degree of membership in the set MEDIUM for 2.5 of price sensitivity is 1.

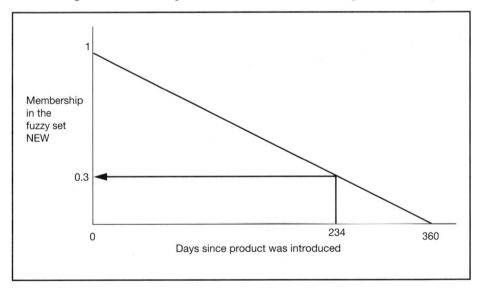

FIGURE 8.5 The Fuzzy Set NEW Product. 225 days has membership 0.3 in the fuzzy set.

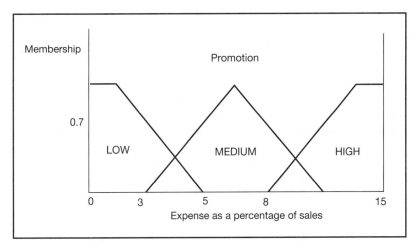

FIGURE 8.6   Fuzzy Sets LOW, MEDIUM, and HIGH for Promotion

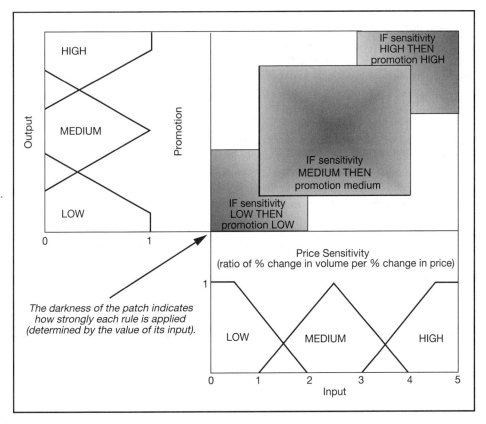

FIGURE 8.7   Fuzzy Rules: The Relationship between Inputs and Outputs as Fuzzy Patches

You can also see that an input value between 1 and 2 falls into an overlapping fuzzy patch (LOW and MEDIUM), meaning that values in this range have membership in both sets. As a result, both rules (low-price-sensitivity and medium-price-sensitivity) will fire with intensities corresponding to their respective memberships.

This is all well and good, but you might be wondering whether the above rules are oversimplistic. Maybe the rule that says that if price sensitivity is high then promotion should be high is too naive and does not capture the various complexities involved in determining promotion levels.

In a sense the rule doesn't. But it isn't supposed to, at least not all by itself. Rather, each rule expresses an *influence,* providing a "tug" toward the final answer that is, in effect, a combination of each of these individual tugs.

To understand this, let's work our way through the consumer products example. (Remember, William Tell is trying to figure out what percentage of estimated sales should be allocated to promotion of each product.)

Assume that based on an analysis of the database, William Tell generates summary data about each product as shown in Figure 8.8.

Let's work out the answer for product ABC.

Product ABC has an age of 234 days. Looking this value up in the set NEW (see Figure 8.5), you can see that it maps to a membership of 0.3. In other words, this product is not considered very new from a promotional perspective.

Applying **new-product-rule** ("IF product is new THEN promotion is high"), you can infer that the promotion for ABC should be HIGH to degree 0.3. (Recall that you *only* apply a rule *to the degree* that its LHS, the "IF" part, is true.) That means that you will only apply the **new-product-rule** to the degree 0.3.

To account for the fact that **new-product-rule** does not apply fully, you need to cut down its influence. If the rule were 100% true, you would fully apply the fuzzy set HIGH for promotion expense. Since this is not the case though, you need to cut the HIGH part of the set NEW for down to 0.3 of its full force. Thus, instead of applying the whole HIGH set, you only apply the first 0.3 of it. (Figure 8.9, top, shows this. The influence of HIGH is shown as shaded.)

Likewise, for product ABC the price sensitivity of 3 has membership 0.6 in the set MEDIUM. Applying **medium-price-sensitivity-rule** ("IF price_sensitivity of a

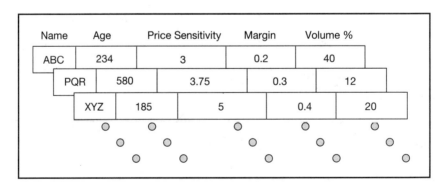

Name	Age	Price Sensitivity	Margin	Volume %
ABC	234	3	0.2	40
PQR	580	3.75	0.3	12
XYZ	185	5	0.4	20

FIGURE 8.8 Database Records Showing Summary Information for Each Product

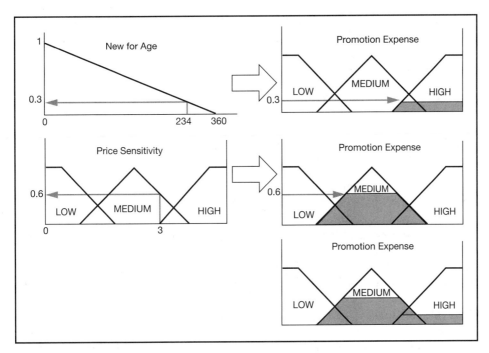

FIGURE 8.9   The Composite Region from Applying the Two Fuzzy Rules

product is medium THEN promotion should be medium"), the promotion expense should be MEDIUM to degree 0.6 (Figure 8.9, middle).

To figure out what all of this means to William Tell, you need to look at the fuzzy set that was formed by the application of the first two rules. The bottom part of Figure 8.9 shows this set. It is called the *consequent fuzzy region* since it is a region that is formed as a consequence of the application of the fuzzy rules. This region is a "combination" of the two individual regions on the top right of the figure.

Note that the contribution of the set HIGH for promotion expense is significantly smaller than that for MEDIUM, which takes up a much larger area. This makes sense, since MEDIUM was more "strongly" established than HIGH. It therefore tugs the final result more toward itself.

In this example, there was only one rule applicable for MEDIUM and HIGH. It fired to the degree 0.6. However, there could have been several rules, which could also have fired based on other data.

Suppose we had another rule that also referred to MEDIUM for promotion, but it had only fired with a strength of 0.4. Which value would we now choose for MEDIUM, 0.6 from the first rule or 0.4 from the second? A little thought should convince you that 0.6 would make more sense. In general we should take the *maximum* membership of the results of each of the rules.

Why?

The basic reasoning is that when you combine the rules, you let the truth of the "truest" rules dominate.

To understand why this makes sense, consider the following example, this time combining two *crisp* rules:

birth-rule
IF a man is born in America
THEN he is an American citizen

marriage-rule
IF a man marries an American citizen
THEN he is an American citizen

Assume a man is unmarried and that he was born in Little Rock, Arkansas. Firing the rule **birth-rule** you establish that the man is a U.S. citizen. However, when you fire the **marriage-rule,** you cannot establish anything new based on this rule since the membership of the LHS is 0. When you combine the results of these two rules, do you determine that the man is a citizen? Of course you do. Even though the **marriage-rule** could not be applied, you know that you can make truthful statements about the citizenship of the man. The result of all of this is that you determine that the man's membership in "American citizen" is equal to the *maximum membership* of all of the rules relating to citizenship that fired.

Now let's get back to our marketing promotion example because we still haven't nailed down how much William Tell's client should spend on promoting product ABC. To finish out the example, however, we'll add another rule into the picture: Promotion should be LOW for products that are HIGH margin *and* have HIGH sales volume:

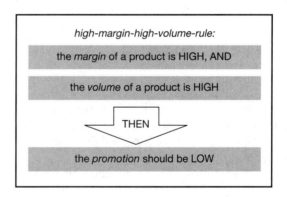

To apply this rule, you need to note that product ABC's membership in HIGH margin is 0.3 and its membership in HIGH sales volume is 0.6. To what degree should promotion be LOW?

This depends on how you combine the two memberships contained in the LHS. One generally accepted method is to assume the "weakest link in the chain" principle, which says that the "composite membership" of the LHS is the minimum of the memberships of all of the conditions on the LHS. In this case, this membership would be 0.3. Thus promotion would be LOW to degree 0.3.

Again, this makes sense. The right hand side (RHS) or action part of a rule is only executed to the degree that the left-hand side (LHS) or condition part *as a whole* is true. Think about the following crisp rule:

IF the car has gas
AND the car has an engine
THEN the car will run.

Assume that we have a car with a full tank of gas but no engine. Note that the first part of the LHS is true (membership = 1). But the second part of the rule is false (membership = 0). The overall result is that the RHS will not fire. Said another way, in evaluating the rule, we chose the *minimum* truth from the LHS and applied that to the RHS.

In summary, we take the *minimum* value when computing the intensity of the LHS of the rule since no condition can be stronger than its weakest link. We take the *maximum* value when multiple rules establishing the same consequent have fired. This inferencing and combination scheme is called *MIN-MAX* combination, and is one of the most commonly used methods of combination.

Now we're finally in a position to determine exactly how much to spend on promoting each product. At this point, it is actually straightforward. Since each of the fuzzy rules tries to "shift the balance" of the consequent fuzzy region, we determine the outcome by "balancing" the consequent fuzzy region.

In technical terms, we calculate the center of gravity, the point at which the region would balance, of the fuzzy set. This operation, which converts a composite fuzzy set to a crisp value, is called *defuzzification*. There are many methods for doing this, but the one we just described, called the *centroid* method (or the *gravity* method), is one of the most common.[2] Figure 8.10 shows an example of centroid defuzzification.

Based on the simple analysis of our toy system, William Tell would see that 8.58% of product ABC's estimated revenue should be spent on promotion.

You may have noticed that we have been doing something a little sneaky. In our first example, the values of ABC lined up exactly on the boundaries of fuzzy sets. This meant that each value only had *one* (non-zero) membership in *one* fuzzy set. As a result, *only one* of our rules ever fired for each variable. We have yet to show a case where a variable's value occurs *between* two fuzzy sets. This would necessitate firing more than one fuzzy rule dealing with the same variable.

Let's look at the next example from our database, product PQR. Since the basic inferencing is similar to the ABC case, we won't go through it all. Instead, we'll just look at **price sensitivity** whose value is 3.75. Examining Figure 8.11 you can see 3.75 has a membership of 0.2 in the set MEDIUM for price sensitivity, but 3.75 also has a membership of 0.4 in the set HIGH for price sensitivity. What this tells you is that 3.75 is more HIGH than MEDIUM.

---

[2]This method basically comes down to taking a weighted average of all of the possible values of promotion expense. The weighting is done based on the degree of membership in the consequent fuzzy region. The more the rules added weight to a particular value (the "truer" the rules supporting it were) the more influence it is given in dictating the output.

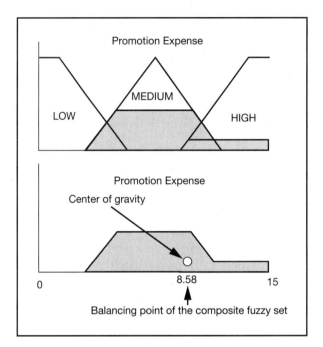

FIGURE 8.10 Defuzzifying the Consequent Fuzzy Region

Turning back a few pages to our price sensitivity rules, you can see that there is a rule for cases where the **price–sensitivity** is HIGH and another rule for when it is MEDIUM. Which rule do you use? The answer highlights the flexibility of fuzzy logic: BOTH!

We already know that we are going to apply the RHS of a rule to the degree that the rule's LHS is true. It becomes a simple matter now to apply the MEDIUM rule to the degree that 3.75 is MEDIUM for **price–sensitivity** (0.2) and to apply the HIGH rule to the degree that it is HIGH (0.4). We can see this in Figure 8.11.

It's easy enough to see the dynamics of what is happening when you fire the rules for **price–sensitivity**, but what are the implications of this? What does the ability to apply several similar rules buy you?

Think about what happens as **price–sensitivity** moves from 3.0 to 4.0. At 3.0, the only rule governing the behavior of the system is the MEDIUM rule. As you move from 3.0 to the right, the effects of the MEDIUM rule gradually decrease, and the HIGH rule starts to have an effect as well. Finally, as you move past 4.0, the MEDIUM rule stops having any impact and all of the behavior is controlled by the HIGH rule.

What this means conceptually is that the behavior of the system changes gradually and smoothly. There is no sudden jump from a MEDIUM value to a HIGH value. Using only two rules and a few fuzzy sets, you have accounted for a very wide variety of possible system inputs. This is what we meant earlier when we said that fuzzy rules are powerful: A single rule applies to a variety of situations, but the *degree* to which it applies depends on the context.

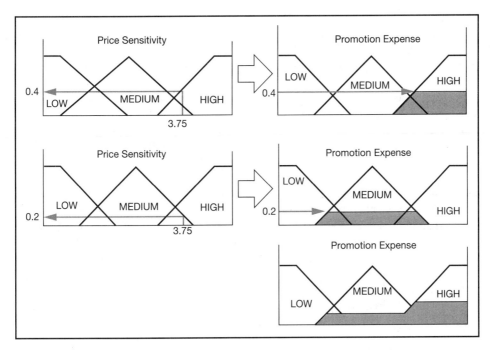

FIGURE 8.11 Two Rules, High- and Medium-Price-Sensitivity Rules Firing Simultaneously

This is also one way of thinking of how a person might apply knowledge about price sensitivity to the problem in similar circumstances. A person might weight feelings about medium values and high values and come up with some sort of mix that was appropriate in the context of the situation.

As we have been running through our example, we have been implicitly taking advantage of another property of fuzzy sets. All of the fuzzy sets we have been using have been *context sensitive*. For example, the set *NEW for Age* was a set ranging from 0 to 360 days. The designer of the fuzzy set determined that this was the appropriate set to describe a "new" product in the marketing database.

However, consider how different the set NEW might look if it were instead describing *NEW for News Story*. In the later case the set might range between 0 and 2 days. Or what about the case of *NEW for Species of Animal*. In this case, the fuzzy set might have boundaries at 100,000 years and 1.5 million years. When you build fuzzy reasoning systems, the implicit assumption is that the sets are context sensitive containing knowledge about the characteristics of the various concepts you wish to manipulate. The rules, therefore, do not need to describe what *New* means in a given context, because the sets already "know" this.

Finally, we need to clarify one more point. There is often confusion regarding the distinction between *fuzziness* and *probability*. The two concepts have much in common. Both deal with uncertainty. Both are measured on continuous scales that range from 0 to 1. However, there are also some fundamental differences between fuzziness and probability.

To understand what these differences are, consider a deck of ordinary playing cards. Let's assume you want to perform an experiment where you draw a card at random from this deck. You want to know the probability of drawing a high card, where a high card is either a jack, queen, king, or ace. For a standard deck, the probability is 16/52 or about 30%.

Once you have drawn the card, you can look at it and you can know for certain what the value of the card is. Let's say that you have drawn the nine of hearts. At this point, there is no uncertainty about the outcome of our experiment, in terms of *whether* you will draw a specific type of card or not. You have already drawn it. That is, the probabilistic component of the uncertainty is no longer present.

Fuzziness seeks to answer a different type of question about a different type of uncertainty. You can look at the nine of hearts in your hand and ask the question, *"Is this a high card?"* Note that this does not have anything to do with the *probability* of the card being high, since we already know the card's value. Rather, fuzziness asks to what *degree* is the nine of hearts high? If you rate the highness of the cards linearly on a scale of 1 to 13, the highness might be 9/13. If, on the other hand, you assumed that only the picture cards and the ace are high, then the nine of hearts' degree of "highness" would be 0.

To further drive this point home, consider the probability of drawing any heart from the deck (0.25). Then you might ask *"to what degree is this (the probability of drawing a heart) LOW?"* The answer might be that the probability of drawing a heart, 0.25, is LOW to the degree 0.65, say. The actual probability of drawing a heart is clear, but our evaluation of the *degree* to which this probability is LOW is subjective. That is what fuzzy logic deals with: the degree to which something has a property, not the probability that it has that property.

INTELLIGENCE DENSITY ISSUES

So, when is it a good idea to use fuzzy reasoning?

It's worth asking why fuzzy logic has proved to be a tremendous success in consumer electronics and industrial control applications. What properties of the technique make it suitable to these problems? What can we learn from these successes in order to understand when fuzzy reasoning is a good approach to try?

The nice thing about rules as a whole is that they allow you to state relationships very *generally* and *compactly,* as associations. On the other hand, they do not require you to be as precise as, say, mathematical models. Why is that a good thing? Recall Zadeh's comment from the beginning of the chapter:

> *As complexity rises, precise statements lose meaning and meaningful statements lose precision.*

What does it mean for a system to become complex? Complexity arises when variables begin to interact in non-linear ways. For example, in an automobile, friction increases non-linearly with speed. So does the amount of fuel required. So does wind resistance. Likewise, in weather prediction, the relationships among wind speed, sunlight, temperature, humidity, etc., tend to be highly interactive and non-linear. Chemical reactions, aircraft dynamics, etc., tend to involve highly non-linear (or discontinuous) relationships among variables. The same is true for financial markets: variables such as interest rates, currency rates, commodity prices, etc., interact in a large number of ways.

The bottom line is that the overall behavior of such systems is complex. Sometimes, you can describe this behavior mathematically in terms of differential equations. Sometimes you cannot. Fuzzy logic provides another, more intuitive and often more flexible, way to describe these behaviors.

Rules are approximations, but they're simple. And fuzzy rules can offer an attractive tradeoff between accuracy, compactness, and scalability. Think back to the rule-based chapter, where we discussed the fact that experts use *abstraction* as a way of simplifying the problem domain. The abstraction consists of *categorizing* variables into intervals, where the intervals actually stand for something meaningful, like *high fever.*

Fuzzy rules generalize the concept of categorization since an object belongs to any set to a certain degree; if something absolutely does not belong to a set, the degree of membership is 0. So, for example, high fever doesn't have to be defined crisply as being between 102 and 108 degrees Fahrenheit; rather, *any* temperature is high, just to a greater or lesser degree.

This property makes fuzzy rules highly compact. A single statement can cover a wide variety of situations and process dynamics. It also gets around the problems that rule-based systems have with borderline cases. In fuzzy systems, there is no such thing as a borderline case. As objects move between sets their membership declines in the first set and increases in the next. The net result is that fuzzy systems tend to be more accurate than rule-based systems when continuously valued variables are involved.

Fuzzy rules also let you break down a complex system into "local" pieces. These local pieces, when taken collectively, can then model the domain of interest. So, for example, a rule that says "if you push the accelerator a little, the speed will increase a little" focuses on a *local region of behaviors*, in this case, a *little acceleration*, and a *little increase in speed.* By expressing enough rules and covering enough intervals using meaningful categories, you can cover the range of behaviors of interest, however non-linear they might be. Figure 8.12 shows how, in principle, enough fuzzy rules, each of which defines a "fuzzy patch," can model a highly non-linear relationship.

You might have realized that the ability of fuzzy rules to approximate non-linear functions makes them sound very similar to neural nets. In a sense, neural nets and fuzzy systems are two sides of the same coin. They both attempt to approximate non-linear relationships that characterize complex systems. But they do it in very different ways. Neural nets make sense when you have access to *lots of data* and you're not in a position to articulate relationships among variables with confidence. In fact, when you've got lots of data of reasonable quality, neural nets will *generate* the non-linear relationships that "fit" the data.

Fuzzy rules make sense in just the opposite type of situation: where you don't have lots of data, but you do have experts who are able to describe pieces of the

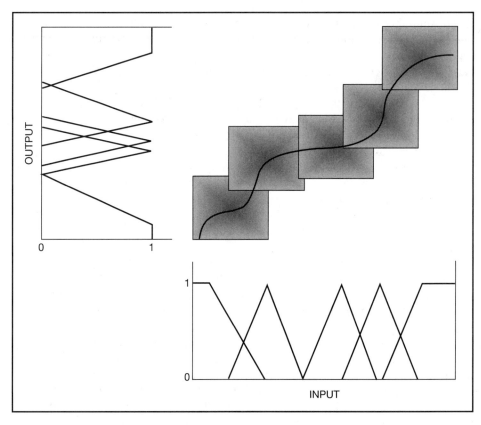

FIGURE 8.12 A schematic of how a large number of fuzzy patches can approximate non-linear relationships.

behavior in terms of rules that cannot be disputed. This enables you to make use of expertise in the problem area, expertise that is the result of trial and error and difficult or impossible to model mathematically. If you've got access to expertise that can help you achieve accurate results, it makes sense to use it! Rules, and especially fuzzy rules, make this expertise usable.

The fact that you represent knowledge *explicitly* with fuzzy rules also provides a degree of comfort to the user. One of the major drawbacks of a neural network is that the knowledge is *implicit* in the network; it is hard to understand the mechanics underlying its decisions. Fuzzy systems have much greater face validity. You can peruse the rules and assure yourself that they make sense.

From Figure 8.12 you can see that fuzzy reasoning can produce accurate results as long as you can define a sufficient number of fuzzy sets and rules. As the figure shows, the larger the number of sets, the more accurately the system reflects the true relationship among variables. Of course, this also increases the complexity and decreases the robustness of the system. Increasing the number of rules also makes it more difficult to modify the system.

Another interesting aspect of fuzzy systems is that knowledge is *distributed* between two parts of the systems: the rules, and the fuzzy sets. If a system produces an incorrect answer, the cause can be either a rule or the fuzzy sets it uses. We have already talked about the fact that fuzzy rules tend to be very general. If they make sense, chances are that you'll spend most of your time eliciting information from experts on the boundaries of the fuzzy sets and tweaking them until they produce the right answers.

Think back to the William Tell example we used in the last section. The rules were quite evident from the two small paragraphs. The real action was in deciding how many fuzzy sets we needed, their boundaries, and their shapes. But this tends to be much less complicated than the knowledge engineering process in crisp rule-based systems in which every case needs to be explicitly treated. It also makes fuzzy systems much more compact.

It is a far simpler knowledge engineering exercise than that required to build rule-based systems.

At this stage you might be wondering why anyone would want to use a traditional rule-based system. It turns out that for problems that involve a lot of branching decisions fuzzy systems can be more difficult to use, for example, problems that involve many rules of the type:

IF <something is true>
THEN <do set of actions A>
ELSE <do set of actions B>

Rules like this tend to lend themselves very naturally to a crisp reasoning system. For instance, an expert system that advised lawyers about which legal statutes applied in different situations would probably involve crisp reasoning since a statute either applies or it doesn't. Crisp concepts are less easily expressed in a fuzzy environment.

On the other hand, you can often express rules that deal with the qualities and attributes of objects in the problem domain more easily in terms of a few fuzzy rules instead of many detailed crisp rules. An expert system that predicted foreign exchange prices might be an example of this. The concepts involved in currency trading, as *high, declining,* and *favorable,* etc., are all somewhat vague in nature and span ranges of meanings.

Fuzzy reasoning offers an attractive tradeoff between accuracy and compactness. The technique encourages you to express relationships in terms of simple rules, each of which provides its own little "tug." This modeling method ensures that the overall result will be an aggregation of these smaller influences. If you can ensure that each of the smaller influences makes sense (expresses an accurate relationship), you can be confident that the overall result will be accurate.

At the same time, the system is not as computationally intensive as standard rule-based systems. Since the number of rules is typically relatively small, the effort required for pattern matching and evidence combination is lower than with traditional expert systems. For this reason, the response time is typically very fast.

Furthermore, remember that we said that all objects belong to their corresponding fuzzy sets to varying degrees. What this means is that a fuzzy system fires *all* of the fuzzy rules each time you execute the fuzzy system.[3] The natural result of this is that, in addition to being fast, the response time for fuzzy systems tends to be very stable.

Fuzzy reasoning sacrifices some explanation for accuracy, reliability, and compactness. Since degrees of memberships of objects in sets is the end result of a process of massaging numbers into an average (such as a centroid), you can't really identify *why* an inference was made as easily as you can with rule-based systems. There is no concept of a *justification* for a fact as in rule-based systems. Rather, incremental changes in inputs produce smooth changes in outputs instead of discontinuous ones. So you can easily see how outputs change in response to inputs, but not necessarily *why*.

While it is possible to see which rules influenced the output of a fuzzy system most heavily (as measured by the compound membership of the LHS and the corresponding magnitude of the fuzzy sets on the RHS), this tends to be less satisfying than the crisp line of reasoning that might be produced by a rule-based system, or the highlighting of similar cases that might occur in a case-based system.

Fuzzy systems deliver some of the goals of many symbolic knowledge representations (rule-based systems, case-based systems, etc.) in that fuzzy logic allows you to add knowledge incrementally to a system without thinking about *how* the knowledge will be used. In this respect, they are highly scalable. Remember that one of the drawbacks of rule-based systems is that people often specify rules with the conflict resolution strategy already in mind. This leads to tweaking of the rules to get the system to behave correctly. Over time, tweaking rules artificially just to get them to fire at the right time erodes the modularity of the knowledge base. That's why rule-based systems aren't always as scalable as they're supposed to be. You can't do these kinds of tricks with fuzzy systems even if you try. There's no question of getting rules to fire at the right time—all the rules relating to a particular concept fire simultaneously. (Flip back a few pages to Figure 8.11.)

The fact that you can truly specify small pieces of knowledge without regard to how the system will use them makes fuzzy systems well suited for modeling complex or changing systems. It makes such systems scalable and flexible in that adding new rules is natural and unlikely to have completely unforeseen consequences.

However, this simultaneous firing of rules can also have a down side as you add more and more rules. A phenomenon that can negatively impact scalability is often referred to as "saturation" of fuzzy sets. This means that a fuzzy set gets so full of inferences that the consequent fuzzy regions are overloaded. The end result is that the system loses the information provided by fuzzy rules and the entire fuzzy region balances on its center point (Figure 8.13).

To understand how this occurs, consider that the more rules that we add that deal with, say, HIGH for promotion expense, the more likely it is that one of them will be satisfied to a high degree. The MIN-MAX and centroid methods suffer from the fact that you take only the maximum of each fuzzy set when you apply them to

---

[3]Certain fuzzy systems, however, take advantage of optimization methods that eliminate the need to fire rules whose consequence will not affect the outcome.

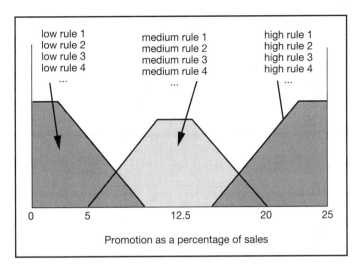

FIGURE 8.13   A Saturated Fuzzy Region for Promotion Expense.

the consequent fuzzy region. And therefore, given enough variables and enough rules, eventually every set could be satisfied to a high degree. Fuzzy systems designers often get around this by sub-dividing concepts and incrementally approaching the output of interest.[4]

Finally, fuzzy systems tend to be moderately embeddable, although not always to the same degree as neural nets or genetic algorithms. As with rule-based systems, you still need an interpreter for doing the pattern matching and evidence combination at run time. However, because much of fuzzy inference involves lots of lookup type operations (i.e., looking up the *membership* of an object in a fuzzy set, looking up the *value* associated with a particular fuzzy membership function, etc.), researchers have developed techniques to make fuzzy systems both more compact and more embeddable.

A fuzzy associative map (FAM) is one example of this. A FAM replaces the rules of a fuzzy system with a simple table that maps the LHS of a rule to the RHS. By doing this the need for rule interpreters can be greatly reduced. There has also recently been a good deal of activity in the area of fuzzy chip design. Fuzzy chips allow fuzzy rules and sets to be embedded in their architecture making fuzzy systems very compact and portable.

In summary, the table that follows shows how fuzzy systems look in terms of the dimensions of the stretch plot:

---

[4]Alternative combination and de-fuzzification methods can also be used. The product-sum method is an example of a combination method in which consequent sets are added together and then re-normalized during de-fuzzification. Consider the following two cases: A: a fuzzy set that has had, say, three LOW rules and one MEDIUM rule satisfied to a medium degree; and B: a fuzzy set that has had only one of the LOW rules and the one MEDIUM rule satisfied to a medium degree. The product-sum method would interpret the outcome of consequent fuzzy set A as lower than that of consequent set B.

Dimension	Fuzzy System	But...
Accuracy	High	Need to be able to describe fuzzy sets and rules in enough detail to "cover" domain
Explainability	Moderate	No "chain" of reasoning, but rules and relative influence of each rule are visible
Response Speed	High	—
Scalability	Moderate	Depends on ability to control fuzzy set saturation by limiting the number of rules that have similar RHS
Compactness	High	—
Flexibility	High	—
Embeddability	Moderate	Depends on rule structure and inferencing mechanism
Tolerance for complexity	High	Depends on ability to decompose problem into smaller sets of variables; ability to describe relationships linguistically
Ease of use	Moderate	—
Independence from experts	Moderate	Still need well-understood general heuristics and expert availability to tune fuzzy sets
Development speed	Moderate	Depends on understanding of process; on complexity of process
Computing resources	Low	—

Suggested Reading

Cox, E., *The Fuzzy Systems Handbook: A Practitioner's Guide to Building, Using, and Maintaining Fuzzy Systems,* AP Professional, MA: 1994.

Kosko, B., *Neural Networks and Fuzzy Systems: A Dynamical Systems Approach to Machine Intelligence,* Prentice-Hall, Engelwood Cliffs, NJ: 1991.

Kosko, B., and S. Isaka, "Fuzzy Logic," *Scientific American,* July 1993.

McNeil, D., and P. Freiberger, *Fuzzy Logic: The Discovery of a Revolutionary Computer Technology and How It Is Changing Our World,* Simon & Schuster, New York, NY: 1993.

von Altrock, C., *Fuzzy Logic and Neuro-Fuzzy Applications In Business and Finance,* Prentice-Hall, Englewood Cliffs, NJ: 1995.

Yager, R., and L. Zadeh, ed., *Fuzzy Sets, Neural Networks, and Soft Computing,* Van Nostrand Reinhold, New York, NY: 1994.

Zadeh, L., "Fuzzy Sets," *Information and Control,* Vol. 8., 1965.

Solving Problems
By Analogy

Case-Based Reasoning

It was déjà vu all over again.
—Yogi Berra

Few things are harder to put up with than the annoyance of a good example.
—Mark Twain

*The key to understanding must be...an organization of the new information
in such a fashion as to seem to forget the unimportant material and to
highlight the important material.*
—Roger Schank

*Case-based reasoning (CBR) is a problem-solving approach that takes advantage of
the knowledge gained from previous attempts to solve a particular problem. A record
of each past attempt is stored as a case. The collection of historical cases, the case
base, then becomes the model. When a CBR system solves a problem, rather than
starting from scratch, it searches its case base for cases whose attributes are similar
to the problem that it is being asked to solve. The CBR system then creates a solution
by synthesizing the similar cases and adjusting the final answer for differences between the current situation and the ones described in the cases. As the case base
grows, the accuracy of the system should improve.*

*In this chapter, we introduce the concepts that form the foundation of CBR. We
look at how it differs from some other approaches, and how and when it makes sense
to consider CBR for a particular problem.*

INTRODUCTION

Think about the last time you went to a new supermarket. Even though you had never been in the store, you probably found your way around pretty easily. Why? Because you've been in other supermarkets. For instance, you know that the household goods would be separated from the food products, and that the meat section would probably be along the back of the store. You were able to apply that experience to the new supermarket. You did not need to study the layout of the new supermarket in detail to learn how to get around.

Or think about how you might pack for a vacation. Chances are you would compare it to previous vacations. Are you going to Europe, Asia, the U.S., or the Caribbean? How will this vacation be similar to the others you've taken in terms of duration? Climate? Did you take the right quantity and variety of clothes last time? Will you have problems with the language?

Rarely do you solve a problem from scratch. Instead, what you often do, loosely speaking, is compare the current situation with previous ones and judge which of them are most similar. You *remember* previous experiences and then look for connections. You see what's different about the current situation, make *adjustments,* and fashion a new solution.

But what defines a "situation" or an "experience"? What makes two *similar*?

In broad terms, you can think of an experience as a "bundle of attributes." A *case*. For example, a 4-day vacation to Puerto Rico might be a case of a trip, as would a 2-week European holiday. Relevant attributes to describe each vacation might be weather, language spoken, the geography, and the duration of stay.

Attributes don't all play exactly the same role. Some of them describe the "situation" but others describe an "action" or a "solution" or a "result." For example, a construction company might want to know the amount the firm should bid for a particular contract based on attributes such as style, architecture, completion time, and so on. The result part of the case would be the price of the bid and whether the bid was won or lost. A collection of bids would be a "case-base." The case-base could be used to find cases similar to the one for which the company is interested in making a bid. After finding one or a few similar cases, an expert could make adjustments to the bid in order to account for the differences.

The process of finding similar cases and making adjustments to account for the differences between them is called *case-based reasoning* (CBR). Typically, the adjustments are made to the solution part of a case due to the differences in the situation part, but the reasoning could well proceed the other way, that is, you could *fix* the result and ask what situation could *lead* to it. This distinction is similar to the forward and backward chaining in rule-based systems. Just like you can use a rule to reason forward or backward, you can use a case to make adjustments to the solution or to the situation.

One of the big benefits of case-based reasoning is that it lets you solve problems without having to work out the solution from scratch each time. It encourages you to make good use of your past experiences. By looking at previously solved problems, you avoid having to encode rules describing *how* the details of each problem affect the proposed solution.

Recall that a rule-based system builds custom-made solutions each time, first breaking the problem down into smaller pieces, solving each piece, and then reassembling the result. CBR, on the other hand, takes an entire completed solution template and modifies it to account for differences. The case is, in a sense, an "off-the-shelf" solution to a particular instance of a problem. In some situations this can result in a tremendous savings in time and effort.

Another benefit is that CBR gives you a better chance of *improving* performance over time. A rule-based system cannot "learn" from its mistakes. If an RBS proposes a solution that is unsatisfactory, it has no way of changing its behavior next time a similar situation arises. It is destined to repeat its mistakes over and over until you add to or modify the rules in the rule base. A CBR system, on the other hand, keeps track of new cases and of errors that old cases produced. As a result, CBR systems tend *not* to produce the same errors over and over.

Examples:
- Foundation Construction is a contractor that specializes in public construction projects. Foundation has a database of information about bids and projects which the firm has participated in. The firm would like to use this information to help draft bids in the future. While many jobs share similar attributes, they are always unique.
- Global Consulting has a worldwide staff of thousands. The firm encourages new consultants to meet with other associates during engagements in order to encourage discussions and experience sharing. Due to rapid growth and internationalization of the firm, knowledge of experiences is becoming more and more distributed. The firm would like to provide associates with a way of finding examples of similar engagements and using them to help form strategies.
- WorkWare is a software manufacturer, specializing in business software. The firm would like its help desk staff to be able to respond more quickly and accurately to customer questions. The firm keeps a record of each call that is reported and hopes that these can be used to help its staff.

THE ABCs OF CASE-BASED REASONING

So, what exactly is a case?

Simply put, a case is a collection of attributes. Together, the attributes describe a scenario involving a situation and an action or solution.

Let's consider the example of Foundation Construction. Say that the firm specializes in bridge design. A bridge construction company needs to make critical design decisions early in the design process based on specifications such as the *purpose* of the bridge, *length, volume of traffic* the bridge is supposed to handle, the *geology* of the location, the *horizontal clearance* and the *vertical clearance* required, and the *number of lanes*. Each bridge that the company has designed in the past would have values for these attributes. The attributes make up what we're calling the "situation" part of the case.

Figure 9.1 shows fragments from two cases using three of the attributes mentioned above: length, number of lanes, and horizontal clearance.

Specific design choices lead to specific outcomes. For example, the *vibration* of the bridge depends on the material from which the bridge is made, the length, and

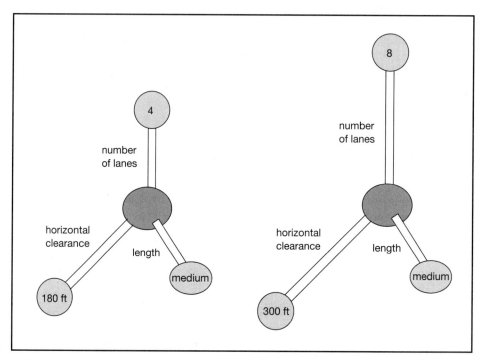

FIGURE 9.1   Fragments of two cases. Sticks represent attributes for specifying a bridge. For numeric attributes, the length of the stick is proportional to the value of the numeric attribute it represents. Collectively, the attributes specify a "situation."

so on. Other "outcome" properties of the bridge are the *deflection* in the middle (the less bowed the span of the bridge, the better), and resistance to earthquakes (higher is better). Similarly, cost is another outcome that depends on a number of related factors. These outcome attributes make up the "solution" part of the case as shown in Figure 9.2.

Figure 9.3 describes a "complete" case. It indicates the outcome (shown in the center sphere) corresponding to the situation as specified by the design decisions (in the little spheres).

In order to be able to deal with a wide variety of situations, it is useful to collect *many* different types of cases. A collection of cases is called a case base. Each case is a snapshot of the solution space. It represents one particular combination of attributes and one particular set of outcomes. The more cases in the case base, the more complete the coverage of the solution space.

Storing cases is well and good, but how can you *use* all this information?

In order to make sense out of a large number of cases, you need to develop a way to "remember" or recall them at the appropriate time. You need to be able to retrieve them in the same way that people remember their past experiences. For example, a doctor who sees a set of symptoms can often recall the few most pertinent cases where patients had similar symptoms. The doctor then weighs the cases based on their similarities with the current symptoms.

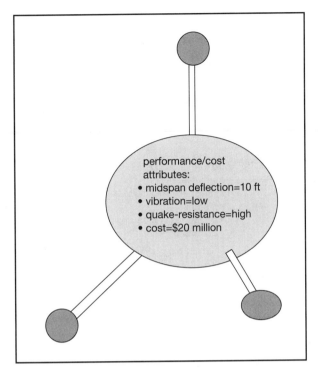

performance/cost
attributes:
• midspan deflection=10 ft
• vibration=low
• quake-resistance=high
• cost=$20 million

FIGURE 9.2 The "Solution" or "Action" Part of a Case. In this figure, the solution part of the case is represented by attributes in the sphere.

The trick is to look only at the few cases that give you the most insight into whatever problem you are trying to solve at a particular time. In this way, the system can provide the decision maker with information that maximizes the decision-making ability.

To find useful information in the cases, a CBR system sends a *probe* into the case-base. The probe describes the situation you're interested in matching. A probe consists of a subset of the attributes, either situation *or* outcome, that is used to describe a state of affairs.

For example, the bridge construction firm might be bidding on a bridge for a highway. The firm might be interested in finding cases that are "similar" to bridges that are used for auto traffic; are of medium length; are three lanes wide; have a concrete deck; and that cost under 20 million dollars.

These specifications can be represented as a probe as shown in Figure 9.4. Notice how you are trying to find cases that match both situation (auto traffic, medium length, four lanes, concrete deck) and outcome attributes ($20 million). In CBR, for probing purposes, all attributes are created equally.

At this point, you might be wondering whether CBR is any different than a simple database query or an OLAP system. While there are similarities between executing a database query and a case-base probe, there are some important differences that have practical implications. These differences, which we will discuss in detail in the next pages, relate to *how smart* the judgment of similarity is, and *what* a CBR

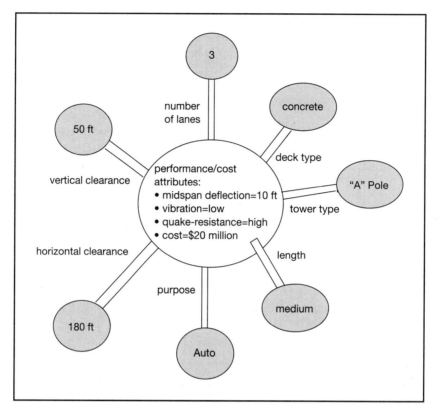

FIGURE 9.3 A Complete Case Consisting of a "Situation" and a "Solution" Part. This case describes a particular bridge.

system does with the cases it finds. In fact, it is these differences that make CBR such a powerful modeling tool.

To appreciate these differences, consider first what a CBR system does with retrieved cases.

Once the probe hits similar cases, the system can use the cases in one of a variety of ways. On one end of the spectrum, the initial probe might only serve as an entry point for similar cases. The user would be more interested in *browsing* the case-base with the objective of finding something interesting. The consultants in the Global Consulting example might use their system that way to let associates find cases of similar consulting engagements.

In this model, a consultant would make an initial rough cut with the probe, use the information in the retrieved cases to construct a new probe, find more cases, examine them for interestingness, modify the probe, and so on. The user would be *collecting further information from matched cases,* successively refining the search.

By using the intelligent matching features of case-based reasoning, systems can be used in a mode that can be thought of as "intelligent browsing." This process is shown in Figure 9.5. Notice that the probe has four situation attributes. The

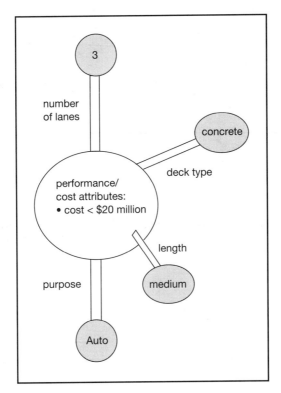

FIGURE 9.4 A "probe" is a kind of query which is used to find "close" cases.

"matching and retrieval" component of the system finds a number of cases. Each case includes not only those attributes that are in the probe but *all* of the attributes in the case. These are shown by the solid black spheres. These new attributes can then be used to construct a new probe, and the matching process is repeated until the user finds what he or she wants.

In browsing mode, a CBR system doesn't necessarily *do* much with the re-trieved cases. In fact, even though it is acting much smarter than a database system in how it *retrieves* cases, the system is acting very similarly to a database or OLAP sys-tem, with respect to what the system *does* with retrieved cases.

(Later on, we will describe how CBR systems judge the *similarity* of a case to the probe. The similarity judging process is much more intelligent in a CBR system than with a database system. This is what makes the CBR system more powerful than a typical database or OLAP system, even for browsing.)

On the other end of the spectrum, though, a CBR system behaves much differ-ently. The system finds cases that are similar to the specified probe, as above, but in-stead of just presenting the cases to the user, the system automatically makes *adjustments* to the "solution" part of the closest cases found. These adjustments take into account the differences between the situation part of the current problem (the probe) and the situation part of the retrieved cases. The system synthesizes the results into a new solution.

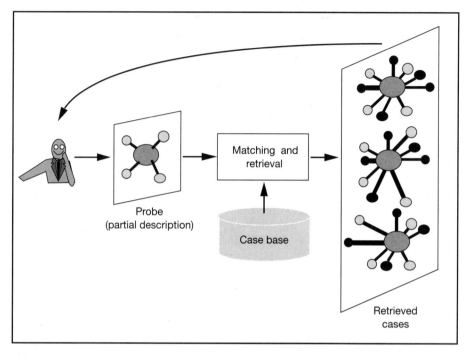

FIGURE 9.5 Case-Based Reasoning. A case fragment can be used as a probe to find similar cases in a case base.

In the bridge example above, the system might find cases most similar to the probe and modify their costs and performance properties using some specified formulas and rules. For example, it might add $50,000 to the cost for every 10 additional feet of length per lane. Or, it might compute the deflection by interpolating between values obtained from cases that "bound" the current one.

So, if a 1000-foot bridge in the case base has a deflection of 20 feet and another that is 1500 feet long has a deflection of 25 feet, the system might be designed to assume that a 1200-foot bridge will have a deflection between 20 and 25 feet. Alternatively, the system might calculate deflection using a specific engineering formula based on other variables like width and so forth.

But we also said that CBR differs from database systems in the way that similarity is judged for retrieval. The important point to keep in mind is that it is a continuous metric, not an all-or-nothing match as in database systems, that is, a query like "all customers where zip = 10010" or "all customers with purchases > $500." Instead, CBR matches are *graded* by how similar they are to the probe.

For CBR, similarity depends on the type of attribute we're comparing. If an attribute is numeric, the similarity for that attribute might be calculated fairly simply, say as the difference between the case attribute value and the probe attribute value.

As an example, look at the top part of Figure 9.6. In this example, suppose you are trying to probe for a bridge with two towers. With this probe, A, the case of a bridge with three towers (Bridge B) is more similar to the probe than is the case of a bridge with four towers (Bridge C).

But what if you were concerned about *both* the number of lanes on the proposed bridge (in this case, one) *and* the number of towers (two)?

Bridge C has one lane, but *four* towers. On the other hand, Bridge D has two towers, but *four* lanes. And what about B with three towers and three lanes?

Now, determining whether B, C, or D is closer to A has gotten a little more complicated. Some of the bridges match better on the number of towers, but others match better on the number of lanes. Similarity must now be based on a *combination* of attributes. Closeness now depends on how heavily you weigh the various attributes in making the comparison.

Let's say you considered the match on the number of lanes to be a lot more important than on the number of towers. This might be the case when the highway that connects to the bridge being designed has a fixed number of lanes, say, one, that cannot be changed. You would be much more interested in cases where the number of lanes was closer to one. For the sake of the example, let's say that a match on the number of lanes was five times more important than that on the number of towers.

The bottom part of Figure 9.6 shows how similarity might be calculated for this example. We have a probe being compared to three cases, B, C, and D (same as in the above example). The top part of the figure shows distances where the two attributes are weighted equally. You can see that case C is "closest" to the probe. However, in the lower part of the figure, where closeness on lanes is far more important than closeness on towers, the more important attribute is, in effect, stretched.

The effect is that even a slight difference in values between the case and the probe on this attribute results in a much larger distance. In other words, the probe becomes more sensitive to this attribute in computing similarity. In this scenario, case C is closer to the probe than case B.

But how can you decide how the attributes should be weighted in the first place?

One way is to specify the importance of the attributes *a priori,* based on your intuition or expertise. This is what is often done in practice. However, while this intuitive approach works well for some attributes, it's a cumbersome and inflexible method if you've got a lot of attributes. You would like the system to have the intelligence to assign the appropriate importance to attributes, depending on what you're probing for and the contents of the case base.

But how?

We'll show you one general approach, variations of which are also used in practice. To see how it works, suppose each bridge in the case base were classified as having high, medium, or low maintenance expenses and you wanted to predict the maintenance expense of a new bridge that you are proposing. Let's assume that maintenance depends, among other factors, on the length of the bridge and the number of lanes.

You can design a probe that automatically uses these two attributes to find good cases. Figure 9.7 shows a scatter plot of cases plotted on these two attributes. The "X" indicates the probe.

The probe describes a four-lane bridge that is 450 feet long. That's the description of the bridge that you want to evaluate. In the figure, the number of lanes is shown in the vertical shaded bar, and the length is shown in the horizontal bar. Look-

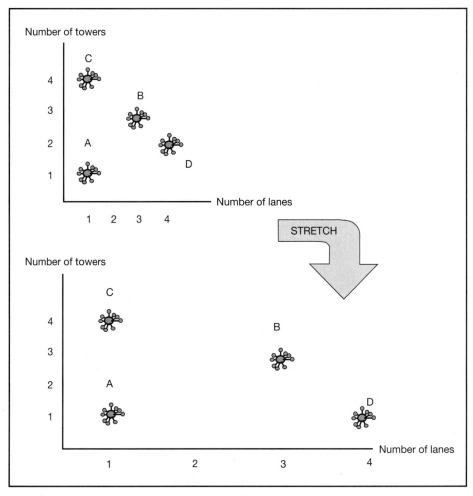

FIGURE 9.6 What is "similarity" with numeric attributes? The top figure shows four cases, plotted on two of their attributes. In the top figure, A and B are closest. In the bottom figure, similarity on the number of lanes attribute has been considered five times as important as that on the number of towers attribute. In effect, this "stretches" the horizontal axis fivefold. Now, C is closest to A.

ing at the lanes attribute, we see that there are three cases where maintenance is low, one where it is medium, and three where it is high.

It looks like when the number of lanes is four, that attribute doesn't provide much *discriminatory power* since it is difficult to tell what the outcome variable, maintenance cost, is going to be just by looking at the number of lanes.

On the other hand, note that 80% of the bridges around 450 feet in length had high maintenance costs associated with them. In other words, the length attribute provides more discriminatory power in this situation, that is, when it is about 450 feet.

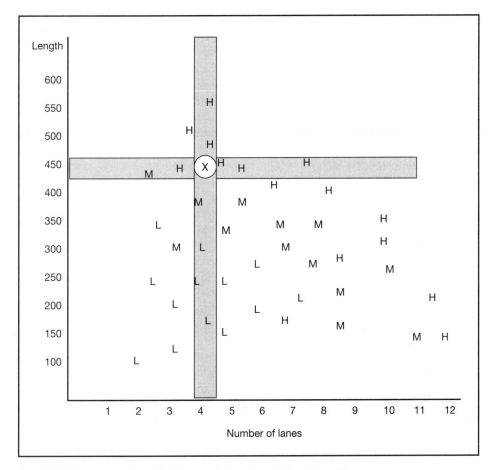

FIGURE 9.7 Cases Plotted in Terms of Length and Number of Lanes.

A similar analysis can be applied across other attributes. The objective of the analysis is to assign weights dynamically to the attributes based on their discriminatory power *as they apply to the case under consideration,* the probe. The weights are assigned in proportion to the discriminatory power of the attributes for the case under consideration.

Once you know how to weight a particular attribute, the last step is to use those weights to calculate the distance between a probe and a case. A popular algorithm for determining the *distance* between cases is the *nearest-neighbor algorithm.* This method works by calculating the geometric distance between a case and the probe, as we showed in Figure 9.6.

Nearest neighbor works well for situations in which attributes represent numeric values. But what do you do for symbolic attributes such as deck type and tower type? How close is a "pre-cast deck" to a "cast-at-site deck?"

It's a lot harder to measure. However, one method for dealing with such attributes is to represent set/subset relationships among the values of the attribute. For example, the set of bridges with *concrete decks* is a subset of all bridges with *decks*. Likewise, *pre-cast* and *cast-at-site* are subsets of *concrete decks*. For such attributes we end with a class hierarchy like the one in Figure 9.8.[1]

How is similarity computed for this type of attribute? Well, you can see that if bridge A has a pre-cast deck, B has a cast-at-site deck, and C has a steel deck, B is more similar to A than C since A and B have concrete decks. That is, they have a *common parent*. The higher up the common parent, the larger is the distance between the probe and the case. CBR systems use a type of nearest-neighbor algorithm that deals with symbolic attributes by heuristically quantifying the distances that attributes have from the common parent.

The matching component of a case-based reasoning system employs a combination of the nearest-neighbor for numeric attributes and "symbolic" nearest-neighbor similarity calculations. "Distance computation" modules do not necessarily have to use straightforward mathematical calculations, though. These modules can take many forms: statistical models, a rule-based system, a neural network, etc. In other words, judging similarity can itself be viewed as a knowledge-based activity. For example, in adjusting the cost of constructing a concrete deck bridge versus a steel deck bridge, a CBR system might employ its own rule-based model of the world of construction materials. Such an RBS, for example, would be able to reason about the design modifications that would be required to use concrete and about the quantities of concrete needed to execute these modifications.

In concluding this section, we should clarify one general point about similarity: As the number of attributes becomes large, computing similarity becomes very (very) hard. It is generally *not* a good idea to use a naive distance computation method such as one that computes the value differences for all attributes and adds them up. This will almost invariably provide bad results.

Why? There are two important reasons. One is that when many attributes are involved, the amount of data you have *relative to the entire space of possibilities* is very small. This makes sense. As you increase the number of attributes, your space of possibilities explodes. The upshot of this is that you cease to have a representative sample.[2] If you don't have a representative sample, chances are a new case will not have *any* similar case in the case base. In other words, to find a similar case you end up *extrapolating* rather than *interpolating*. Interpolation is generally safe. Extrapolation is usually risky.

The second reason is that with a large number of attributes, it is more likely that a data point will not have any other data point next to it, but instead, will be closer to one of the edges (the dimensions). Again, to find a neighbor you can end up doing extrapolation instead of interpolation.

The upshot of all this is that you have to be clever about matching cases in a high-dimensional space. One way of doing this is by letting the context determine

---

[1]Appendix A (on object representations) describes in more detail how hierarchies like this might be developed and work.

[2]Jerome Friedman summed up the reason for this as follows (clarifications are in parentheses): "the topology of a high dimensional space (many attributes) is very different from that of a low dimensional space. In a high dimensional space any sample (case base) is too small. Also, in a high dimensional space, a data point (a case) is likely to be closer to an edge than it is to another data point."

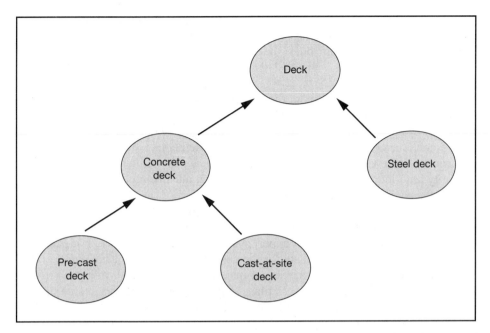

FIGURE 9.8 Case attributes can be hierarchical. The attribute deck is defined in terms of the hierarchy above.

which attributes to use in computing similarity. The method we described in Figure 9.7 is one where the "neighborhood of the case" is used to determine the discriminatory attributes. The scheme we described is a simple way of implementing this basic idea.[3]

INTELLIGENCE DENSITY ISSUES

So when is it a good idea to use CBR?

To understand when CBR makes sense, it is worth asking why cases are used so widely in instruction. Why have we used them in this book?

There are a number of reasons that people like to use cases to explain things. Cases transform abstract concepts into real images. Seeing a concept in use enhances your understanding of it. Having seen cases, you get a better sense of what solutions work under different conditions. You can formulate and solve future problems better and faster. A case provides some inherently useful information because of how it organizes information and accesses it.

But there's another reason why cases are popular, especially in areas such as business and policy analysis. There are no clear-cut theories in these areas. Rather, a case provides a "representative example," or more practically, a good starting point

---

[3]For pointers to other approaches, see the Trevor and Hastie article listed in the suggested readings at the end of this chapter.

from which to begin the search for a better or more detailed solution. It forces you to consider explicitly the similarities and differences between different situations in a structured way, along the attributes that are used to describe the cases. At the same time, it provides a degree of open-endedness to the exercise, allowing us to think creatively about new solutions.

It is important to underscore the fact that CBR is, at least conceptually, quite different from database querying. CBR is used to *solve a problem,* not answer a query. For example, you might use a CBR system to figure out how much you should pay a potential employee. This isn't a query itself. Remember, the system first generates a query-like event such as "find me people that are similar to this employee." The similarity criterion used in doing this kind of search must be highly flexible. In CBR systems the similarity metric is adjustable.

But CBR systems also provide a hook for plugging in the logic needed to modify the *action* part of the matched cases. The logic can be a simple formula, or something more complex, like an expert system or a neural network. For example, coming up with a ballpark estimate for the cost of a project might involve a simple linear interpolation. On the other hand, making a gourmet dish might involve a fairly elaborate sequence of steps, a plan, to do it right. Modifying such a plan to take into account a new ingredient might require another plan to take into account the properties of the new ingredient. It could require a significant amount of domain knowledge: The ingredient adjusting module could be an expert system in its own right.

By enabling such knowledge to be pluggable into a CBR system, the action modification part of the CBR system can be as sophisticated as necessary. In essence, a CBR system provides an open-ended "shell" into which other systems can be integrated.

CBR systems also enable *navigation.* This is useful when the user wants to browse a complex domain in a focused manner. In such situations, the user might not have a specific question at the outset of the interaction. Instead, the user might want to specify some situation and *find* additional information for that situation that might be useful for subsequent probing. For example, the user might specify a profile for a client and want to know what additional information is "typically" associated with the specified profile. This additional information can be used to direct further browsing as we showed in Figure 9.5. In this mode the CBR system becomes a decision support tool.

What characteristics about a *problem* might make CBR a candidate approach? Or, conversely, when is it advantageous to use CBR over other techniques?

CBR is useful when there are *discontinuities* in the relationships between variables. That is, a relationship might hold between variables but only within some range of values. A CBR system can enable a user to uncover these discontinuities. For example, the size of a company, measured in terms of various ratios of asset and liability types, might be one determinant of financial strength *for small companies* but not as important for very large ones. In other words, strength might increase with size, but only up to a point. A well designed case-based reasoning system can *figure this out.*

While CBR handles discontinuities well, it does not work as well when the complexity of the interactions among problem variables rises. In other words, the influence of variables on the solution should be moderately separable, not highly inter-active as in very complex systems.

When you have lots of subtle interactions among continuous valued variables, cases are not likely to sample an adequate part of the solution space. Also, if the classes of cases are not easily separable, as shown in Figure 9.9, it becomes harder to find discriminating criteria among them, and finding meaningful "neighboring" solutions becomes more of a hit-or-miss kind of thing: Small changes in the similar-ity criterion can cause significant changes in the result, the matched cases. This hap-pens in situations where the relationships among variables cease to be *monotonic* (for example, if income increases initially with education but then *drops* as educa-tion level increases).

CBR also works best when an approximate solution is better than none at all. The flip side of the coin is that the quality of output of a CBR system degrades smoothly. Unlike rule-based systems which degrade badly in areas not covered by the rules, a case-based system will almost always give you *something,* however crude. And the better the case base, the better that something is. For this reason, the better the quality of the data, the better the chances of a good match.

Case-based systems also turn out to be highly scalable and flexible since they are typically built with the expectation that cases will be added to the system over time and that this will enhance the scope and accuracy of the system. If new variables or attributes are added to the system, however, older cases that do not have them will

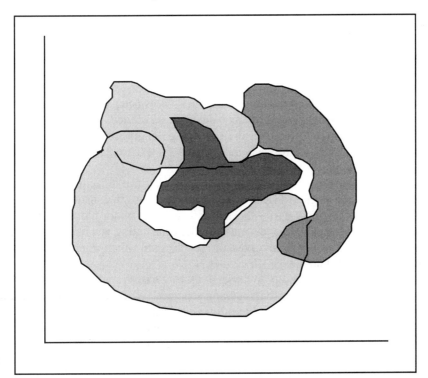

FIGURE 9.9   Classes That Are Hard to Separate

not be part of similarity matches on those attributes. This can be avoided if the new attributes are also added to old cases.

Because a CBR system allows you to add a case when the system makes a mistake, it is less likely to make the same mistake twice. Contrast this with rule-based systems. If an RBS reaches an incorrect conclusion, the only way to fix it is to modify the rules. This can be a highly time-consuming and painful exercise requiring an expert's time and effort. In contrast, with a case-based system, *the process of using a CBR system can result in the generation of a new case.* The next time the system encounters a situation where it failed previously, it is more likely to find the new case instead of the old one that didn't work. However, you have to be careful not to be too liberal about adding new cases, otherwise the case base can grow quickly and the cases will overlap redundantly. You should ensure that there is in fact no old case that matches the situation of interest before adding a new case.

The improvement over time in performance in CBR systems comes with only a modest reliance on experts. In other words, the knowledge-engineering component of the system development life cycle is small, as long as there is an adequate quantity and quality of cases to get started. The role of the expert is in designing the structure of the case and in providing heuristics or rules that can be used in determining similarity and adjusting cases.

On the other hand, *in the absence of a good database of cases,* the burden of constructing the cases by interviewing experts can be time consuming. For example, if your firm is a service organization wanting to leverage your past experience, it is useful to have this experience recorded in a form that is directly usable. A database containing all calls with detailed descriptions of the problem and its resolution would provide a good starting point in defining the structure of a case. It is then easy to use experts to *validate* cases that you construct for them instead of requiring them to help you *build* the cases from scratch.

It is worth pointing out, however, that even if cases need to be constructed from scratch and you don't need more than a few dozen to get started, the effort involved in doing so is significantly lower than the knowledge-engineering effort required in building rule-based systems. It is generally easier for experts to recapitulate stories than it is to provide rules.

For example, a real estate appraiser would have little difficulty remembering the salient aspects of cases of high-value homes. Likewise, a construction engineer would probably recall fairly easily those projects where major plumbing problems occurred. These experts might have a much harder time telling you rules than abstract relationships among variables involved in the cases. In other words, cases can be more natural "units of knowledge" than rules.

Experts also have the ability to retrieve relevant cases rapidly. One popular theory is that experts employ effective indexing schemes. When a case is recorded, the expert somehow indexes it using a set of attributes; the more important and multifaceted the case, the larger the number of indexes the expert is likely to use to record the case. These indexes serve as "handles," making retrieval fast. If the case is not richly indexed, chances are that the expert will have to "think harder" to remember the details. In other words, the expert would have to search more.

This makes sense. When you record an experience in your mind, you are seldom thinking about how that experience will be used later. However, if the experience seems like an "important" one in some way, chances are that you will unconsciously record more aspects of it than for a seemingly incidental event. If that seemingly incidental event turns out to be important, you'll have to search your memory even harder to dredge up its details.

With case-based systems, you usually have to make the decision about which attributes to use for indexing when designing the case base, although there is nothing to prevent you from adding additional indexing attributes later. This decision must be based on prior experience with the problem domain.

In a library system, for example, commonly used indexes are author, title, and subject. If for some reason you wanted to do retrievals based on the number of pages, you'd be out of luck. Without an index for this attribute, it is simply infeasible to perform such a search. The analogy applies to current-day CBR systems, whose success ultimately depends in large part on how appropriately you index the cases.

To what extent is CBR opaque like a neural net or transparent like a rule-based system?

Think about how similarity is judged. Isn't that a black box? To some extent, it is. After all, taking a weighted average of distances for each attribute and aggregating it into a number introduces a degree of opacity into similarity judgment much like neural nets do in attaching weight to links between nodes.

On the other hand, however, a matched case does stand for an explanation in itself as long as the user understands the similarity metric. A CBR system says "here's a solution that can be applied to your situation, because it worked in a situation similar to yours." The closer the example to the current situation and the clearer the similarity judgment, the more comfort associated with the explanation. And you can get a feel for how closely the solution matches the probe by examining the distances between the probe and the cases that were used to build the solution.

A CBR system does not present the user with an audit trail of a reasoning process. It gives cases. The user must examine the matched cases and their solutions and judge whether they are appropriate for the current situation. For example, the CBR system might say something like "For this set of symptoms, in 27 cases operation X was successful and in three cases it resulted in complications." This is an empirical or evidentiary kind of explanation. It is *driven by the data*. The better the quality of the cases, the better the quality of the explanation.

In contrast, a rule-based system provides a much more abstract or theory-based kind of explanation. As we saw in the RBS chapter, an explanation in an RBS results from an instantiation of the rules. As rules fire, inferences are made, and chains of inferences ultimately link outputs (like conclusions) to inputs (like facts). To get the most out of this kind of explanation, the user must understand the basis for the rules.

In summary, a CBR system is both transparent and opaque. The similarity judgment part can be cloudy, like a neural network. On the other hand, the matched examples are natural units of knowledge that are explicit and provide an empirical depth to the explanation, kind of like an RBS.

The intelligence density issues can be summarized according to the following table:

Dimension	CBR System	But . . .
Accuracy	Moderate to High	Improves over time as more cases are added
Explainability	Moderate	Transparency of the system is limited by how opaque the similarity judgment metric is
Response Time	Moderate to High	Depends on number of cases, complexity of matching, adjustment algorithms, and efficiency of indexing scheme
Scalability	High	—
Compactness	Low to Moderate	Depends on the implementation; entire case base is required for execution
Flexibility	High	—
Embeddability	Moderate	—
Tolerance for Complexity	Moderate	Good for discontinuities, but less useful when the interactions among variables become non-monotonic and complex
Tolerance for sparseness of data	Moderate	Depends on the number of variables and complexity of the problem
Tolerance for noise in data	Moderate	If case base is large, individual anomalies will not affect matching and adjustment as much
Independence from experts	Moderate to High	Need expert input to develop matching, adjusting techniques

Suggested Reading

Hastie, T., and Tibshirani, R., "Discriminant Adaptive Nearest Neighbor Classification," *Proceedings of the First International Conference on Knowledge Discovery and Data Mining,* Montreal, August 1995.

Kolodner, J., *Case-Based Reasoning,* Morgan Kauffman, Los Altos, CA: 1994.

Riesbeck, C., and Schank, R., *Inside Case Based Reasoning,* Lawrence Erlbaum Associates, Hillsdale, NJ: 1989.

Schank, R., *Tell Me a Story: A New Look at Real and Artificial Memory,* Scribner, NY, NY: 1990.

10

Deriving Rules from Data

Machine Learning Algorithms

*In our description of nature the purpose is not to disclose the real essence
of the phenomena but only to track down, so far as possible, relations
between the manifold aspects of our experience.*
—Niels Bohr

*We should be careful to get out of an experience only the wisdom that is in it—
and stop there; lest we be like the cat that sits down on a hot stove-lid.
She will never sit down on a hot stove-lid again, and that is well;
but also will she never sit down on a cold one any more.*
—Mark Twain

*[On inductive learning:] Los Angelenos know that one hot high pollution
day is followed by another. Doctors know that elderly heart attack
patients with low blood pressure are generally high risk.*
—Breiman *et al.*

*Machine learning algorithms create rules and rule-trees by searching through data
for statistical patterns and relationships. The algorithms use information about the
distribution of the data to try to cluster records into specific categories. Machine
learning algorithms can be particularly attractive since, in addition to providing
good models for prediction and classification, they also abstract clear rules from
data. This can help explain the process that generated the data. This type of analysis
can in itself be a valuable business tool.*

*In this chapter we explore a particular class of machine learning algorithms
called* recursive partitioning algorithms, *and we discuss what factors can make them
good solutions for certain problems.*

INTRODUCTION

Suppose your company had a database of sales data. Lots of sales data. How could you go about using this database to help figure out an effective marketing strategy?

You'd be interested in knowing about the statistical averages and distributions of the variables in order to get a basic feel for what the data showed. These kinds of statistics provide a thumbnail sketch of large amounts of data. They are the first step in increasing the intelligence density of the data.

The problem with a thumbnail sketch is that it's just a sketch. In order to go beyond this you need to probe the data. You might think about doing some specialized queries such as: "Show me how many widget buyers also bought doo-hickies within a week of their widget purchase." You might even use an OLAP system to dive into the data and follow up hunches.

But the problem with doing queries is that you have to already have some idea of what you are looking for before you start. You have to have a *hunch,* for example, that there's some relationship between buying widgets and buying doo-hickies.

What if you don't *have* those hunches, though? What you really need then is a way to query the data intelligently so that you can uncover useful relationships among the variables quickly; relationships that you might not have known even existed.

This is where machine learning algorithms can help you.

While database queries answer the question, "What are the data that match this pattern?" machine learning algorithms answer the question, "What is the pattern that matches these data?" Machine learning (ML) employs search heuristics to uncover interesting and systematic relationships in data.

We discussed how neural networks provide one way of finding relationships between inputs and outputs. The relationships in a neural net are not explicit; they are implied in the weights among neurons and the transfer functions of the neurons.

We also discussed how rule-based systems encode knowledge in explicit chunks of expertise called rules. These rules must be elicited from experts and encoded manually.

The machine learning algorithms we describe in this chapter learn from data like neural networks, but attempt to find explicit rule-like relationships among the variables, like rule-based systems.

Figure 10.1 shows where machine learning algorithms fit in the intelligence density increasing process. The first step, as shown in the figure, is to specify the problem: What are you trying to find out? What are the relevant variables? How should the data be prepared?

Once the data set has been prepared, the machine learning algorithm takes this selected data as input and produces a set of rules that describes how certain variables (*dependent* variables) are related to other variables (*independent* variables). You can view this relationship as a decision tree, a rule, a chart, an equation, etc. It is a high-level distillation of the data, or a model of the problem. The challenge for the machine learning algorithm is to focus its statistical analyses so that the interesting relationships bubble up to the surface as fast and as clearly as possible.

Two of the techniques we discussed in earlier chapters can be used as machine learning techniques, that is, to produce models from data. Genetic algorithms, for ex-

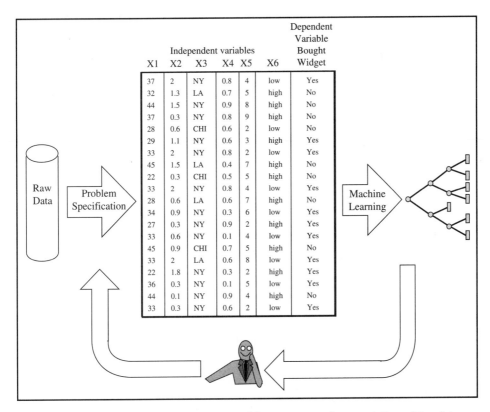

| | | | | | | Dependent Variable |
| | Independent variables | | | | | Bought |
X1	X2	X3	X4	X5	X6	Widget
37	2	NY	0.8	4	low	Yes
32	1.3	LA	0.7	5	high	No
44	1.5	NY	0.9	8	high	No
37	0.3	NY	0.8	9	high	No
28	0.6	CHI	0.6	2	low	No
29	1.1	NY	0.6	3	high	Yes
33	2	NY	0.8	2	low	Yes
45	1.5	LA	0.4	7	high	No
22	0.3	CHI	0.5	5	high	No
33	2	NY	0.8	4	low	Yes
28	0.6	LA	0.6	7	high	No
34	0.9	NY	0.3	6	low	Yes
27	0.3	NY	0.9	2	high	Yes
33	0.6	NY	0.1	4	low	Yes
45	0.9	CHI	0.7	5	high	No
33	2	LA	0.6	8	low	Yes
22	1.8	NY	0.3	2	high	Yes
36	0.3	NY	0.1	5	low	Yes
44	0.1	NY	0.9	4	high	No
33	0.3	NY	0.6	2	low	Yes

Raw Data → Problem Specification → Machine Learning

FIGURE 10.1   The tree toward the right provides a compact interpretation of the data.

ample, can be used to represent patterns. These can be matched against a database, evaluated for "goodness," modified through mating with other patterns, which are in turn evaluated, and so on, until interesting patterns are produced.[1] Neural networks also produce models that are "learned" from data, storing the learned patterns as relationships between weights. There are also many other types of machine learning algorithms that use logic, Baysian probabilities, fuzzy logic heuristics, and so forth.

In this chapter we focus on another class of machine learning techniques called *recursive partitioning algorithms*. Recursive partitioning algorithms split the original data into finer and finer subsets (recursively), resulting in a decision tree, like the one on the right of Figure 10.1. The tree is a compact explanation of the data. Given the data in Figure 10.1, the tree would tell us the profile, if one exists, of the typical widget buyer. For example, it might show that most widget buyers live in New York and are less than 35 years old.

The tree is a useful abstraction of the data. It can be used for classification, prediction or estimation. The decision tree in Figure 10.2a is used for classification. The

---

[1]A special type of genetic algorithm called a *classifier system* is often used for genetic machine learning. Classifier systems work by creating populations of messaging units that communicate among each other to make predictions or classify data. The messaging units compete to be able to classify a piece of data, with the most successful ones getting the classification.

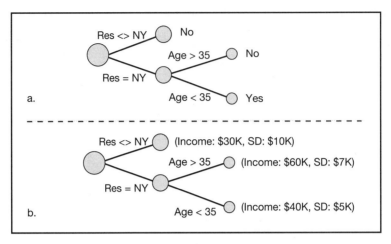

FIGURE 10.2a A Classification Tree **b** A Regression Tree

nodes at the tips of the tree designate categories into which the cases that trickle down the branches are classified.

The tree in Figure 10.2a shows the rule "*IF Age is less than 35 and Residence = New York THEN widget buyer.*" This type of tree is called a *classification* tree. The decreasing size of circles toward the right indicates the decreasing number of cases of data that fall into each successive cluster.

On the other hand, when the dependent variable is continuous, like an employee's income, you're usually interested in estimating or predicting its value. Figure 10.2b shows such an example. In this tree, each branch partitions off a subset of the data and the last node indicates the value of income for that subset of the data. The tree in Figure 10.2b shows the following types of rules: "*IF Residence = New York and age is less than 35 then Income is $40K on average with a standard deviation of $5K.*" More generally, the tree tells us that average incomes are higher in New York, and that, within New Yorkers, incomes are higher for people above the age of 35. When the dependent variable is continuous, the decision tree is called a *regression tree.*

The two best known and perhaps most widely used recursive partitioning machine learning algorithms are called ID3 (and its successor, C4.5) and CART.[2] The algorithms both try to create clusters like the ones shown in Figure 10.2. The goal of the algorithms is to make the clusters at the nodes purer and purer by progressively reducing the "disorder" in the original data.

The search heuristics used in ID3 are based on concepts from information theory: The algorithm tries to reduce the information disorder (called *entropy*) in each cluster of a data set through a series of successive splits on the independent variables. This technique is used to create classification trees.

The CART family of algorithms, on the other hand, is a natural extension of statistical techniques such as regression, factor analysis, and cluster analysis. CART

---

[2]CART stands for Classification And Regression Trees.

algorithms try to reduce the statistical disorder (or *variance*) of the data at each cluster and separate the clusters as much as possible by maximizing the distance between them. CART can produce both the classification and regression type trees shown in Figure 10.2.

Examples:
- Victory Loan Corp. makes over $3 billion in home equity loans a year. The firm hopes to be able to convert its large database of borrower profiles and loan performance into a competitive advantage by developing a model to predict loan default and delinquency.
- Widgitco Inc. makes a variety of novelty items. The firm would like to be able to predict which types of customers are likely to purchase various products by looking at the demographic data associated with its mail order sales database. The firm hopes that its sales force can also use this information to determine how to better market novelty items.
- Bull Bear Investments has a database of trades for each of its bond traders. The investment bank would like to use these data to understand its traders' successful and unsuccessful transactions. The firm is hoping to determine what combinations of market conditions and trading strategies led to good versus bad trades. The firm's goal is to determine what its most successful traders do to be successful.

THE ABCs OF MACHINE LEARNING

Let's look a little more closely at the snapshot of data shown in Figure 10.1. The dependent variable on the far right column is binary: a *yes* or a *no*. It describes whether one of Widgitco's customers bought a widget or not. In this case, the independent variables represent demographic information. The dependent variable could also be ordered (high, medium, low) or numeric. Likewise, the independent variables can be of any type.

The question in this problem is the following: How can Widgitco divide up the original data along the independent variables so that the cases form clusters where each cluster contains predominantly a YES or NO as the response?

Take a look at Figure 10.3. The leftmost cluster in the figure shows only the dependent variable from the data set in Figure 10.1. The crosses and circles denote the yes and no responses. The objective in building a tree is to determine which strategic questions we can ask about the other variables that will separate the original data into homogeneous groups in as "simple" a way as possible. Simple means getting the most useful discrimination of the data by asking the fewest questions. In Figure 10.3, the tree discriminates by splitting on two variables, *residence* and *age*.

But how did the algorithm decide to split on these two variables and how did it determine the boundaries for the splits?

In order to answer this question, you first need a way of *measuring* the degree of "impurity" or "disorder" in a set of data. With such a measure you have a yardstick for comparing the impurity of clusters generated by alternative splits. Then all you need to do is find which split results in the largest reduction in impurity.

To understand what we mean when we say "disorder," think about what a disorderly group of people is like. When you think of a disorderly group of people, you

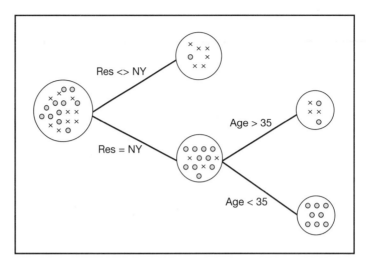

FIGURE 10.3 ML algorithm attempts to split up the data (examples) into more homogeneous subsets (cross = yes, circle = no).

probably think of a mob of individuals each doing their own thing. In a sense, this is what disorderly data are. It is a collection of data in which each data record is different from those in the cluster.

Clearly, the more disorder there is, the harder it is to interpret the meaning of the cluster or to describe it simply. For example, in your marketing strategy, it is clearly more useful to know (and easier to describe) that a particular cluster of customers (from a certain city, for instance) *all* bought widgets than it is to know that the same group had 50% widget buyers and 50% non-widget buyers.

To get a clearer picture of how data can be "purified," look at the rightmost cluster at the bottom of Figure 10.3. What is its disorder? Intuitively, you can see that since all the data in this cluster are uniform (all circles), the disorder is 0: It is as pure as you can get. What about the cluster on the far left? It seems much more impure since there are almost an equal number of circles and crosses (9 and 11). Knowing that a customer is in the leftmost cluster doesn't tell you much about the propensity to buy widgets or not.

There are many ways to quantify this intuitive feeling about impurity. For expediency, we'll skip a lot of the details of how the math is actually done. However, if you want a deeper understanding of how impurity is computed, see the appendix to this chapter. It describes one approach for measuring the impurity of a sample. The approach is motivated by a field of mathematics called information theory and involves a concept known as *entropy*. (If the details don't interest you, skip the appendix and just assume that there are formulas for determining how pure a cluster of data is.)

The one detail that will make it easier to understand how these algorithms work is that entropy uses a function called a logarithm to calculate impurity.[3] The math

---

[3] The expression $\log_2(\cdot)$ is just a function like, say, a square root. The function $\log_2(x) = y$ is the solution for the equation $2^y = x$. For example, since $2^3 = 8$, $\log_2(8) = 3$. Tables exist for looking up the logs of most numbers.

ends up showing that the highest possible impurity for a cluster that contains K possible outcomes or categories is $\log_2(K)$ bits,[4] which is just the number of bits it takes to describe K categories in a computer.

For example, if there were two categories, "YES" and "NO," you could code the two categories with a single bit in a database; either 1 for records in category "YES" or 0 for records in category "NO":

```
NO      0, or
YES     1.
```

Likewise if there were four categories A, B, C, and D, you could code all four using two bits:

```
A       00,
B       01,
C       10, and
D       11.
```

And so forth.

This is exactly what the entropy formula shows: When there are two equally likely outcomes, "YES" or "NO," the maximum entropy possible in the data is $\log_2(2)$ or 1 bit. With four equally likely outcomes, the maximum impurity is $\log_2(4)$, or 2 bits, with eight outcomes it is $\log_2(8)$, or 3 bits, and so on. This makes sense. When there is maximum entropy, you don't save anything. You still need exactly the same number of bits to describe a category in a cluster as you would without any information about which cluster it is in.

With no information content, you need the full number of bits to describe each category. If you have some additional information, though, you can actually describe the data in the cluster with fewer bits. For example, if you knew that a cluster contained only categories A and C instead of all possible categories A, B, C, and D, you could use only 1 bit to describe the possible outcomes of that cluster instead of 2 bits.

There is maximum disorder in data when there is an equal probability of each category, and minimum disorder, 0, when all the cases belong to a single category. Knowing this simple relationship will make it a lot easier to follow the discussions in the rest of the chapter.

Figure 10.4 shows two clusters of the sales data with different amounts of disorder. In cluster A, which corresponds to the original data, there are 11 widget buyers and 9 non-widget buyers. The probability that a customer picked at random will belong to the widget buyer class is therefore 11 out of 20 (0.55) and the non-widget buyer is 9 out of 20 (0.45).

The impurity of this data set computed using the entropy formula in the appendix is 0.993 bits. How pure is this? Since there are two possible outcomes (widget

---

[4]The units of impurity are bits. Bits are like binary choice questions. The number of bits can be viewed as the number of binary choice questions necessary *on average* to identify the category of a case picked at random from a data sample.

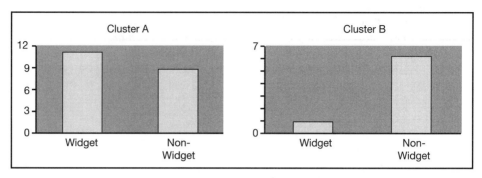

FIGURE 10.4 Two Clusters with Different Degrees of "Disorder"

buyer/non-widget buyer), the *maximum* possible impurity when there are two possibilities involved is 1 bit ($\log_2(2) = 1$), so this data set is almost as *impure* as it could be. (The maximum possible impurity of 1.0 would occur when the two outcomes were *exactly* equally likely.)

Now suppose that we take a subset of the original data, namely all those who do not live in New York. This subset has one widget buyer and six non-buyers. The impurity associated with this cluster is much lower since it consists predominantly of non-widget buyers (6 out of 7 cases).

Using the entropy formula in the appendix, Cluster B's impurity is only 0.207. The reason that cluster has such a low impurity is because just knowing that a person is in Cluster B tells you a lot about whether he was likely to have been a widget buyer or not. (Chances are he wasn't!)

Figure 10.5 shows how impurity is removed from the data. Cluster A is the original data. The top node after the first split is Cluster B. The first split is on variable X3. What does splitting the data this way buy you? Look at the resulting data clusters more closely.

The first cluster that results from this split has 7 cases and 6 of them are *yes* responses. The second data set has 13 cases and 10 of them are *no* responses. Intuitively, it seems like a pretty good split since both of the new clusters seem much purer than the previous one.

In fact, you've already computed the impurity of the first cluster (Cluster B in Figure 10.4). It has an impurity of 0.207 bits. Using the formula in the appendix, the other half of the split has an impurity of 0.506 bits.

A nice feature of entropy is that the total entropy of two clusters is just the sum of the entropy of each one. You can add the two impurity measures to get the total impurity of the data after the split:

```
0.207 + 0.506 = 0.713
```

Remember that the original sample (on the far left of Figure 10.5) had an impurity of 0.993 bits. How much better is the new split at increasing purity? We say that the *gain* from this split is the difference between the original total entropy and the total entropy after the split ($0.993 - 0.713 = 0.280$ bits).

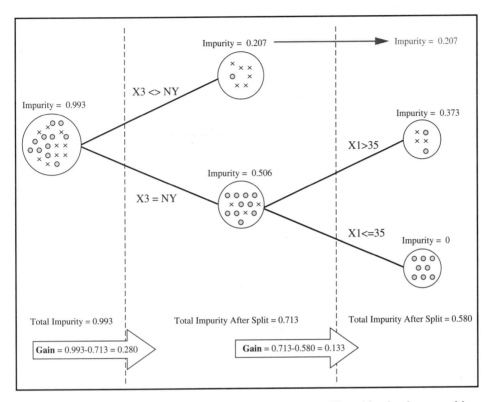

FIGURE 10.5 How "Impurity" is Removed from the Data. The objective is to partition some independent variable that maximizes information gain.

The second split (on the second sub-sample at the bottom) splits the data into clusters where the variable X1 (*age*) is less than or equal to 35, and greater than 35. The gain from this second split is 0.133 bits.[5]

Looking at these data from a business perspective, identifying these splits is a good start for the marketing team at Widgitco since it shows that New Yorkers over the age of 35 have a pattern of buying widgets, but that the team might need to focus more on customers outside of the New York area as well as on younger New Yorkers.

To get another perspective on what this splitting is actually doing, look at Figure 10.6. A split is basically a line drawn perpendicular to the axis of a variable. The dotted vertical line labeled "Split 1" partitions the data on either side of 0.5 for the variable X2. Likewise, the dotted horizontal line splits the first sub-sample in Figure 10.4 into the "pure" one with seven *no* responses (labeled 2) and one with two *no* responses and three *yes* responses (labeled 3). It is difficult to visualize how the splitting would look if you included all of the variables (there would be many dimensions), but it works identically.

---

[5]We arrived at an overall impurity of 0.580 by splitting one cluster to get two new ones with impurities of 0 and 0.373, and leaving the other untouched with an impurity of 0.207.

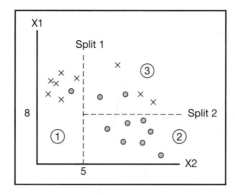

FIGURE 10.6 The recursive partitioning algorithm draws lines that are perpendicular to an independent variable's axis.

By now you are probably wondering how the partitioning algorithm decides where to split the data at each point. This is actually very simple: Most algorithms test all possible splits on all possible independent variables. They then compute all the resulting gains in purity, and pick the split that maximizes the gain. This is done over and over again on each resulting cluster (*recursively*) until a tree is built. In practice, the more sophisticated algorithms implement a variant of picking the split that maximizes gain. This makes sense since it means that each split will be as efficient as possible at increasing the gain.

For example, the algorithm that produced the tree in Figure 10.5 determined that the variable X3, when split on the value NY, gave the highest gain of all possible splits on the variables in the data. Furthermore, once the data were split at X3, the new cluster formed by all of the NY records could be further purified. The algorithm did this by testing all of the variables again, but only using the data in the new cluster. This time the algorithm determined that X1 was a good discriminator when divided at 35.

But how much splitting is appropriate? Figure 10.7 shows two different partitionings of the widget sales data. The one on the right contains just one split, which still leaves a good deal of impurity in the resulting clusters. The one on the left contains seven splits, where ultimately each resulting partition is pure.

Which one is better?

The approach on the right with just one split seems somewhat coarse: After all, the two resulting sub-samples are still quite impure. On the other hand, in the approach on the left, there seem to be too many splits: The model has become very complicated. When a model is very complicated, in addition to being hard to understand, another problem may creep in: *overfitting* the data.

We discussed overfitting when we talked about neural networks. What overfitting means is that the algorithm does a great job of finding a model that fits the data on which it was trained (also referred to as *in sample* or *training* data), but in the field, the model will probably perform badly on new data it hasn't seen before (on *out of sample* data).

The problem arises because, like a neural network, the ML algorithm may have

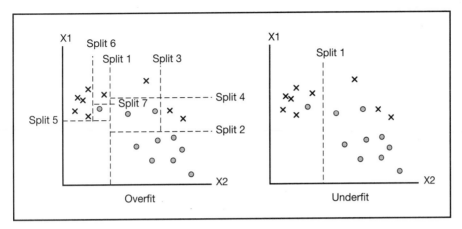

FIGURE 10.7   The extreme case of overfitting is one where each data point has its own terminal node. Underfitting means that the algorithm has not become meaningfully specific.

inadvertently picked up on details in the data that are characteristic of the training sample, but not of the actual problem being modeled. It is easy to "overtrain" ML algorithms and neural nets so that they perform really well on training data but badly on data they haven't seen before.

One common way of avoiding overfitting, especially when data are limited, is to do what is referred to in statistics as *cross-validation*. What this means is that you break up the training data into several parts, say 10, and use all but one of these parts to build the model. You can then use the leftover part for testing. By doing this several times and varying which of the parts you pick for training and testing, in effect, you can test the splits on several different combinations of the training and testing data.

For example, with 10 parts, 9 of which are used for training and 1 for testing, there is a total of 10 combinations of training and testing data sets. Cross-validation helps you get more mileage out of the data when the quantity of available quality data is limited. This technique is useful in many modeling situations, machine learning or otherwise.

Besides careful testing procedures like cross-validation, ML algorithms themselves can be engineered to minimize overfitting. To protect against overfitting, the algorithm must construct a model that generalizes the data "just the right amount." Typically, the more complex a tree becomes, the more likely it is that some overfitting has taken place. On the other hand, if it becomes too simple, it will be inaccurate.

Figure 10.8 is typical of what happens to the accuracy of a model on out of sample data as the model size increases. As the figure shows, the error rate of the model initially decreases as you add more splits, but starts increasing after a point. The trick is to find the optimum number of splits, that is, where the error rate on out of sample data will be the minimum.

So how can you get to "right-sized" trees? There are two possible ways to control the size of a tree. The algorithm could limit the number of splits it explores as it is

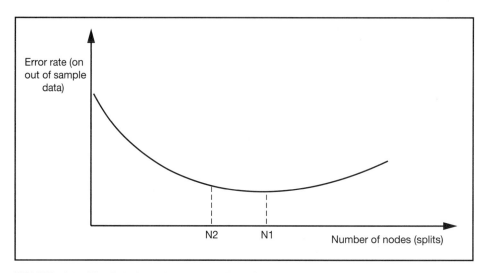

FIGURE 10.8   The Relationship between Tree Complexity and Error Rate

building a tree, stopping when they get to be too many. Alternatively the algorithm could try all of the splits possible and grow the complete (overfitted) tree, and then selectively "prune back" the useless branches, that is, the ones that *increase* the error rate on the out of sample data.

It turns out that deciding when to stop while going forward (constructing the tree) is very hard to do. On the other hand, researchers have found that constructing the entire tree first and pruning it results in much more robust trees.

The process of growing and then pruning the tree is shown in Figure 10.9. First, a highly overfitted tree is constructed. Then the tree is iteratively pruned, and with each pruning, the error of the pruned tree is computed. (The most heavily pruned tree would end up with 0 splits and contain just the original data.) The rightmost tree in Figure 10.9 corresponds to the best overall tree.

The "right" size depends on certain parameters that you set before the ML algorithm starts building the tree. These parameters describe things like how complex a tree you are willing to tolerate, and the allowable error (or conversely, accuracy). In machine learning, there is a constant trade-off between simplicity and accuracy.

This brings us back to what we mean by "simplicity." One way to view simplicity is that the clusters should be derived based on as few splits as possible. This makes the results easier to interpret. To appreciate this point, consider the two following, alternative partitions of the data:

1. "If X3 is *NY* then customer is a *widget buyer.*"

2. "If X1 greater than 35 and X4 is less than 0.3 or greater than 0.8 then customer is a *non-widget buyer.*"

All other things being equal, the first rule provides a simpler explanation for the dependent variable. Another way of looking at it is that rule 1 tells you directly vari-

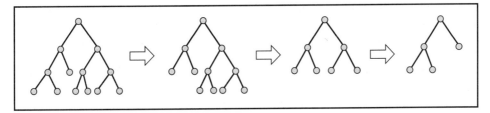

FIGURE 10.9 A large tree is first grown that overfits the data and then pruned back to a "right-sized" tree.

able X3's role in determining widget buyers. In rule 2, the roles of the variables are somewhat less clear.

The fewer the questions (splits), the more understandable the output. Accordingly, an algorithm needs to find the questions that "weed out the impurity" from the data set using the fewest number of splits. The parameters we mentioned can help control the number of splits by imposing penalties on the evaluations of more complex trees.

To end up with a tree that reflects a user's trade-off between accuracy and complexity, many algorithms include a penalty factor that you can adjust. This factor handicaps the tree on a per node basis.

So, for example, if the penalty term were set to 0, it would mean that complex, hard to interpret trees would *not* be penalized. This type of treatment might make sense in applications where you're interested in the accuracy of the tree more than anything else. On the other hand, if the penalty factor were greater than 0, and you were to examine two trees with equal impurity values but different numbers of nodes, the tree with the smaller number of nodes would be favored. These types of trees would be more useful for interpreting data in a database. By varying the interplay between the penalty factor and the accuracy, you can tailor a tree to your specific needs.

One other item before we conclude this section. So far we've focused on classification trees where the dependent variable was *categorical:* yes/no. The techniques that we have been discussing for measuring disorder in data clusters would work equally well if instead of the two classes (bought widgets/didn't buy widgets) we had four classes (bought widgets/bought doo-hickies/bought widgets and doo-hickies/ bought nothing), and so on.

But you've probably been wondering what happens when the dependent variable is not categorical but continuous, like *income*. The regression tree corresponding to this type of problem was shown in Figure 10.2b. For such problems, the notion of a "pure" partition doesn't really exist since there is an infinite number of values possible for the dependent variable (it is continuous). So, what do you measure in order to determine how to split the tree?

With continuous data, it makes more sense to think in terms of a cluster's average value and its "dispersion." In statistical terms, these are quantified by parameters such as the mean (or median) and standard deviation (or absolute deviation) of the cluster. Data clusters with a wide range of values will have a wide dispersion and this will be indicated by a large standard deviation. A cluster containing both very high and very low incomes would be an example of this. On the other hand, if the values are all close to each other (fairly homogeneous), the standard deviation would be quite small.

Despite the fact that you are measuring the dispersion differently for continuous variables than you did for the categorical variables, the objective in both cases is exactly the same: Keep splitting the data into more and more homogeneous clusters. However, you need a slightly different way of measuring impurity and gain. Specifically, you want to develop clusters where the average value in each cluster is as far away from that of the other clusters as possible, and the dispersion of values within each cluster is as small as possible.

Figure 10.10 shows what this means (no pun intended). The first split shows the means of the two resulting sets whose averages are on either side of the original one. The second split is similar. As we move toward the right, the resulting distributions of the dependent variable become successively tighter and their averages move farther apart. As in the discrete case, the best tree is the one for which the error on out of sample data is minimized.

Figure 10.11 shows part of a decision tree constructed from a customer database containing approximately 2000 records, one per customer for a software company that sells packaged PC software. The dependent variable in this case is the total annual sales made to the customer.[6] There were approximately 30 independent variables in the data. The partitioning algorithm found only three of these variables to be relevant for classifying customers: the number of users in the customer's organization, the number of inquiries they made about the products they purchased, and the number of product licenses they purchased.

Figure 10.11 shows a tree built from the data. The tree was built using CART and, since the dependent variable (*sales*) is continuous, the clusters are identified by the average sales of each customer and the dispersion (standard deviation) of this estimate. Lower dispersions mean that you can be more confident that the results are near the average. The averages and standard deviations are shown in the boxes representing the actual clusters.

INTELLIGENCE DENSITY ISSUES

So, when is it a good idea to use recursive partitioning machine learning algorithms?

A strong point in favor of these algorithms is *explainability*. We mentioned earlier that you're not always interested in the most accurate tree, especially when your objective is not prediction but interpretation.

The best way to illustrate this is through an example. The tree in Figure 10.11 while not completely overwhelming, is not easy to interpret. If we expanded the top branch further, there would have been six additional nodes. In practice, it is possible to end up with trees with hundreds of nodes. Such large trees are usually quite diffi-

---

[6]This tree was constructed using actual data and the CART algorithm. The dependent variable, *sales,* is continuous. The real variable names have been disguised as have the values.

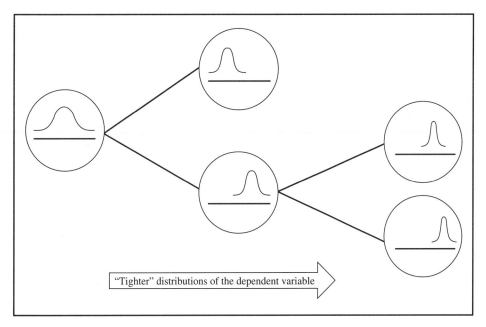

FIGURE 10.10 How Partitioning Works with a Continuous-valued Dependent Variable. When the dependent variable is continuous, the algorithm attempts to split up the data (examples) into more homogeneous subsets that are far apart from each other.

cult to understand. If the objective is to get an overall interpretation of the data, it is often worth sacrificing accuracy for parsimony.

Now, take a look at Figure 10.12. This tree shows what happened when we specified that we were willing to accept a slightly less accurate but simpler tree than the one in Figure 10.11. This tree provides an easy to interpret snapshot of the data. Essentially, it splits the original data into four types that could be classified into a 2 by 2 matrix: large customers who make a large number of inquiries, large customers who make a few inquiries, and, likewise, small customers making large and small numbers of inquiries, respectively.

The nice thing about the classification in Figure 10.12 is that its simplicity makes it more actionable. It makes the dividing lines between the categories easier to interpret. In other words, the rules that the tree in Figure 10.12 implies are more concise and intuitive than the one in Figure 10.11. Users can understand and use the output more easily.

But this ease of interpretation does not come for free. We also mentioned earlier that there is a trade-off between explainablility and accuracy. The more explainable the tree becomes the less accurate it will tend to be.

To understand exactly why, consider Figure 10.13, which shows the sales data again. The dotted lines show how the data were partitioned by the algorithm: Each split inserts a surface (in Figure 10.13, a line) that is parallel to one of the axes and perpendicular (or *orthogonal*) to the others. As a result, the outputs are very rule-like and easy to interpret.

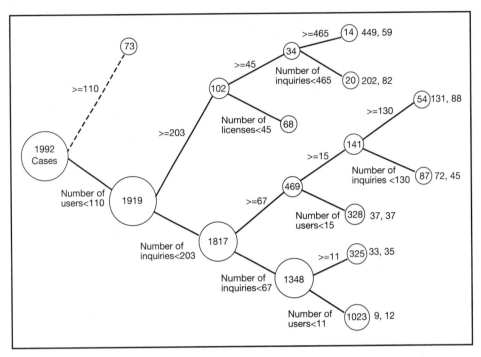

FIGURE 10.11 Part of an "Optimal Tree." Numbers in circles denote number of cases; at leaf nodes, pair is mean and SD.

Contrast this with how a neural net might partition the data (the heavy line). In general, neural nets are more powerful approximators since they can construct arbitrarily complex, non-linear partitions around the data. However, this extra power comes at a price: reduced explainability. Partitioning algorithms, on the other hand, while usually more interpretable, cannot divide data as subtly. In fact, these algorithms need many more partitions to describe the same data.

Another way of contrasting the techniques is to think in terms of their abilities to handle interactions among the variables, what we call the problem *complexity*. Again, Figure 10.13 is an interesting illustration of the limited ability of recursive partitioning techniques to deal with some types of complex interactions among variables.

Essentially, while recursive partitioning works by splitting one variable at a time,[7] neural nets are much more *multivariate* in character: They can model subtle and complex interactions *among* variables.

While recursive partitioning algorithms can, to some degree, model complex problem domains, they do this by "adding up" many linear splits, rather than as is the

---

[7]Some implementations of machine learning algorithms, notably some implementations of CART, allow for multivariate splits that are linear combinations of variables, but these techniques become very slow under these circumstances. The trees are also much harder to interpret.

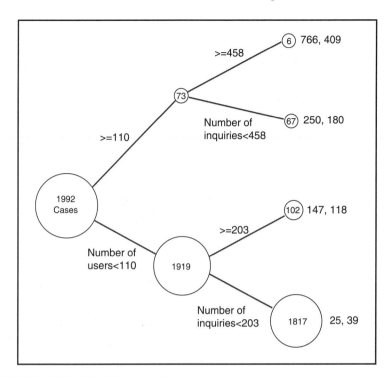

FIGURE 10.12   A Simplified Decision Tree

case of neural networks and fuzzy logic, fitting smooth surfaces over a multidimensional space.

For example, consider what a recursive partitioning algorithm would have to do to represent a relationship between two variables, say a simple ratio of x/y. Let's simplify the problem a bit and assume x could only take on the three values 1, 2, and 3, and y could only take on the same three values. To describe this very simple relationship, the algorithm would have to create a tree that looked like the one in Figure 10.14.

This tree is pretty complicated when you consider that it only describes a very simple function with only two variables and seven possible values. Furthermore, it would be very difficult to know, by looking at the tree, that the tree actually described the x/y function.

Like neural networks, recursive partitioning techniques "learn" from data, so you might expect the need for expert consultation to be low. However, our experience is that experts can and do need to get fairly involved in interpreting the outputs, separating outputs that make sense from the coincidences. More importantly, the process of discovering relationships is an iterative one as we showed in Figure 10.1: Outputs from one run generate insights used for the next run. Experts can play a significant role in this iterative exercise. For this reason, the dependence on experts can be fairly

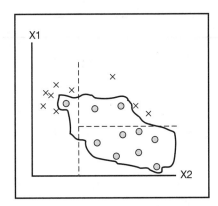

FIGURE 10.13   The split used by an ML algorithm is very different from the way in which a neural net might construct a surface around the data.

substantial; however, it is still far lower than it might be for developing a rule-based system.

Because recursive partitioning techniques base their splits on general properties of the data, they perform best when there is abundant data. Otherwise, the results can be *unstable:* Running the algorithm by tweaking the parameters (such as complexity and error rate) can yield very different trees from one run to another. It is hard to be confident about the results when there's no stability between different runs of the algorithm.

The nice thing about recursive partitioning algorithms, however, is that they are also fairly robust even with noisy data. The reason for this is that since the splitting happens at key points on individual variables, it is more unlikely to be affected by a few values being erroneous than if the technique looked at all of the variables at once.

For instance, say you had a database of sales data and one of the records was entered incorrectly so that instead of reading "$100" it read "$1,000,000." If you took the average of these, which is what many statistical methods like regression do, you might end up with very skewed results.

On the other hand, if you instead calculated the median (middle value) of all of the records, the erroneous record would not have much influence, since the median only calculates a splitting value in the data. It splits the data so that there are an equal number of records with values above the median and below it so the bad record would only move the median at most one notch up. Recursive partitioning algorithms are similarly robust with respect to erroneous values since they too rely on splitting data sets. Even more importantly, outliers or noisy values tend to get split off into their own clusters.

The fact that recursive partitioning algorithms learn from data makes them fairly adaptable. Like neural networks, these algorithms can be reapplied if conditions change. For example, if the demographics of a sales region shift or the profitability of a type of customer base changes, a new decision tree can be developed by taking the new data and building a new tree. Of course, sufficient new data about the process must be available to do this.

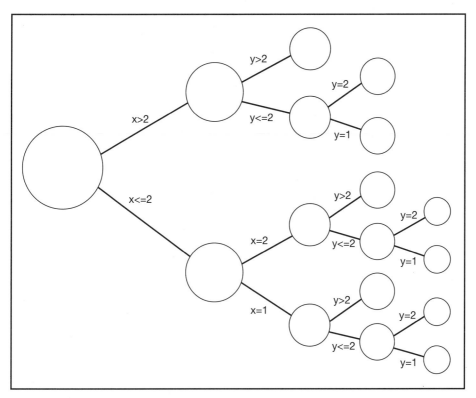

FIGURE 10.14   A Very Complex Tree. It describes z = (x/y) when x and y can only take on values of 1, 2, and 3. If x and y took on more values, the tree would become much more complex.

In addition, as the number of variables in a problem increases, recursive partitioning algorithms are able to adapt by increasing the number and diversity of the splits in a tree. What this means is that the algorithms scale nicely. The downside of this increase in splits is that the trees become more and more "bushy," which makes them harder to interpret.

Recursive partitioning algorithms are surprisingly fast in terms of response time. Once the tree is developed, finding out which cluster a new piece of data belongs to is usually just a matter of a few comparisons (one for each split until you get to the cluster). Since in most cases you only need to follow one branch of the tree, the number of comparisons is usually quite small.

The fact that the tree is just a set of comparisons makes it easy to encode compactly since the rules themselves define the model and no other type of inference engine is required. This fact also makes ML-produced trees easily incorporated into larger systems.

The intelligence density considerations can be summarized as follows:

Dimension	ML Algorithm	But...
Accuracy	Moderate to High	Depends on parameter settings to adjust for trade-off between tree size and accuracy; overfitting must be controlled
Explainability	Moderate to High	Depends on parameter settings to adjust for trade-off between tree size and accuracy
Response speed	High	—
Scalability	Moderate to High	Time to build tree increases as data sets get large
Compactness	Moderate	—
Flexibility	High	Depends on availability of data representing changes in process
Embeddability	Moderate to High	—
Tolerance for complexity	Moderate	Some complexity can be captured but only through increasingly complicated trees
Tolerance for noise in data	Moderate	—
Tolerance for sparse data	Low	—
Development speed	Moderate	Depends on understanding of process; on computer speed and memory
Tolerance for independence from experts	Moderate	Users may wish to have expert audit developed rules
Computing resources	Moderate	Scale with respect to amount of data

Suggested Reading

Breiman, L., J. H. Friedman, R.A. Olshen, and C.J. Stone, *Classification and Regression Trees,* Wadsworth, CA: 1984.

Golomb, S. W., R. E. Peile, and R. A. Scholtz, *Basic Concepts in Information Theory and Coding: The Adventures of Secret Agent 00111,* Plenum Press, NY: 1994.

Hawkins, D.M., and G. V. Kass, "Automatic Interaction Detection," in D. M. Hawkins, ed., *Topics in Applied Multivariate Analysis,* 267-302, Cambridge Univ. Press, Cambridge: 1982.

Michie, D., D. J. Spiegelhalter, and C. C. Taylor, eds., *Machine Learning, Neural and Statistical Classification,* Ellis Horwood, Chichester, West Sussex: 1994.

Quinlan, J.R., *C4.5: Programs for Machine Learning,* Morgan Kauffman, Mountain View, CA: 1992.

APPENDIX TO CHAPTER 10:
Entropy as a Measure of Disorder

In information theory, the concept of measuring the "amount of information" conveyed by a message forms a central theme.

For example, if you were to tell a friend the number that would *definitely* win the state lottery tomorrow, there would be a *lot* of information associated with this message. Why? Because there are many, many numbers that *might* win the lottery, but only one that will *definitely* win.[8]

The qualifier *definitely* is an important one: If the lottery number above has a 50% chance of winning as opposed to being a sure bet, the amount of information would be reduced by half. If it has the same chance of winning as any other number, the amount of information reduces to 0.

On the other hand, if you were to rush over to your friend and tell him that the sun would *definitely* rise tomorrow, the information content of this message would be very low: It's a highly likely event and the message is unnecessary. Even without your message, your friend knows that the sun will rise. Unlike the case of the lottery number where you are singling out a specific number as very different from all other numbers, in the rising sun case you are not telling your friend anything interesting that distinguishes tomorrow from every other day (when the sun rises).

In the same way that you might send a message to your friend about the lottery, ML algorithms send messages to users by indicating in which cluster a piece of data belongs. As we've discussed, the goal of many machine learning algorithms is to increase the *information content* in data by segmenting the data into more and more definite categories.

In essence, ML algorithms allow users to play a game of 20 questions with the data to try to narrow a piece of data down to a particular category.

To understand how this works, you need to first see how to measure how much "information" you get by knowing that a piece of data belongs to a certain category. Once you can do that, you can determine how much information you have about a piece of data's category when you know that a piece of data is in a particular cluster. This is a measure of how pure a given cluster is.

In information theory, the formula for measuring the amount of information in data (measured in *bits*) is based on the probability of receiving the message (classifying the data as belonging to a particular category) given all of the other messages (categories) you *could have gotten.*

The measure essentially tells you how many bits (1s and 0s) you would need to uniquely describe every possible category. Data involving very complicated messages (lots of possible categories) would require many bits, while simple ones need fewer. Another way to think about this is that this formula measures how hard it would be to guess the message if you were not told it.

While the actual formula is a little more complicated, you get a good intuitive feel for how the measure works by thinking of the information content as a simple

---

[8]Say you were entering a lottery in which you had to match five numbers and there were 50 possible numbers from which you could choose. Of the 2,118,760 numbers you could choose, only one would be *definitely* the winner. Such a message would be a very rare occurrence.

probability. The value of the message will be higher if the probability of getting the message is lower. Thus, you can crudely value the information content as the probability of *not* getting the message, or 100% minus the probability of the message. You would expect signals for very likely events (the sun rising) to need a low amount of information to describe them (100% − 99.99999999%) and signals for extremely improbable events to need high levels of information to describe them.

It turns out that for theoretical reasons which we won't go into here, a better measure of the information required to code a message is

$$-\log_2(p),$$ **(Eq. 10.1)**

where p is the probability of a message's occurrence.[9]

Thus, for a message about events occurring that have a probability of 1 (the sun rising tomorrow), the amount of information is 0 bits since,

$$-\log_2(1) = 0.$$

In other words, you don't need to bother sending the message.

Likewise, if the probability were 1/2, the amount of information is 1 bit (-$\log_2$ (0.5)), and so on.

At the other extreme, as the probability approaches 0, as in the lottery case, the amount of information grows much larger.

For instance, for a lottery in which you have to choose the correct combination of five numbers from a possible 50, there are 2,118,760 possible combinations. Therefore, the probability of guessing the correct number is

$$\frac{1}{2,118,760} = 0.00000047,$$

so the information content of a correct signal (the winning number) is

$$-\log_2(0.00000047) \approx 21.$$

That single message contains about 21 bits of information, since it eliminates all of the other (losing) numbers.

If you had a machine learning algorithm that could somehow classify your lottery pick as a winner or a loser, it would be very valuable, and this is reflected by the very high information content.

How can you use knowledge about the information content of a particular category to determine how much *disorder* there is in one of the clusters formed by an ML algorithm?

Information theory uses the term *entropy* to describe the information content in a cluster of data. A high degree of entropy implies a low amount of information in the cluster of data. The formula often used to measure entropy is based on information content formulas like Eq. 10.1.

To think of this another way, entropy measures, on average, how much additional information is needed to identify the category of a piece of data once you know

---

[9]Remember that the function $\log_2(x) = y$ is the solution for the equation $2^y = x$.

it is in a particular cluster. This type of analysis essentially answers the question, "If I know a customer is in this cluster, how certain am I that he is a widget buyer?" The more mixed the cluster is, the harder it is to answer this question, and the more additional information you need.

Entropy is described as:

$$H = -\sum_i p_i \log_2(p_i), \qquad \textbf{(Eq. 10.2)}$$

where p_i is the probability of the ith message occurring in a particular cluster.

Notice that the information provided by each category in a cluster is weighted by its representation in the cluster. Therefore, if a cluster is evenly dispersed with different categories, each will be weighted similarly. On the other hand, if the distribution is weighted heavily toward one category, that category influences the entropy more.

This average number, the entropy, is a measure of disorder. The higher this number is, the more information you to describe the cluster. The more information you need to describe the cluster, the less certain you can be of what the cluster contains.

An easy way to see this is that Eq. 10.2 would go to 0 as the probability of a single category got close to 1. What this means is that the most valuable type of cluster is the type that has only a single category in it. The disorder in this cluster is 0, and its entropy would correspondingly be 0.

Saving Time and Money Using Objects

The beginning of wisdom is the definition of terms.
—Socrates

For, of course, the true meaning of a term is to be found by observing what a man does with it, not what he says about it.
—P. W. Bridgeman

INTRODUCTION

The notion of software systems as being composed of "objects" was introduced in the early 1970s. The AI community referred to these as *frames.* In the 30s, cognitive psychologists had used a similar notion, called *schema,* to describe how we mentally represent real-world objects or abstract concepts.

The schema *ball,* for example, would describe something round *shaped,* smooth *surfaced,* and so on. The italicized words are the *attributes* that make up the structure of the object. The values, such as round and smooth help us describe the "state" of an object.

Why is it useful to understand objects?

The answer is simple. Systems will continue to become more sophisticated and complex. In order to keep a lid on complexity, the building blocks of these systems, which can be viewed as "software parts," will have to be transparent and malleable. This means that developers need to be able to pick up a software part that someone else created, modify it to fit their own needs, and add it to a system that they are building—all without needing to worry about how the part is built or the details of how it works. That's what objects bring to the table.

One way objects promote malleability is by making the building blocks of the system similar to the thing being modeled. The software part should have the same attributes as the thing it represents in the program. To describe an electrical circuit, for example, the software objects would represent things like transistors, power supplies, connectors, and so on. Objects in a naval fleet might represent things like helicopters, aircraft carriers, jets, marine crafts, and so forth. These software objects should behave in the context of the program in the same way that their real-world counterparts behave in the real world.

■ 191 ■

In reality, there's a trade-off between how malleable and pluggable an object is on the one hand, and its value added on the other. This makes sense. Instead of thinking about software, think about an automobile for a moment. You might think of an auto part at the level of a gear or a bearing. Such parts would be highly pluggable: Many automobiles would be able to use them. On the other hand, gears and bearings don't really do much by themselves. In contrast, if the auto part were an engine or an entire body for a specific car model, it would help the manufacturer build quickly the type of car that used these complex parts; however, the parts wouldn't be usable in other car models.

In the world of software, businesses confront this basic trade-off. On the one hand, low-level parts such as lists, arrays, dialog boxes, and other types of graphical user interfaces are highly generic and reusable. However, there's a limited bang for the buck at this level. That's why many organizations are trying to get to the next level and build "business objects" where the value added is high. Figure A.1 illustrates this basic trade-off.

To see why objects are useful, consider the characteristics that drive costs in the existing software infrastructure:

1. A lot of software is redundant. The same data structures and subroutines, adjusted slightly, are replicated in many systems.
2. Software systems are invariably too opaque and brittle. Making changes and maintaining them costs too much.
3. Too often, software takes longer to develop than it should.

Objects are appealing because they address the three cost drivers directly.
Think first about redundancy and opacity.

Most systems have common low-level functionality. It is hard to come across a system that doesn't sort things or store things in a list,[1] yet most programmers rewrite the sorting logic and list structures over and over again with slight variations. All of this leads to a tremendous amount of redundancy.

The costs of redundancy add up in two ways. First, it's a waste of time and money to do things over again if you don't have to. Why reinvent the wheel? But far more significantly, making changes and improvements to these systems requires a lot more effort. Each time you want to change a sorting routine, you have to find all the different versions of it. Once you find an occurrence of the routine, you have to figure out what little twists it has that might make it different from other sorting routines. The object concept, on the other hand, promotes a centralization of modular and reusable parts. They can be maintained in one place and application programmers can dip into the parts warehouse whenever needed.

---

[1]For example, the two PC applications that you probably use most both store data in lists and have sorting routines. Spreadsheets store data in lists that are organized into a sheet, and allow users to sort data in a number of ways. Word processors store the letters and words of a document in lists and, although you might not realize it, whenever you use the spelling checker you are using a sorting routine to organize the spell check. By the way, whenever you open a file by selecting from a list of files, you are using a sorting routine to put the files in alphabetical order, and you are probably storing the file names in a list. These routines and structures show up everywhere.

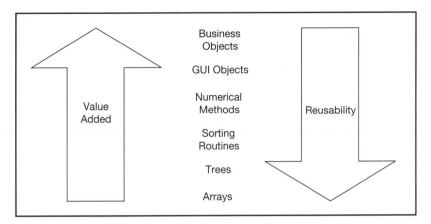

FIGURE A.1   The Trade-off between Reusability and Value Added

Second, many systems are highly *opaque*. The logic and data structures are convoluted, especially if the programs have been modified over time. It's hard enough for a person to understand a well-designed piece of software written by someone else (or even written by themselves several years earlier), but making sense of enigmatic "spaghetti code" is a nightmare. It's usually less risky to leave it alone if it works rather than to try to modify it.

Opaqueness is caused by interaction among pieces of software at a low level. In part, this happens as a consequence of separating the procedural part of a system, the logic or behavior, from the data part of the system. Making changes to procedures or data is a tricky business since procedures call each other and share data. A small change to a data structure could mean changing all subroutine that use that structure . . . if you can identify them.

How do objects help you overcome this convolution?

The object paradigm promotes modularity and transparency by providing "self-sufficient" building blocks called *classes*. A class is the definition of how an object will act and store data. In a very loose sense, the class is the mold, and the object is the part it creates.

In object-oriented terms, objects are *instances* of a class. In a class, data (like traditional data structures) and behavior definitions (like traditional subroutines) are wrapped into a single unit. The set of behaviors of the class forms its *interface*. All instances of a class, objects, *inherit* the data structures and behavior from the class.

For example, let's say you define a financial class called *stock*. You will need to define places to hold data such as price, volume, etc. Calculating the volatility of a stock would be part of its behavior. IBM, Apple, Motorola, etc. are all objects that belong to the class stock and the same volatility calculation would be inherited by them. This makes sense. If you know how to calculate the volatility for IBM, you probably know how to calculate the volatility for all stocks that are like IBM.

Furthermore, the data and behavior are not visible to other parts of the software. Rather, the system only deals with an object (requesting it to behave a certain way or to show its data) through its interface. How the behavior is implemented is wrapped up within the object. Figure A.2 shows the basic idea behind the concept of a class. Figure A.3 shows a class called Account, like a bank account.

The account object has two data storage locations, one for the balance, and one for the customer id. It also has two types of behavior associated with it: withdrawal and deposit. Programs using the object would increase or decrease the balance by using the services of the object (withdrawal and deposit), but they would not be able to directly modify the balance.

While it might seem odd that "hiding" internal details makes things more transparent, it makes a lot of sense. For example, bonds and stocks might be two common types of objects in a financial trading system. Each object would have a price and, for each object, you could compute standard things like volatility of prices, annual return, and so on. The internals about how return is calculated would be hidden within each type of object. (Fixed rate bonds make periodic fixed interest payments whereas stocks may or may not make dividend payments.)

The thing to note is that a programmer who uses the object doesn't have to worry about *how* the return is calculated. The programmer just accesses the information through the object's interface. It's up to the object to figure out how to calculate return. The fact that the details are hidden actually makes it easier to see what the overall system is doing.

It also makes systems more stable to changes. Tomorrow, if you replace the logic involved in calculating stock returns with a more accurate or efficient method, it will not affect any other part of the system.

Why?

The system only deals with the interface. If you change the internals of a class, it shouldn't affect the interface. In other words, an object's interface tells you everything about what it represents *and* about what kinds of things you can do with it. Objects are the knowledge equivalent of one-stop shopping. This property of "encapsulating" or "hiding" the details of objects promotes modularity and transparency.

This explains how objects can be less opaque than traditional programming approaches, but what about malleability?

Object classes can be organized into class hierarchies. The nice thing about hierarchies is that they allow you to modify an object to make it more specific to your needs. As we mentioned, objects that are instances of the lower classes would inherit data and behavior from the higher classes.

Let's say that you have a generic checking account object (which is itself a special case of the generic account object). Since the account object has a balance and a customer ID, the checking account will inherit this as well. (In object-oriented terms we would say that a checking account has an IS A relationship with account. In other words, a checking account "is a" account.)

In addition, you might add the behavior to "write–check" which would allow a customer to write a check against the checking account. The savings account class wouldn't have this feature, but it would have "calculate–interest" behavior. If, a few years later, you started offering NOW and Checking Plus accounts, you could allow them to inherit the behavior of checking accounts, but also add additional data and behavior that are specific to NOW accounts. Figure A.4 shows a class hierarchy of different types of accounts.

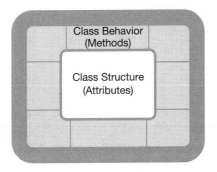

FIGURE A.2   The Anatomy of a Class
Attributes are used to describe the structure of a class. Methods describe things that can be done to all members of the class.

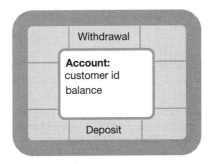

FIGURE A.3   A Class Called **Account**
Its structure is described in terms of customer id and balance. The two things you can do to *any* account are make withdrawals and deposits.

So interfaces make objects pluggable and transparent, and hierarchies make them malleable. Now think about the last driver of costs in software development: development time.

Since objects are malleable and pluggable, the object paradigm encourages you to build or buy reusable libraries of objects. Why build it from scratch when you can buy it off the shelf? If object class libraries have been thoroughly tested, buying object libraries speeds development tremendously.

But object hierarchies also help you think about and structure problems more naturally and logically. As we showed in Figure A.4, class libraries are arranged in logical hierarchies with the most general things at the top and specific things at the bottom. This lets you more easily build up the structure of a system.

There's a real parsimony associated with organizing the building blocks in terms of hierarchies: Lower categories "inherit" information from the more generic ones. Software works the same way. Organizing the building blocks into a hierarchy and allowing developers to dig into this toolbox gives them tremendous leverage. Software development becomes more of a process of gluing prefabricated parts together, occasionally adding on new branches to a hierarchy.

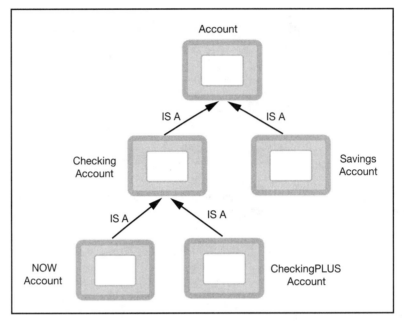

FIGURE A.4   An ISA Hierarchy
In this example, there are two types of accounts, checking and savings. Checking is further specialized into NOW and CheckingPLUS. An object that belongs to the class **NOW Account** also belongs to **Checking Account** and **Account**.

Interestingly, hierarchies bring together all three of the benefits of objects. As we just discussed, they allow rapid development. As we showed earlier, they allow malleability. Finally, object hierarchies reduce opacity. They allow you to understand very easily how related objects differ from each other. Essentially, an object that inherits the properties of another object says to a programmer, "I am exactly like that other object except for these explicit differences." For example, the only thing that makes a checking account object different from an account object is that it has "write–check" behavior. This makes determining how software has been modified much simpler.

Of course, nothing comes for free. One of the major impediments to object-based systems is that people are still getting used to thinking in terms of objects. On the face of it, the idea is deceptively simple. In reality, however, many systems that are supposed to be object based end up looking like traditional systems that just happen to be programmed in an object-oriented language such as C++[2]. Most people still struggle with thinking through a complex design in object-oriented terms. A high level of skill is required to do good object-oriented development in C++. Currently, these skills are scarce and expensive.

---

[2]And as many people would argue, C++, the industry standard, is not a "pure" or the best implementation of the object concept.

A CASE

It's worthwhile to look at a brief example of an object-oriented toolkit that shows the power of the object approach. What is interesting about this case is that it involves the design of the techniques we've discussed in this book in terms of objects.

Moody's Investors Service, a Wall Street firm specializing in fixed income analysis, is now using an object-oriented library that was developed privately by one of the authors of this book. Moody's now has access to an object-oriented "toolbox" for modeling complex problems. This toolbox is called ENIGMA (ENvironment for Investigation and General Modeling Applications).[3]

What does ENIGMA do and why is it useful?

At Moody's, the ability of analysts to understand and evaluate the credit issues surrounding institutions and industries benefits from the use of quantitative tools from the fields of statistics, mathematics, finance, and AI. Developing these analytic tools, especially when they involve complex mathematics, neural nets, genetic algorithms, etc., can be a time-consuming complicated process, since many times developers need to combine several of these methods to solve a problem.

For example, a developer might want to use a genetic algorithm to select the variables that produce the best predictions for a neural network model, as we discussed earlier in the text.

Although this sounds easy conceptually, getting all of the data and the GA and the neural network programs to talk together using a standard procedural language can be difficult. This is especially so when a developer wants to experiment with several different approaches to see which solution might be most effective. This trial-and-error process can be time intensive and costly.

Moody's uses the object library to try out modeling ideas quickly. Each type of tool is an object class. ENIGMA contains neural network objects, fuzzy set objects, fuzzy rule objects, genetic algorithm objects, graphical visualization objects, and various types of statistical and financial modeling objects.

Any type of basic object (neural network, genetic algorithm, etc.) can be glued together by creating it as an instance of an existing object class. So, instead of creating a specialized program to implement a back-propagation neural network, and a specialized program for choosing variables using a GA, a developer can create an instance of a neural network object and an instance of a GA object and then tweak each one to make it fit his needs. The two objects would then be stitched together with some additional programming.

How would a developer do this using ENIGMA?

What the developer wants to do, in this case, is create a genetic algorithm to experiment with and test out different neural network models. The hope is that the genetic algorithm will use its optimization power to select a very good set of variables for the neural network. In order to do this, the system needs to let a GA create different neural networks and evaluate their performance based on how well they predict, using a set of variables that the GA's chromosome selects.

---

[3]Portions of ENIGMA were implemented by Spencer Kimball of the Computer Science Department at U.C. Berkeley.

A developer could start by defining the fitness function of the GA. Since the goal would be to decide which variables produce the best predictions from a neural network, the fitness function would need to be able to decide which variables a particular chromosome recommends. It would then train its individual neural network using these variables, and evaluate the performance of that individual neural network. In other words, each chromosome will have its own neural network and each one will train its net using its subset of the variables.

The GA would need to create a population of chromosomes, each representing a possible set of variables (columns in the data). The GA's fitness function would decode each chromosome by converting it into a set of variable recommendations. (For example, a 1 in position 3 of the chromosome might mean include variable number 3 and a 0 in position 4 would mean exclude variable 4.) The fitness function would then use the selected variables to train its individual neural network. Since the neural network is a self-contained object, it only takes a single line of code to include it in a fitness function (which is itself an object).

Once the neural network has been trained, the GA would test it using hold-out data, and the prediction error term would be passed back to the GA as the fitness of the chromosome. The lower the error of the network using the variables selected by the chromosome, the higher the fitness of that chromosome. This process would be done for each chromosome in the population and repeated in each generation until the GA halted.

Compared to the use of traditional procedural programming, the flexibility and speed of the object-oriented environment is much more efficient. It is also a lot more flexible than trying to patch together tools from different vendors. As a result, Moody's is able to develop and test new modeling approaches more quickly than in the past. Furthermore, approaches that would have been considered too costly can now be explored.

AI Software Products

The following is a list of vendors of software products for experimenting with and developing AI-based applications. In addition to the products listed here, there are extensive libraries of public domain software and applications available at many university internet sites. We recommend that the reader explore these as well. (We haven't listed these since the Website and ftp addresses change frequently.)

We have only listed a few of the many vendors in each category. Some of the vendors produce more than one product as well. For a variety of reasons, we have not commented on or reviewed the individual products, although their quality and robustness do vary considerably. This appendix is provided as an aid and does not represent an endorsement for any of the products listed. We have attempted to present information which is timely and accurate at the time of this publication.

Data Warehouse / OLAP
(Many major DBMS vendors now offer some form of data warehousing functionality. In addition, the companies listed below are a few of those that offer specialized data warehousing and OLAP solutions.)

CrossTarget
Dimensional Insight, Inc.
111 South Bedford Street
Burlington, MA 01803
(617) 229-9111

DSS Agent and *DSS Server*
MicroStrategy, Inc.
8000 Towers Crescent Drive
Vienna, VA 22182
(703) 848-8600

Essbase
Arbor Software
1325 Chesapeake Terr.
Sunnyvale, CA 94089
(408) 727-5800

Light Ship Suite
Pilot Software
One Canal Park
Cambridge, MA 02141
(617) 374-9400

PLATINUM Repository
PLATINUM Technology
1815 South Meyers Rd.
Oak Brook Terrace, IL 60181
(708) 620-5000

Redbrick Warehouse VTP
Red Brick Systems
485 Alberto Way
Los Gatos, CA 95032
(408) 399-3200

Genetic Algorithms

Evolver
Axcelis Corp.
4668 Eastern Ave. N.
Seattle, WA 98103
(206) 632-0885

GeneHunter
Ward Systems Group, Inc.
Executive Park West
5 Hillcrest Drive
Frederick, MD 21702
(301) 662-7950

GenSheet
Inductive Solutions, Inc.
380 Rector Pl.
New York, NY 10280
(212) 945-0630

Neural Networks

BrainMaker
California Scientific Software
10024 Newtown Rd.
Nevada City, CA 95959
(916) 478-9040

Neural Network Toolbox
The Math Works, Inc.
24 Prime Park Way
Natick, MA 01760
(508) 653-1415

NetSheet
Inductive Solutions, Inc.
380 Rector Pl.
New York, NY 10280
(212) 945-0630

NeuralWorks Professional
NeuralWare, Inc.
202 Park West Dr.
Pittsburgh, PA 15276
(412) 787-8222

NeuroShell 2
Ward Systems Group, Inc.
Executive Park West
5 Hillcrest Drive
Frederick, MD 21702
(301) 662-7950

Rule-based Systems

Exsys Professional
Exsys, Inc.
1720 Louisiana Blvd N.E.
Alburquerque, NM 87110
(505) 256-8359

Level5 Object
Information Builders, Inc.
503 Fifth Ave.
Indialantic, FL 32903
(800) 444-4303

Nexpert Object
Neuron Data
156 University Ave.
Palo Alto, CA 94301
(415) 321-4480

Fuzzy Systems

CubiCalc
HyperLogic Corporation
Suite 210
1855 E. Valley Pkwy.
Escondido, CA 92027
(619) 746-2765

Fuzzy Logic Toolbox
The Math Works, Inc.
24 Prime Park Way
Natick, MA 01760
(508) 653-1415

fuzzyTECH
Inform Software Corp.
2001 Midwest Rd.
Suite 100
Oak Brook, IL 60521
(708) 268-7550

TILShell
Togai InfraLogic
Distributed in the US by:
Ortech Engineering Inc.
17000 El Camino Real #208
Houston, TX 77058
(713) 480-8904

Case-based Reasoning

CBR Express
Inference Corp.
550 N. Continental Blvd.
El Segundo, CA 90245
(800) 322-9923

Esteem
Esteem Software, Inc.
2016 Belle Monti Ave.
Belmont, CA 94002
(415) 596-9275

Induce-It
Inductive Solutions, Inc.
380 Rector Pl.
New York, NY 10280
(212) 945-0630

Machine Learning

CART
Salford Systems, Inc.
5952 Bernadette La.
San Diego, CA 92120
(619) 582-7534

C4.5
Morgan Kaufman Publishers
2483 Old Middlefield Way
Suite 103
Mountain View, CA 94043
(415) 578-9911

S-PLUS
Statistical Sciences
1700 Westlake Avenue N.
Suite 500
Seattle, WA 98109
(800) 569-0123

SYSTAT
SPSS, Inc.
444 North Michigan Ave.
Chicago, IL 60611
(312) 329-2400

APPENDIX

General Reading

The following is a list of books that are geared toward the general reader. Some are classics in the AI field, some are histories of AI or related topics, and some are interesting discussions of related topics like decision making or evolution.

The level of these works varies considerably, but all are geared toward the intelligent layperson and avoid technical discussions and mathematical treatments, favoring instead intuitive presentation of material. We have enjoyed reading each of the texts listed here for different reasons and each has been rewarding.

Calvin, W. H., *The Ascent of Mind: Ice Age Climates and the Evolution of Intelligence,* Bantam Books, NY: 1990.

Campbell, J., *The Improbable Machine: What New Discoveries in Artificial Intelligence Reveal About the Mind,* Touchstone, NY: 1990.

Casti, J. L., *Searching for Certainty: What Scientists Can Know About the Future,* William Morrow & Company, NY: 1990.

Crevier, D., *AI: The Tumultuous History of the Search for Artificial Intelligence,* Basic Books, NY: 1993.

Dawkins, R., *The Blind Watchmaker: Why the Evidence of Evolution Reveals a Universe Without Design,* W. W. Norton & Company, NY: 1987.

Franklin, S., *Artificial Minds,* MIT Press, Cambridge, MA: 1995.

Gleick, J., *Chaos: Making a New Science,* Penguin, London: 1987.

Hodges, A., *Alan Turing: The Enigma,* Vintage, London: 1992.

Hofstader, D. R., *Godel, Escher, Bach: An Eternal Golden Braid,* Vintage, NY: 1989.

Kahneman, D., P. Slovic, and A. Tversky, *Judgment Under Uncertainty: Heuristics and Biases,* Cambridge University Press, NY: 1982.

Levy, S., *Artificial Life: The Quest for a New Creation,* Pantheon Books, NY: 1992.

Lewin, R., *Complexity: Life at the Edge of Chaos,* Macmillan, Toronto: 1992.

Minsky, M., *The Society of Mind,* Simon and Schuster, NY: 1985.

Penrose, R., *The Emperor's New Mind: Concerning Computers, Minds, and the Laws of Physics,* Penguin, London: 1989.

Simon, H. A., *The Sciences of the Artificial,* MIT Press, Cambridge, MA: 1969.

von Neuman, J., *The Computer and the Brain,* Yale University Press, New Haven, CT: 1958.

Waldrop, M. M., *Complexity: The Emerging Science at the Edge of Order and Chaos,* Simon and Schuster, NY: 1992.

Case Studies

The following appendix contains a collection of seven cases taken from the experiences of businesses that have successfully applied the techniques in this book.

Each of the cases is analyzed using the framework that we presented in the first three chapters. The cases assume that you already understand something about the techniques used and the framework itself.

The cases were written based on our own experiences, discussions with our colleagues, and published reports describing details of some of the work. We used the framework in interviewing developers and analyzing their work while we were writing the cases.

The main point we hope to convey is not that the approaches that these organizations took are the ones that should be used by developers in other situations. There is no one "right" approach. Rather we hope to show that each organization and problem is different and as such requires a unique perspective.

What is interesting about the cases is the way in which each organization uniquely crafted a solution that fit its needs, and the way these solutions changed its business.

C A S E

Quality Control and Monitoring of Suppliers

Kaufhof AG, Germany

THE ORGANIZATION

Kaufhof AG was founded in 1868, and is a large German "superstore" chain. Kaufhof's stores are somewhat similar to very large U.S. department stores. Unlike American department stores, however, Kaufhof has a much broader range of products and services, carrying goods extending from foods and delicacies, to clothing, to durable goods, and to service bureaus providing services like travel planning.

Typically, these stores are located in the heart of large metropolitan areas. Not long ago, the firm also expanded into the territories of the former East Germany. In addition, Kaufhof has recently acquired Horton, one of the other major German department store chains. Prior to the acquisition, Kaufhof maintained 93 stores, but with the addition of Horton's outlets, Kaufhof now boasts 164 department stores.

Kaufhof handles very large volumes of merchandise, so much so that the firm maintains 16 of its own warehouses on the outskirts of major German cities. Manufacturers deliver orders directly to these warehouses. The warehouses themselves then route and deliver orders to specific stores. The logistics involved in this distribution system can become very complex and Kaufhof has recently re-engineered its logistical infrastructure to cut costs and improve efficiency.

Logistical management is critical to Kaufhof's continuing operation. In view of the very large number of items that the stores must stock, the firm cannot afford to spend too much on storage and shelf space. Kaufhof prides itself on the high quality of its goods and services. This means that the firm must continually monitor the quality of suppliers and products in order to ensure against quality problems. With thousands of suppliers, this can be very time and labor intensive.

Inspection and quality control are where intelligent systems came into play at Kaufhof.

THE PROBLEM

Kaufhof deals with a total of about 14,000 suppliers. Each day these suppliers make over 7,000 deliveries to each warehouse. That means on an average day, the company receives about 112,000 deliveries. The superstore chain employs a staff of quality assurance personnel whose job it is to ensure that the merchandise meets Kaufhof's standards.

Individually checking the quality of each delivery is very time consuming and labor intensive. As a result, the firm wanted to develop a system that would reduce the labor involved in quality control.

However, this can be tricky. The severity of an error can sometimes be difficult to assess. For example, let's say the firm ordered 100 pairs of black socks. There is a difference between a delivery that contains *96* black socks, and one that contains 100 *blue* socks or 100 *white* socks. Depending on the store, the time of year, etc. one type of error might be far less severe than the other. Or consider a shipment of fine china in which one of the sets has a chipped cup.

Kaufhof wanted to develop a system that would allow its inspectors to concentrate on the more risky shipments, thus reducing, overall, the need to examine each shipment as it came in to the warehouse.

While there are legal reasons why firms do not report headcount reduction statistics in Germany, Kaufhof estimates that its savings in labor would be about proportional to its savings in capacity. In other words, doubling the number of shipments inspected per hour would be expected to free up the labor involved by about half.

Kaufhof wanted complete control over the quality of the goods on the shelves of its retail outlets. Currently, testing all shipments results in about a 1% error rate. In other words, 1% of the shipments accepted are later found to be erroneous.

The factors that help determine whether a delivery is likely to be bad interact in complicated ways, though. Affecting the shipments are such things as:

- *the nature of the items being delivered.* Some items are more prone to errors and breakage than others. Crystal, for example, is riskier to ship than blue jeans. But what about power tools?

- *the past performance of the supplier.* Certain suppliers have better internal quality control, shipping practices, and so forth than others.

- *the recent performance trends of the supplier.* Suppliers' performances are non-stationary: They change over time as new management practices are introduced by suppliers, and their own input quality and client bases change. In addition to looking at overall historical experience with the supplier, it is important to consider more recent trends in performance.

- *the size of the order.* Larger cash value orders pose relatively larger risks to a retailer, so the size of the order is important for assessing the risk potential of a shipment.

Kaufhof decided that the proposed system needed to be adaptable enough to deal with new products, new suppliers, and new types of quality control policies. Furthermore, it had to be convenient for use in a warehouse. Kaufhof currently employed an inventory control system by which workers could scan bar-coded labels on each box that arrived at the warehouse. It would be nice if the new inspection advising system made use of this procedure.

The problem of inventory quality control is a common one. In Germany, as elsewhere, there are typically three approaches to inspection and quality control: no-inspection, the brute-force approach, and the threshold approach.

The policy of no inspection is simple: The retailer depends on the supplier for all quality control and just accepts all orders without checking them.

The brute-force approach is also simple. A company checks every shipment for damage and accuracy. Needless to say, this is very costly and reduces the speed with which orders can be processed and passed on to outlets. This, in turn, increases inventory carrying costs and the amount of time that goods sit on warehouse shelves.

The threshold approach is less costly. It involves checking orders that are larger than a certain cash "threshold" value. Smaller orders are passed without inspection. This approach is less than desirable for several reasons. First, erroneous smaller shipments will always be passed on to the stores, thus necessitating correction further downstream with associated costs, or worse, resulting in dissatisfied customers. Second, as suppliers gain more experience dealing with a retailer, the suppliers may discover the threshold point, and therefore take less care in preparing shipments of lesser value.

Brute-force is attractive since it ensures that very few bad shipments make it through to the store shelves. On the other hand, the threshold approach is attractive since it is much less time intensive.

Kaufhof decided to try to combine the two methods. The firm needed a system that could allow an inspector in the warehouse to scan the label of a shipment and, based on the factors discussed above, determine how likely it was that testing would find a problem in the shipment. Shipments that had high-risk scores would be inspected by hand, and those shipments with sufficiently low scores would be passed without inspection.

In order to evaluate a system, Kaufhof decided to use as a benchmark the error rate obtained when brute-forcing the shipments (1%) versus when using the system. If the system's performance were sufficiently close to the performance obtained by the brute-force method, then Kaufhof would consider the system successful and roll it out on a larger scale.

Since Kaufhof wanted to match the accuracy of the brute-force testing method, the system would need to be very reliable. A 1% error rate is a pretty high standard.

Although the firm had data about orders that had been processed, it did not have any data about which orders were historically bad. What this meant was that there would need to be a fair amount of interplay between the system designers, the purchasing department, and the quality assurance staff in order to understand the process better. This would necessitate explaining what factors of the model would produce which types of behavior so that the experts could perform "tweaking." Furthermore, over time, users of the system would need to make changes to reflect new products, inspection policies, and so forth, so the flexibility would need to be fair. This was particularly true since most users would not be very familiar with the technology.

Since Kaufhof wanted to incorporate the new system into the current inventory control system, any new quality control system would need to "work and play well" with the inventory system. It also had to be able to deliver very fast responses so as not to disrupt the workflow at the warehouses.

Finally, nobody at Kaufhof could articulate, exactly, the rules of thumb that should be used for spotting potentially risky shipments. What this meant was that much work would have to be done developing the rules. But the rules themselves would not be exact. There would be ambiguities involved and no one knew exactly how all of this fit together in risk assessment. Any system would have to be able to deal with this domain.

THE SOLUTION

The problem requirements are as follows:

Dimension	Target Solution
Accuracy	High
Explainability	High
Response Speed	High
Flexibility	Moderate
Embeddability	Moderate
Tolerance for Complexity	High

When thinking about problems that involve such things as historical performance, recent trends, and so forth, it is not uncommon to consider statistical approaches. Unfortunately, in Kaufhof's case, this did not make sense. Why? As mentioned, while Kaufhof had quite a bit of data relating to the shipments, cash amounts, dates, and so forth of shipments from its suppliers, the firm had no data about whether inspecting those shipments actually turned up errors or not, or whether inspection was warranted for those cases. In other words, there was no dependent or decision variable to add meaning to all of these data.

What this meant was that whichever approaches the firm considered, it didn't have any data that related outputs to inputs. This ruled out all "bottom-up" approaches such as neural networks and other machine learning algorithms such as clustering techniques. It also ruled out statistical techniques such as Principle Components Analysis.

Problem formulation with statistical methods also requires a fair amount of expertise. The same is true for changing the problem formulation. Since the inspection policies needed to be modifiable over time and across stores, Kaufhof was looking for a solution that was easy to understand and modify by businesspeople.

On the other hand, quality control expertise (the business knowledge) was available. Experts could, for example, articulate criteria under which they would want to inspect shipments. For example, if a supplier had been making bad shipments recently, it made sense to inspect; if the dollar value of a shipment was high, it made sense to inspect, and so on. Since the experts could articulate this general knowledge, Kaufhof decided to explore expert systems. These did not generally require large amounts of data and they tended to be fairly intuitive. In addition to conventional rule-based systems, Kaufhof also considered fuzzy systems, thinking that these might require fewer rules and allow more flexibility.

These two approaches then, RBS and fuzzy systems, were the serious candidates for solving Kaufhof's problem.

Consider the rule-based system approach: One of the most powerful features of an RBS approach is its ability to explain its decisions. This is due to the explicit chaining that occurs in the inference engine. This, and the interpreter machinery in general also make the RBS approach one of the slower ones, especially if there is a fair amount of complexity in the problem. In addition, as a result of the inference engine, RBS almost always require some sort of proprietary software and databases. In some cases these special systems can cause problems with respect to integrating RBS into established environments.

As far as complexity goes, rule-based systems tend to do better with categories and logical tests than with continuous variables. This is because rules tend to produce behavior that "jumps" as the system moves from using a rule that applies to one data range to a rule that applies to the next. The resulting output from an expert system is correspondingly limited, leading to results that are sometimes rough for numerical predictions.

On the other hand, because of the rule structure and the way that an RBS allows designers to partition knowledge into manageable chunks, modifying rules or policies is fairly straightforward.

Now consider fuzzy systems: Fuzzy systems allow processes to be modeled using gradations of truth as opposed to all or nothing rules. Fuzzy sets and rules are consequently more able to deal with complex interactions among variables since they do not require complex branching logic. This lack of branching also makes fuzzy systems very fast.

Since fuzzy systems do not rely on chaining to execute their rules, they do not need to maintain an inference engine and can often be rendered easily into standard computer languages like C or FORTRAN. Fuzzy systems are also easily modified to accept new rules or new fuzzy sets.

Fuzzy systems do have drawbacks as well. Because they avoid the chaining of rules, applying all of the rules simultaneously, it is more difficult to understand how a particular decision is reached. Nonetheless, since the rules, as well as the degree to which each is fired, are explicit, a user can get a rough feel for what caused the output.

Finally, since fuzzy sets are able to more finely define subtle changes in variables and processes, they tend to produce very accurate output.

We can summarize the comparison as follows:

Dimension	Target Solution	RBS	FUZZY
Accuracy	High		✓
Explainability	High	✓	
Response Speed	High		✓
Flexibility	Moderate	✓	✓
Embeddability	Moderate		✓
Tolerance for Complexity	High		✓

Solving the Problem

Kaufhof decided to pursue the fuzzy rule-based approach. Not being experts in fuzzy systems development, the retailer enlisted the help of INFORM GmbH, a firm specializing in the development of fuzzy systems and tools.

INFORM developed a system for Kaufhof that was compact and easy for the Kaufhof staff to understand and modify. The system was integrated into the COBOL-based inventory management system which runs on Kaufhof's mainframe computer. The system is called Invent/W.

The fuzzy system takes a series of inputs from Kaufhof stores in the inventory system and ancillary databases, as well as taking inputs from special tables used only by the fuzzy system. When a delivery arrives at one of the warehouses, a Kaufhof employee scans the bar-coded label that is attached to the shipment. This code supplies the system with the information it needs to evaluate the content of the shipment, the supplier, and so forth.

With this information, Invent/W is able to access historical data, trend data, product type data, etc. The fuzzy system then analyzes all of these data and comes up with a fuzzy score between 0 and 100. The lower the number, the more the shipment should be inspected.

The entire analysis process usually takes less than a second. After scanning the label, the employee receives output that tells him or her in which area of the warehouse to put the shipment. Quality control personnel inspect shipments in one area, and the warehouse stores or distributes those in the other areas.

How is this determination made?

First the system needs to compute the fuzzy score. There are 164 rules in Kaufhof's system. In addition, there are tables that allow the system to determine the risk profiles of various products and suppliers. The rules take advantage of data about the supplier's past performance and recent performance. These data deal not only with the values of shipments and so forth, but also with fuzzy concepts such as quality.

For example, using a hand-held data input device, quality assurance inspectors record every type of supplier problem when it is discovered. The characteristics of a problem are broken up into three categories: INACCURACY (the wrong item was shipped), SHIPMENT PROBLEM (something was broken or damaged), and VALUE (the value of the shipment was different than it was supposed to be). The quality assurance inspector inputs values from 0 to 100 for each of these categories. For instance, a shipment of crystal that was broken would get scores of 0 for INACCURACY and VALUE, but a score of 100 for SHIPMENT PROBLEM. On the other hand, the shipment of 100 blue socks (instead of 100 of the more expensive black socks) might get a score of 0 for SHIPMENT PROBLEM, but scores of 60 for INACCURACY and 25 for VALUE.

The system then uses this information in assessing the supplier's historical performance. A typical rule might conceptually take the form of:

IF *recent–SHIPMENT–PROBLEM* HIGH
AND *item–shipment–risk* HIGH
THEN *risk* is HIGH

Such a rule would determine that a shipment of crystal from a careless supplier should be a high candidate for inspection.

But such rules can be hard to manage since there tends to be a lot of them. Furthermore, controlling interactions among such rules can become difficult. To control this, INFORM decided to break the problem into smaller pieces using *rule blocks*. A rule block is a set of rules that go together. For example, if three rules define what to do if *shipment–value* is HIGH, MEDIUM, and LOW, and all take the same variables as input, they would be considered one rule block. INFORM partitioned the problem into five rule blocks, which made it much more manageable. The rule blocks, in turn, interact to determine the shipment's score.

Once the system generates a score, it must still decide whether the score warrants inspection. Invent/W handles this in a surprising manner. For each shipment, the system also generates a random number between 0 and 100. If the random number is larger than the fuzzy score, the shipment is inspected.

At first, this may seem like an unusual way to inspect shipments. *Randomly!* But consider that a shipment which is ranked 100 will never get inspected and one that is ranked 0 will always be inspected. On average riskier shipments will be inspected more often than less risky ones. Furthermore, if the inspection threshold were fixed, then shipments with high scores would never get inspected, even though they could also have problems. By using a random approach, even very good suppliers are checked from time to time. Finally, consider what would happen if a supplier sent 10 shipments of the same product. The scores would be identical for each of the shipments. Let's say the system scored the shipments at 51, but the cutoff for inspection was 50. This means that *none* of the shipments would be inspected. On the other hand, using the random approach, about half of the shipments would be inspected.

In order to allow businesspeople to modify rules or add new products, INFORM provided Kaufhof with a Windows™ based graphical environment called *fuzzy*TECH® with which users could easily define rules and the shapes of fuzzy sets by pointing and clicking. Once a user is satisfied with the modifications, the system can generate COBOL code for Kaufhof's mainframe. In this way users do not need to be technical experts to make changes to the system.

Results

So, how did Invent/W perform in actual use? To test the system, Kaufhof decided to roll it out to a limited number of warehouses. Kaufhof used the system to evaluate shipments, but it also used the brute-force testing approach in parallel.

To test a typical shipment after it arrived at a Kaufhof warehouse, the bar code would be scanned, Invent/W would evaluate the risk, and the resulting score would be recorded. After this, *regardless* of what the score turned out to be, the shipment was inspected. Kaufhof evaluated the contents of the shipment for errors, and then determined whether the fuzzy system's score would have predicted the error.

The results may surprise you. In the first 4 months of testing, Invent/W identified 98.5% of all erroneous orders. (The score might have been higher, except that a series of new suppliers was added in the third month of testing bringing the average down as information was being input into the system about these suppliers.) Invent/W was modified to allow management to vary the random number generator so when a large number of new suppliers is added to the system, the system will request more inspections.

The firm was so pleased with the results that it has rolled the system out to all of its storage facilities. The system is now performing at about a 99.5% level, and inspection capacity has been reduced by more than 50%.

There is nothing fuzzy about numbers like those.

Lessons Learned

The developers of the system say that they have learned an important lesson from this case: that the fuzzy system developed for this application has widespread applicability for inspection problems in general. INFORM GmbH has developed several systems since Kaufhof's that focus on other problems such as the checking of invoices. For instance, Volkswagen AG is currently using a version of INFORM's software for its invoicing processes.

This is a generic problem across business organizations, which is traditionally carried out by back office employees (in accounts payable departments). The problem is very similar to Kaufhof's problem: Which invoices should be "flagged" for further review by experienced people and which ones should be skipped?

The great flexibility of the fuzzy system seems to make modifying it to solve similar but different problems much easier than might be expected with traditional RBS.

Suggested Reading

von Altrock, C., *Fuzzy Logic and Neuro-Fuzzy Applications in Business and Finance,* Prentice-Hall, Englewood Cliffs, NJ, 1995.

-------------------------------- **C A S E** ---------------------------------

Workflow Monitoring and Improvement for Rapid Customer Service

U S WEST Communications, Englewood, Colorado

THE ORGANIZATION

U S WEST, Inc. is a provider of domestic and international telecommunications, cable and wireless networks, directory publishing, and interactive multimedia services. U S WEST was formed in 1982 as a result of the divestiture of Bell Telephone. The break-up separated local and long-distance telephone services into distinct businesses. The parent company, AT&T, continued to provide long-distance services but the local telephone business was divided into seven regional companies, of which U S WEST was one. Today, U S WEST has about 61,000 employees and revenues of almost $11 billion.

U S WEST Communications is one of the two major groups owned by U S WEST. U S WEST Communications provides commercial and residential telecommunications services to customers in 14 states in the West and Midwest. The firm services 25 million customers from Washington to Montana.

U S WEST Communications considers itself to be a leader in technology, actively introducing Internet-based services, SingleNumber calling, and other innovative offerings. The firm has generally sought to use technology to improve service to its clients. In the highly competitive telecommunications industry, service is one of the only ways that providers can compete. U S WEST Communications has responded with such service-oriented programs as temporary loans of cellular phones for customers awaiting out of the way land-line connections and CustomChoice, a calling plan that allows small businesses to lock in current phone rates for an extended period of time.

THE PROBLEM

U S WEST Communications wants to excel in service. The firm has the eventual goal of being able to deliver phone service within an hour. The firm would like to be able to connect a new customer account so quickly that minutes after the customer finishes placing his or her order, the customer has a dial tone and fully connected service. To do this, U S WEST needs to be able to accurately track and monitor its installation process at all levels from regional managers to quality assurance staff to computer system administrators.

This might seem like it should be easy in today's computerized business environment. But it is more involved than it sounds. U S WEST Communications processes 15 million orders from 14 states each year. Each order passes through an elaborate series of steps on its way to completion. Even simple orders involve eight separate mainframe computer systems. More complicated orders interact with even more systems. Each of these systems was developed independently, and each has its own quirks and data storage conventions.

In the early 1990s U S WEST Communications realized that in order to be able to achieve its one-hour goal, it would need to be able to understand and analyze its installation process to a much higher degree than the current myriad of computer systems and databases allowed. The firm was having a difficult time even following the processing of a single order through the complex system.

U S WEST needed to better understand its process from customer contact to service delivery and billing, and to use its process data on an ongoing basis to monitor and streamline its installation process. Why was this a challenge?

First, the existing computer infrastructure to support the business process was sprawling. As you might imagine, installing and billing for 15 million orders a year involves some pretty powerful computing. In fact, U S WEST had over 30 different computer databases and programs to handle the various aspects of the process. Trying to understand these data was a nightmare due to such things as:

- *data being divided across many systems.* This made it impossible to perform a simple query to unite different data elements if they were stored on different machines.

- *multiple hardware and operating platforms.* Some computers were IBM mainframes running MVS, some were Amdahl mainframes running more UNIX, etc.

- *multiple DMBS environments.* Some of the data were stored in IMS and DB2 databases, some in Sybase or Oracle databases, some in Informix, and so on. In fact, U S WEST had most major DBMS vendors represented somewhere in its infrastructure!

- *different data naming and representation.* Since each system was developed separately, the same variable, say "order–date" might have a different name in each database or might be represented differently.

U S WEST was having a hard time understanding its processes because it was having a hard time understanding its data. It wasn't measuring anything about its current process, so it was hard to improve anything in a well thought out manner.

Second, the problems weren't all technical. In addition to the many mainframe programs that process installations, an order can also go through numerous manual interventions. These typically happen when an order "drops out" of the system. Dropouts happen if the specifications of a service request are incompatible with the data available in the systems or with the business rules for installations.

For example, an order might drop out for something as simple as an erroneous customer address that doesn't match an address in the U S WEST switching database, or something more subtle like a customer who requests CallerID in an area where it is not available.

Orders that drop out are routed to clerks who then manually correct the order and then resubmit it. In addition to being slow and expensive, it makes it difficult to know where in the system a particular order is at any given time. Is it in the processing queue of one of the mainframes? Is it being transmitted between mainframes? Has it dropped out onto the desk of a clerk in one of the regional offices? Maintaining a high level of customer service in this environment is exacting because you're measured by failures, not successes: Even a low proportion of failures can damage reputation and make a service function look bad.

What U S WEST Communications wanted to do was understand the entire process better so that businesspeople and units could respond quickly to snags or recurrent inefficiencies in the installation process. By being able to monitor and identify these rough spots, the firm hoped to be able to direct resources dynamically to where they were needed, when they were needed. Eventually, the organization hoped to be able to reduce the amount of manual intervention by identifying trouble spots in the order process.

The problem was that the current data systems were not talking.

To address this, US WEST needed a way to be able to determine, for any given recurrent installation problem, what was causing delays. The firm wanted to be able to diagnose, on an ongoing basis, whether new training was required, whether new software needed to be written, whether a computer system was malfunctioning, whether particular personnel or groups needed closer monitoring or more resources, and so on.

U S WEST decided that it needed an easy to use, fast system to allow line businesspeople at all levels of the organization to access data about problems in the installation process and analyze the data to determine the causes of the problems. The people responsible for making these decisions need to be able to understand the data as they evolve. The system would need to allow users at many different locations in the firm to access data from many different sources.

How would the system be used?

Managers who use the system need to be able to track trends in data to better understand the business process. This means that they need up-to-date data, although not necessarily in real-time. Managers are also seeking explanations for the problems that they identify in the data and need to be able to understand them in order to figure out remedies.

A manager might be interested in looking at the installations by region one day, and the technicians by installation time the next. The system would therefore need to be able to adapt to the changing needs of uses or changing dynamics of the data. Similarly, a user needed to be able to follow up hunches quickly and easily as one discovery led to another in the data, requiring a fast response. Since so many people would be using the system, it had to be designed in such a way as not to put a drain on the computing infrastructure of the firm, but U S WEST wanted to develop a solution without adding more hardware if possible.

Finally, since there would be many different types of businesspeople using the system and each would have his or her own needs, the MIS group needed to be able to develop the system without taking up a lot of the user community's time. The systems also needed to be developed fairly quickly to meet the overflowing user demand.

THE SOLUTION

The problem requirements are as follows:

Dimension	Target Solution	
Accuracy	Moderate	
Explainability	High	
Response Speed	High	
Flexibility	High	
Independence from Experts	Moderate	
Development Time	Moderate	
Computing Resources	High	

What options did U S WEST consider?

The firm had been limping along on a standard DMBS technique and reporting. The MIS department knew this wasn't working. Programmers were drowning in requests for reports. The reports themselves were getting harder and harder to write because users wanted more and more complicated queries done. Furthermore, each time a report was run, it chewed up valuable computer time and slowed down the rest of the system.

A natural alternative, particularly in the early 1990s when this took place, was an executive information system (EIS). An EIS would allow users to get access to data easily through a friendly interface. It would also allow users to easily get at data in the corporate databases.

Another alternative, which was not so obvious at the time, was some sort of OLAP/data warehousing solution. OLAP and data warehousing systems were still new technology at the time, but U S WEST felt that there might be some potential in the new technology. OLAP and data warehousing technology were promising to allow users to slice and dice data any way they wanted. This sounded good but risky because it was so new.

First consider the EIS approach:

An EIS would interface directly with the transactional databases. As a result, its data would be updated in real-time. Specific reporting functionality would be pre-programmed into the EIS to allow managers to get a better picture of what was going on in the data. An interface would allow users to query for specific items, say the installations for a particular technician, but only those types of items that had been included in the pre-programmed reports.

Since the reports would be pre-programmed, they could be optimized for better performance. The fact that the user would be directly querying the transaction database would also put a load on the mainframes, but no new hardware would be needed.

Lastly, each user's needs would be addressed through specialized reporting features, so each user would need to actively participate in the design of the system to ensure that the reports were what they needed. This also meant that the system might take a while to build.

Next, consider the data warehouse/OLAP approach:

The data in a warehouse are usually updated periodically at the end of the day. The OLAP engine allows users to drill down into the data as they need to or drill up for more perspective. Users can also spin the data around to reconfigure them into a more appropriate format for their analysis.

Since the data warehouse would be optimized for fast data access and querying, users would be able to get answers fast. The separate data warehouse would also reduce the load on the company's main computers but new hardware would be needed to house it.

Since users peruse data at their own pace and according to their needs, no special provisions would need to be made for report writing and so forth. Nonetheless, users would need to be consulted about the meanings of variables in the database or business processes. Since no customized reporting would be necessary, this would reduce development time. On the other hand, work might have to be done to develop the data warehouse itself if one could not be purchased from a third party. Also, being a new technology, there were sure to be unforseen technical and architectural snags.

Taking all of the options together, U S WEST's options look as follows:

Dimension	Target Solution	EIS	DW/OLAP
Accuracy	Moderate	✓	✓
Explainability	High		✓
Response Speed	High	✓	✓
Flexibility	High		✓
Independence from Experts	Moderate		✓
Development Time	Moderate		
Computing Resources	Low	✓	

Solving the Problem

U S WEST Communications' solution bore out the analysis above and the organization developed a combination data warehouse and OLAP solution, although the firm didn't exactly plan it that way at the outset.

Around the end of 1989, U S WEST decided that the current state of its databases was reaching a critical point. There were 30 different databases, each containing different vital data. The MIS department drafted a plan for a data warehouse to unify these databases and to reduce the load on the mainframe transaction systems.

Initially, U S WEST investigated third-party vendors of data warehouses. At the time, though, it was unable to find a product that would interface with all of the different types of systems and databases that the firm needed to unify. In addition, since much of the data were in different formats and used different variable names, extensive work needed to be done by the data warehouse to scrub the data as well. Most early products didn't do this well. (Both of these things are much less true today.) As a result, the MIS department decided to build its own data warehouse.

The system became known as *In Process Measurements* (IPM). IPM works by collecting data from the 30 or so databases that run the business and unifying the data into a single DB2 relational database on a single mainframe computer. The collection process used by IPM depends on which systems are providing data. For example, some of the older mainframes output large files which IPM reads periodically during the day. Other systems have trigger events built into them and they shoot data into the warehouse on a record-by-record basis.

The end result, though, is that the data are collected in a single place where they can all be queried at once. Furthermore, queries to the data warehouse don't slow down the main transaction databases or interfere with other computer processes. It is a much more efficient way to get at the data. U S WEST thought that this reduction in load on the transaction systems more than offset the cost of adding the new hardware required for the warehouse.

Although U S WEST had changed its data infrastructure, its MIS department hadn't yet changed its mind set. Initially the MIS department thought it could use this new consolidated data warehouse in the same way that it had been using the other systems. Programmers saw it as an easier way to do reporting.

For the first 6 months, IPM was used primarily by the report writers to fill management requests for data. Although the group tried to produce these reports, the demand was just too high. A backlog soon developed. Furthermore, even users who got their requests filled were frustrated since they usually wanted to know more about the data as soon as they saw the reports. They wanted *more* reports!

The MIS group quickly realized that they needed a better solution to user queries.

In 1993, U S WEST implemented an OLAP system to give its employees greater data access and flexibility. U S WEST acquired an OLAP product from a third-party vendor specializing in OLAP software. The OLAP tool then became an interface into IPM.

In the course of installing the new interface, the designers of the data warehouse realized that they had made some design decisions about the warehouse that were more suited to the old OLTP way of thinking about data than to a DSS approach. As a result, the team redesigned parts of the data warehouse to make it more flexible. Two months later the OLAP front end was in place.

The system has been introduced throughout U S WEST Communications, and training for the average user only takes about half a day. All types of businesspeople, using PC-based versions of the OLAP engine, access the data using specialized graphical user interfaces.

What kinds of things do they use the system for?

Because the system is set up specifically for analysis, users can access the data along any dimension that will help their analysis. This is a refreshing departure from the traditional pre-programmed DSS approaches that the firm had used in the past.

Users log in to the system through a Windows™ or Macintosh™ based interface that presents the data graphically or in tabular form. Every number or graphical region on the screen is "hot." What this means is that if a user wants to drill up or down into data, he can do so just by clicking on the item he wants to examine.

For example, let's say that a U S WEST manager is using the system to monitor installation times in his region. The manager has asked to see the information in the form of a bar graph of installation times by managerial regions. The manager notices that one of the bars is much larger than the others, indicating that customers in one particular region are experiencing unusually slow installation times. The manager can click on that bar to see the region broken up by switching area. Now maybe it looks like one particular switching area has very long installation times, which is pushing up the average. Click again. Now the manager is looking at installations by service technician. But none of the technicians seems to be taking longer than any of the others in that town . . . they all seem to have slowed down. Click again. Now the manager looks at the installations by problem type. Ah ha! There is an unusually large number of service requests "dropping out" due to requests for CallForwarding, which is not yet available in the area. There's the problem. The manager might now notify the operators who take orders to explain to new customers that they cannot get CallForwarding if they are from the blacked-out area. The manager could check later to see if the number of "drop-outs" due to this problem drops back to normal levels after the new policy is in place.

Before the system was in place it would have been almost impossible to rectify a situation like the one above unless the manager was willing to wait weeks. In fact, because each of the "clicks" above would have had to have been a special report written in a query language like SQL, most managers would not have been able to take advantage of their data to solve the problem. They would have had to rely on a lot of guess work and telephoning to try to get a picture of their business.

A major benefit of the system is that it allows users to interact with the data very easily, but still allows U S WEST to use the mainframe infrastructure that it needs for OLTP types of tasks.

Results

Users embraced IPM enthusiastically. For most of them, it was the first introduction of direct data access. Previously the firm had to go through programmers who would (manually) write reports or use some rudimentary EIS, but these didn't offer the freedom of IPM and its interface.

But there were some significant productivity improvements as well.

Within the first three months, managers using IPM identified many training issues. They could now zero in on the orders for which they were responsible. A manager was now able to spot patterns of unusual orders and determine who had entered them.

For example, one manager discovered that in one of his offices in Minnesota every typist was making the same mistake when he entered data. This simple procedural snag was causing hundreds of drop-outs each day. But the typing errors were so easy to fix that clerks who handled the drop-outs were correcting and passing the orders on without reporting back to their managers on the problem. Management was in the dark!

The manager of the Minnesota office was able to discover the problem by using IPM. The manager was looking at his order data and started drilling down into his drop-outs. The manager saw that all of the Minnesota office's orders were dropping out *for the same reason*: typographical errors. He visited the office and cleared the problem within a day.

Erroneous order flow changed from 30,000 drop-outs a month to almost 0.

In another case, management got an unexpected result. U S WEST was using IPM to measure process order efficiency, but in the course of this, the firm inadvertently discovered something very interesting. In the normal flow of the order process, the customer's phone service is usually connected quite quickly. However, it takes several more steps for the customer's account to get posted to the billing system. The billing system flags errors and creates drop-outs if the data posted to them are erroneous. When this happens a customer will be not billed for any phone usage he or she makes prior to the account being posted to the billing system. So, for example, if the customer got connected on Monday morning and the account wasn't posted until Wednesday morning, the customer would not have to pay for any calls he or she made on Monday and Tuesday.

U S WEST discovered that a single type of error was frequently causing certain orders to drop out of the billing system. What was even more distressing is that when this type of error occurred, the drop-outs would sometimes sit in limbo for up to two months before being resubmitted. Once management discovered this problem and took steps to rectify it, the error rate for those transactions dropped to much lower levels.

Estimates at U S WEST are that catching that one error increased revenues by about $2 million in the first year alone. Other similar problems have also been identified since then, leading to further savings.

Overall U S WEST has had very positive experiences with the system and is looking to expand usage beyond customer service applications into other areas of the business.

Lessons Learned

In developing the data warehouse and OLAP solutions, U S WEST learned some valuable lessons . . . the hard way.

Probably the most important lesson was that it is much easier to do the homework that you need to do to understand the data and business processes *first* before you start developing the system. U S WEST started coding the data warehouse based on assumptions about the data and hearsay about the business processes, and later paid the price for it.

For example, each of the 30 or so systems produces an error if it cannot execute its part of the installation process. As a result of the error, the order it is processing will drop out and be captured by IPM. Some systems can produce hundreds of errors. For instance, if an order goes into the cable pair assignment system, there could be hundreds of possibilities why an error might occur (e.g., address does not match assignment database; the combination of services is impossible like a residential line at a commercial location; etc.).

The MIS department interviewed experts about the conditions under which an error would occur, but it never actually validated what the experts said. It later turned out that the errors were occurring when, according to the experts, it should have been impossible. The members of the MIS team spent hours trying to figure out how their analysis was flawed, when in fact the data were wrong.

Another thing that U S WEST learned was that databases for DSS purposes need to be designed quite differently than those for OLTP systems. The developers who worked on IPM were mostly from OLTP backgrounds. As a result, they did things that would make a transactional database much easier to use and more efficient. As they found out when they tried to use the data warehouse with the OLAP front-end, these were not the best things for a decision support system to have. They eventually involved people with DSS backgrounds as well.

Finally, U S WEST felt that trying to design a data warehouse and OLAP simultaneously would have been difficult for them. Because of the previous two points, it would have been hard to stabilize the warehouse while users were banging away on the OLAP front-end. The six months of query experience on the data warehouse let the developers understand the data much better and adapt the warehouse to what users really needed.

Suggested Reading

Ermish, R., "Improving the Quality of Customer Service at U S WEST," *Phone+ Magazine,* July 1993.

"Software in the Pursuit of Quality: Automated Tools for Better Decision Making," *Quality Observer,* November 1993.

------------------------------ **C A S E** ------------------------------

Help Desk Task Scheduling

Moody's Investors Service, New York

THE ORGANIZATION

Founded in 1909, Moody's Investors Service specializes in the credit analysis and rating of fixed income securities and the analysis of international financial markets. Moody's bond ratings (**Aaa, Aa1**, etc.) are well known by investors, who use them to aid in the evaluation of the credit quality of various financial instruments.

While Moody's is primarily a financial service firm, the company is constantly expanding its computer workstation, database, and wide area network facilities. This expansion is essential due to the vast amounts of information that must be collected, interpreted, and synthesized with the experiences and judgment of analysts around the world to form the firm's credit opinions. New in-house software packages are constantly being developed and refined, third-party software packages and on-line services are introduced regularly, database enhancements are implemented almost daily, and sophisticated econometric modeling and research take place continually. This environment necessitates a broad computational infrastructure capable of supporting such activities.

Like many large organizations with large computer user bases, Moody's has an in-house support group to aid in resolving technical problems. In addition, it has a "help desk" where users can report problems, and, in some cases, get help in resolving those problems over the phone.

The scheduling of problem servicing in the help desk area will form the focus of this case study.

THE PROBLEM

Moody's objective was simple. The firm wanted to increase the efficiency with which computer problems were resolved. It realized it has become virtually impossible for an employee to function well without having a computer running. One way to ensure that people spent less time idly waiting for their machines to be repaired was to effectively prioritize, schedule, and route problems.

Typically in a help desk environment problems are processed in a series of stages. Users usually contact the help desk with a specific problem. If the contact person at the help desk is able to, he or she tries to resolve the problem over the phone. Unfortunately, in many cases, this is not possible. The more complex or time-consuming problems are forwarded to other specialists who visit the user site directly.

Moody's problem was not one of developing a powerful *diagnostic* system that could be used to resolve problems, but a *dispatching* system, such that the right people were sent to fix the various problems. The challenge facing the help desk administrator is to effectively allocate tasks to personnel so that the loss of value by the firm due to computer down time is minimized. But this alone won't ensure that the internal customers are happy. The administrator also needs to be concerned with minimizing dissatisfaction on the part of users due to the timeliness of support.

This might sound easy, but in practice it is complicated by numerous issues. The help desk administrator (HDA) needs to consider the priority of the various tasks in the help desk queue. Is a problem a severe one that seriously prevents a user from doing his or her job, or is it a less serious problem that is more of an inconvenience? The administrator must also consider how long it will take to resolve a particular task and how this impacts the help desk's ability to service other users. The ability of the various customer service representatives (CSRs) to perform the various tasks will also impact schedule design. All things being equal, it makes little sense to have a highly experienced technician perform a relatively simple task while a more complex task remains undone because the other (idle) technicians do not have the skills to perform it.

On top of all of this, the administrator also needs to consider the amount of time that a given task has been outstanding. The longer a problem, even a minor one, is outstanding, the more dissatisfied a user will be.

Moody's help desk was facing a problem common to help desks. The volume of tasks and the task distribution system was such that it was very difficult to prioritize, schedule, and distribute tasks efficiently. This was due to the large number of tasks, the large number of CSRs, the varying capabilities of CSRs, and the very wide variety of task types. In addition, simple, low-priority tasks would tend to get postponed in favor of higher-priority tasks. The result was that these low-priority tasks would be put off indefinitely, sometimes until users were ready to give up.

At the time Moody's was scheduling tasks in a basically ad hoc manner. After tasks were entered into the tracking system, a paper "job ticket" was printed. The job ticket described the task, the time of the call, and had other related information about the user and problem. This job ticket was then inserted into one of a group of folders in a central area in the help desk. The folders were broken out by broad categories of tasks. The administrator, along with CSRs, would periodically check the various folders and try to determine which tasks to do next. A CSR would then take a task ticket and visit the user. The help desk was rarely in a position to be able to tell users *when* they would be addressed.

Finally, the administrator did not have a clear sense of how loaded the CSRs were, or how balanced the loads were across CSRs. Determining how many problems were left unattended at the end of each day was also a time-consuming exercise. In other words, the administrator was not in intimate "touch" with the situation on the front-line.

This system had worked well enough when the number of tasks and CSRs was small, but as the scope of the help desk grew, it became increasingly difficult to come up with efficient scheduling that took all of the factors above into consideration.

The help desk administrator now needed a tool to help with the scheduling and routing of tasks to technicians. The system had to:

- be able to provide outputs that could be used to tell users *when* their problems would be addressed. In order to accomplish this, the system needed to produce good schedules that were efficient.
- be able to assess task priorities based on severity of the problem, number of people affected, etc., and also be able to make adjustments due to various circumstances. The system would also need to know about things like CSR availability and CSR skill sets, and also be able to generate good estimates of how long it would take to resolve a particular problem.
- integrate with Moody's other databases and database systems that were already in place for logging and tracking help desk problems. Moody's had already invested in the development of a system that allows help desk personnel to access a good deal of information about a caller when calls reached the help desk.
- be flexible enough to allow new types of task definitions to be inserted into the system and to accommodate changes in personnel, training, etc.
- also be flexible enough to let the help desk administrator *modify* the solutions it generated. For example, if a certain department was working on a tight schedule, the administrator needed to be able to give its jobs priority.
- be able to generate and reevaluate schedules quickly since new tasks are constantly flowing into the help desk. The developers estimated that the system must be able to generate good solutions in under 15 minutes and do so *consistently*.
- not take CSRs or the administrator away from their work for any extended period of time during development. Since the help desk is a very busy place, the administrator could not spare the resources to undertake a protracted development project.
- be developed fairly quickly.

Moody's decided to measure schedule goodness based on the number of hours of down time each schedule cost the organization. Schedules that resulted in large amounts of down time would be considered bad while those that produced fewer hours of lost time would be considered good.

Over time, Moody's also expected that the number of employees would increase, causing an increase in the number of help desk calls and a corresponding increase in the number of CSRs. The system needed to be able to accommodate reasonable growth of this sort. Furthermore, the help desk staff would be maintaining the system going forward, so a very complicated system would not be useful in the long run.

The administrator would need good schedules, but the schedules did not have to be "perfect." This is both because of the nature of the help desk domain, and because of the fact that there would be oversight on the part of the administrator and CSRs.

THE SOLUTION

The problem requirements are as follows:

Dimension	Target Solution
Accuracy	Moderate
Response Time	High
Scalability	Moderate
Flexibility	Moderate to High
Embeddability	High
Ease of Use	Moderate
Independence from Experts	High
Development Speed	High

It turns out that scheduling is an extensively pursued problem in both operations research and in Artificial Intelligence. A score of numerical techniques (including almost every technique in this book) have been applied at one time or another to solving scheduling problems.

In Moody's case, however, the authors had been independently working on a research paper that explored "job-shop" scheduling problems in general. (The help desk is a variant of this type of problem.) Specifically, they were exploring the merits and demerits of using GA-based versus integer programming (a numerical optimization technique) versus expert system approaches to constrained satisfaction problems.

Integer programming is a well-known numerical technique that is often used for optimization. Expert systems, on the other hand, solve problems through the use of heuristics and have also been applied to solving a variety of optimization and scheduling problems. GAs are very good general optimization systems based on evolutionary principles.

These three approaches, integer programming, expert systems, and genetic algorithms, were considered to be primary candidates for the scheduling system.

How did the RBS stack up?

A primary drawback of an RBS approach can be the need to describe the process of optimization in a series of rules. For some types of problems, this representation of knowledge is ideal. But in the help desk case, the expertise is not exact and it was not clear that a set of optimal rules could be developed by the schedulers. In addition, remember that for the help desk problem the administrator could not spare much time or resources to develop the system. Moody's felt that trying to develop and tune a set of rules could be time consuming since there are so many different types of help desk problems and circumstances in which they arise.

Moody's would need to be careful about choosing or designing an expert systems environment, since some commercial expert system development tools require special "inference engines" and software modules that might be difficult to deal with. However, if it selected an environment wisely, a schedule produced by an RBS could probably be made easily accessible to the current help desk system.

The foundation of RBS, intuitive rules, are easy for most people to understand since most people describe their own knowledge in terms of rules. RBS-based optimization systems also tend toward good solutions, but seldom achieve fully optimal solutions for complex problems. Since the help desk schedules did not need to be perfect, just very good, this was O.K.

RBS generally perform well on small domains, but for problems such as the help desk one, the large number of interactions might make an RBS scale poorly as the domain size increases. For the help desk problem, the size of the rule base would probably be several hundred rules, which is considered a moderate size. Accordingly, interactions among problem variables would be moderate which could cause some scalability problems.

Depending on the architecture of an RBS and the problem domain, it can be either very easy or very difficult to add new rules or constraints; in Moody's case, the rules would probably be easy to modify as long as the rule base was small, but modifications would probably become harder as the size increased.

A small RBS can be developed very quickly, since the most time-consuming aspect of an expert system is usually knowledge acquisition and engineering; for Moody's problem, given the nature and number of rules, *and assuming the expertise were available,* a system could probably be developed and tuned fairly quickly. Unfortunately, the help desk was very busy and experts did not have any free time.

Lastly, due to the need to calculate solutions through an inference engine, an RBS can take a long time to generate good schedules with larger sets of resources and tasks; for Moody's problem size, response time would probably be moderate.

Now consider the integer programming (IP) solution:

Integer programming is a numerical method that is based on the linear programming method. A complete discussion of the technique is beyond the scope of this case. In simple terms, the technique bounds through the search space, repeatedly cutting off sections until it arrives at an answer. It is generally very good at finding an optimal solution in a reasonable time. However, a primary drawback of the method is that it has been found to be very sensitive to changes in the parameters and constraints of the optimization program. As a result, a slight change can increase the execution time from minutes to hours to days. Even worse, such changes can sometimes render a problem unsolvable. If the IP method cannot perfectly solve a problem, then it produces no solution.

Previous research had shown that the integer programming approach is a useful tool for solving a wide variety of optimization and scheduling problems. Schedules produced by IP-based solutions are optimal. In fact, as we just mentioned, the IP method can *only* generate optimal solutions. Period. If it can't find an optimal solution, IP cannot produce anything.

An IP tool would also be able to input and output schedules in a form that could interact with the database already in place at Moody's.

For most IP problems, the coding of the constraints is where the bulk of time is spent in development. This, by itself, generally does not take excessive amounts of time, or require extended discussions with domain specialists.

So where's the concern? Some research *has* shown that small changes in the constraint requirements of a problem can result in large changes in the execution time of an IP program. Thus, while some solutions might be executed quite quickly, similar but slightly different solutions sometimes take much longer to execute. This would mean that Moody's would have to be very careful about how it made changes to schedule and problem requirements.

To make matters worse, for problems involving continuous-type variables (i.e., time) or "soft" constraints (i.e., user satisfaction in the help desk problem), IP solutions can be quite complex to encode and a fair amount of comfort with mathematical constructs and numerical methods is usually necessary to implement or modify the IP solutions.

Such solutions also tend to become much more time intensive with larger data sets than they are with smaller ones; given the number of variables involved in the help desk case (several hundred), scaling further might not be easy.

Lastly, Moody's considered a GA solution:

GAs generally offer fast, consistent response time since they perform the same set of operations each time they are run. Although GAs slow down as the chromosomes and populations get larger, in Moody's case, the number of daily tasks was not expected to grow beyond a few hundred a day, and the number of CSRs beyond two hundred.

The solutions that GAs produce are not optimal but are often close. In addition, GAs often give novel solutions. One nice thing about a GA is that there would always be some answer, even if it were not perfect.

GAs solve problems by trying out different solutions and comparing them to an objective function. The GA would not actually have an internal strategy for manipulating tasks. Since a GA would not need to have explicit problem-solving strategies input, Moody's would not need to spend a lot of time speaking with experts beyond initial discussions about task definitions and scheduling objectives. This also meant that the system could be developed quickly.

The absence of internal strategies would also make it easy to add new types of tasks, as long as their descriptions were consistent with the fitness function. This also meant that the system would not need to be reengineered if Moody's decided to expand the scope of the problems it dealt with, for example, including network problems as well as hardware and software problems.

Finally, since users would concentrate on describing tasks, not scheduling strategies, a GA would be easy for them to use. Like an IP system, a GA would be able to interact easily with the current database.

In summary, we can compare the three techniques with respect to Moody's help desk problem definition in the table that follows. Check marks indicate that the requirement is met or exceeded by a particular approach.

Dimension	Target Solution	RBS	IP	GA
Accuracy	Moderate	✓	✓	✓
Response Time	High		?	✓
Scalability	Moderate	?	✓	✓
Flexibility	Moderate to High	✓		✓
Embeddability	High	✓	✓	✓
Ease of Use	Moderate	✓		✓
Independence from Experts	High		✓	✓
Development Speed	High		✓	✓

Solving the Problem

While each of the techniques offers good solutions, the best in this case seems clearly to be the GA approach. Moody's elected to approach the problem using a GA. The firm began the implementation of the scheduling system in the summer of 1993.

Moody's addressed its scheduling problem by developing a schedule optimizing system that incorporated both a genetic algorithm to deal with scheduling and a fuzzy logic engine to deal with issues of preference. The fuzzy logic portion of the system will not be discussed in detail in this case study.

The system is called SOGA for Schedule Optimizing GA. Moody's adopted the conventions used in several other GA-based scheduling systems and represented each task in the queue as a gene. The entire task list formed the chromosome. In each generation, each chromosome was decoded by feeding the task list into a scheduling module that assigned tasks only to those CSRs that could perform them and were available.

Since an optimal schedule would order the tasks in such a way as to minimize the down time of users while maximizing their satisfaction, the fitness of each chromosome was determined by calculating the amount of time that would be lost while the employees of Moody's waited for tasks to be completed based on the schedule defined by the chromosome. More value was placed on the time of employees who rely heavily on their computers, or whose time is expensive relative to the average user.

These schedules are modified by a "goodwill" function that is used to estimate how dissatisfied each user would be if forced to wait the amount of time prescribed by the schedule. This is where the fuzzy logic came in. Rules such as "IF wait time is long THEN satisfaction is decreased" were used to adjust schedule evaluations.

In addition, user interfaces were designed for both the administrator and the CSRs. The administrator's interface allowed for moving tasks within schedules by picking them up with a mouse click and moving them to the appropriate CSR. This also allowed the administrator to gauge the volume and load on the help desk. The CSR interface allowed each CSR to view his or her own queue from remote PCs.

With the SOGA system and interface, tasks and resources are scheduled as follows:

A call is received by the help desk. As before, where possible, the call is resolved over the phone at the time of contact. In cases where the call is too complex, the contact person determines the *specific* task type category to which the call belongs. SOGA automatically calculates an initial priority for the task based upon the hourly cost of the down time associated with the task to the user community. Background user and task information for this calculation is retrieved from SOGA's proprietary database tables.

SOGA runs in the background behind the tracking system. It updates schedules based upon a predefined time threshold (every 10 or 15 minutes, for example). CSRs access their current job queues through their interface, but are only allowed to accept a specified (small) number (two or three) of tasks at any time.

When the jobs are completed, reassigned, or suspended, CSRs log the status of the tasks either directly or remotely. Since CSRs can only have a limited number of tasks open at any given time, the system requires this logging to take place before assigning new tasks. This encourages CSRs to log tasks in a timely manner, which makes the calls database more accurate.

Results

The SOGA system was well received by the administrators and, after a training period, the CSRs. The Help Desk Administrator (HDA) in particular felt that it provided a good solution.

- The system is timely (schedules could be generated in about 5 minutes).
- The system produces good solutions that made sense to the HDA.
- The system is flexible enough to allow for updating of task definitions, etc.
- The system scaled well from smaller to larger domains (in proportion to number of tasks).
- The system has become an integrated part of the existing call management system.
- The help desk staff are able to understand the schedules and system easily.
- The system was developed in a period of two months using one programmer with oversight from the designers.

The new procedures, as described above, resulted in benefits in several areas within the organization.

Tasks don't fall through the cracks. The SOGA-enhanced system allows task priorities to be assigned automatically and based on a consistent framework. The scheduling is done in a manner so as to favor global minimization of down time while giving consideration to user satisfaction. Since duration in the queue (satisfaction levels) and lengths of tasks are both considered in addition to task priority when scheduling, the tendency for low-priority tasks to be indefinitely postponed is reduced.

SOGA's objective is to optimize in a global sense. The HDA and CSRs provide additional oversight. Because of the interactive interface, the administrator can get a broader and deeper view of the status of the job queue, as well as exercise better control over how and when the tasks are executed. This facilitates planning and allows some estimation of task start and completion times.

Finally, formalizing a representation of the help desk scheduling problem addressed by SOGA and implementing the system have resulted in an unforeseen benefit for the support group in that it has forced the help desk personnel to think carefully about how to categorize user problems into meaningful classes. This process is an ongoing one and the help desk administrator continues to adjust parameters as Moody's needs change.

Lessons Learned

Moody's learned several things in the course of developing SOGA.

First, the firm learned that it could work much more efficiently when the help desk staff didn't need to worry about scheduling and routing calls. Neither the help desk staff nor the administrator realized how much effort they had been spending on prioritizing and scheduling calls.

Moody's also realized the importance of the user interfaces that were designed to sit on top of SOGA. Using the interfaces, the HDA was able to get a much better perspective on the load on the help desk and on individual CSRs. It also became possible to track calls much more accurately.

But because both the CSRs and the HDA had their own interfaces, it meant that both could potentially modify data simultaneously. Moody's needed to think through issues of concurrency and network access carefully to ensure that calls that were closed would be flushed from the queues of all users in a timely manner.

Finally, Moody's realized the importance of giving users partial control over the scheduling process. Initially a CSR would see only his or her own queue and would only be able to accept a single task. Because users were uncomfortable with the idea that a machine was deciding their schedules, and because in some cases users had access to decision factors that were not available to SOGA, the HDA decided to allow users to accept several tasks at once, and then decide in which order they should be done.

SOGA now does the bulk of the scheduling, but now users make the fine adjustments to their schedules. In addition, users can now assign a task to another CSR's queue, if that CSR is more proficient with the problem or more knowledgeable about the user. Giving users the ability to interact with the system, rather than just blindly following it, has improved both the efficiency of the system and the level of user acceptance.

Suggested Reading

Clarkson, Mark, "Moody's Evolving Help Desk," *BYTE Magazine,* February 1995.

Stein, R., and V. Dhar, "Satisfying Customers: Intelligently Scheduling High Volume Service Requests," *AI Expert,* December 1994.

Stein, R., and V. Dhar, "Maximization of Organizational Uptime Using an Interactive Genetic-Fuzzy Scheduling and Support System," Working Paper #IS-93-27, *Information Systems Working Paper Series,* Stern School of Business, 1993.

-------------------------------- **C A S E** --------------------------------

Financial Market Analysis and Prediction

LBS Capital Management, Clearwater, Florida

THE ORGANIZATION

LBS is a management investment firm. LBS began managing investment capital with AI-based technologies in late 1986 because it believed that conventional approaches to money management were having an increasingly difficult time meeting or exceeding benchmarks. Further, it believed that the new generation of modeling techniques had the ability to capture significant non-linear cause and effect relationships for use in forecasting when market and security price behavior is dominated by non-linearity.

LBS manages about $600 million in assets, primarily in stocks and mutual funds, for both institutional and individual investors. This includes a *Fortune* 100 pension fund and a large international bank, making it one of the largest firms in the country managing money with cutting-edge AI technology.

While LBS uses a variety of the technologies mentioned in this text to perform tasks ranging from macro-economic analysis to portfolio optimization, the focus of this case study will be LBS's efforts to create tools that the firm hopes will help better predict the performance of the individual financial instruments in the firm's portfolios.

THE PROBLEM

Simply stated, LBS's objective is to maximize the return on the assets it invests for its clients while minimizing their risk exposure. LBS, like many other asset management enterprises, believes that a key ingredient to successful investing is *timing*. LBS tries to determine whether the market is providing any *signals* about how it is likely to behave in the intermediate term (i.e., a few months), and bases investment decisions on these signals. For LBS, it is not enough just to know *which* securities to purchase. In order to be successful, the asset management firm must also know *when* to buy and sell the securities.

LBS believes that these objectives can be achieved by providing its financial professionals with insight into the financial markets. LBS feels that it can do this through a combination of high-quality analytic tools, highly efficient computer engineering, and market-savvy analysts.

LBS is a small firm comprised of a core group of financial analysts, computer scientists, and portfolio managers. While the firm's analytic staff spend a good deal of time perusing balance sheets, studying market patterns, and so on to better understand factors that influence financial markets, the firm also utilizes tools to help make better investment decisions.

LBS is unique in that it is one of only a few firms using AI technology, combined with statistical and financial analysis, as a primary means to manage its portfolios.

In a field where even a slight advantage can mean millions and any additional market insight can be profitable, LBS continues to search for better tools for evaluating investment scenarios.

But it is extremely difficult to find consistent tools that model financial markets well. These markets are complex and only partially understood. Prediction, even in the short term, is a very difficult exercise. The problem of developing a system to estimate future prices is daunting because financial processes are generally characterized by high levels of non-linearity and complexity, making them hard to model. The amount of data available to an analyst is overwhelming. Furthermore, financial markets are constantly evolving so models must adapt to these changes.

LBS's system needed to reflect these factors:

- The system needed to be able to quickly incorporate knowledge about a domain that often defies explicit definition. The financial domain is characterized by broad micro-economic and macroeconomic relationships among many complex and often poorly understood variables. Furthermore, on a day-to-day basis, random shocks, crowd psychology, and short-lived trends influence financial markets in complex ways. It is not unusual to have widely varying interpretations of the data from different experts even *after* the fact. Even expert traders sometimes have difficulty explaining what general principle led them to make a specific trade.

- The system needed to be able to deal with and analyze complex data. As a result of the interactions among several different market forces, financial markets can exhibit highly non-linear and highly complex behavior.

- The system needed to be able to deal with the *large amounts* of economic and financial data that are generated daily. It is difficult or impossible even for the most skilled expert to assimilate this amount of data accurately and consistently. In the words of one experienced trader, "Even the smartest of us is not as smart as the market. In order to make sense of the data, we have little choice but to turn to the computer."

- The system needed to be able to adapt quickly over time. Financial markets are highly non-stationary: They often change rapidly over time. A trading strategy that worked in a bull market will probably not fare as well in a bear market. But even a strategy that worked well in *last year's* bear market might not do so well in *this year's* bear market. Markets evolve and adapt to different forces over time.

Thus, LBS's research group searches for solutions that highlight possible market opportunities so that analysts could focus more thoroughly on understanding these situations. In essence, LBS wanted models to sift through the volumes of data it has and highlight the more interesting relationships. LBS wanted to increase the intelligence density in market data.

Initially, LBS experimented with a variety of objectives for its models. Over time, however, the objective became more focused: to have a system provide recommendations on individual stocks.

The tool needed to provide insight into the direction and magnitude of price movements over time. LBS felt that correctly choosing a time horizon for prediction was an important facet of setting up the problem. On one hand, making predictions in the very short term is hard due to the high levels of noise and unpredictable factors (i.e., random effects) that are present in financial markets. Paradoxically, however, choosing too large a horizon is equally meaningless due to the high number of uncontrollable large scale exogenous factors (politics, economic policies, etc.). For these reasons, LBS determined that a meaningful horizon was a window of about 12 weeks.

LBS decided to evaluate each stock relative to a fixed market indicator, such as the S&P 500 since the market index provides a general standard of market performance. That is to say LBS is an "active" manager that seeks to outperform the market, as opposed to a "passive" manager that indexes its portfolio with the market and seeks only to match the market's performance.

LBS wanted to be able to integrate the results of the analysis into its then current analytic processes and produce results in reasonable time. The accuracy and consistency of a system would be used as a measure of system goodness. In order to make this realistic, though, LBS would use simulated trading systems to test the models. Models were then also tested (or *validated*) by back testing over several historical years to determine how they would have performed. (This validation process takes into account things like realistic transaction costs, etc.) Models that recommended buying stocks in volumes that were not obtainable or conducting so many trades that transaction fees wiped out profits would not be considered successful.

To be useful to LBS, the system needed to be able to interpret and analyze large amounts of market data and "update its view of the world" frequently and easily. It needed to continually be able to access and assess economic and market data from a variety of sources and, using these data, indicate those stocks that were "likely" to be winners, and those that were more "likely" to be losers over the next 12 weeks.

LBS's data were plentiful, although not necessarily clean. Errors can enter data as a result of a number of problems such as errors that occur when downloading, errors in how the data are recorded at the source, and so forth.

LBS did not need the system to make specific point predictions for prices on a specific date but needed it only to provide the decision maker with estimates of a security's upside and downside potential. On the other hand, since a decision maker (typically a portfolio manager) would be interpreting the results of a prediction, it would be useful if the model could offer some insight into its analysis. It was also important that the system fit smoothly into LBS's workflow and current modeling tools. To do this, the system also needed to interface smoothly with the financial databases where the market data are stored.

Since LBS was interested in a 12-week time horizon, the decision maker was not going to be under second-by-second real-time pressure to make investment decisions so the firm felt that the system need not function in real-time. On the other hand, since there would be thousands of securities to analyze, the system did need to be able to perform the analysis on each individual security in a reasonable amount of time.

The system also needed to be able to be expanded to accommodate additional securities and input factors, which are expected to be added over time. To be practical, the model would also need to be flexible enough to accommodate new market trends, new types of data, and portfolio objectives.

The types of processes that LBS planned to model were highly complex with many subtle interactions. Accordingly, LBS felt that given the inherent uncertainty in the domain, it would be difficult for an expert to specify *all* relevant knowledge accurately. In addition, LBS thought it would be best to take up as little of the firm's expert traders' time as possible. Expert time is valuable; each hour away from market analysis or trading can cost real dollars. Furthermore, and more important, LBS had found that it could be somewhat difficult for their expert traders and analysts to articulate their expertise, especially since the rules are complex and continually evolving.

THE SOLUTION

In summary, each of the modeling options needed to be compared on at least the following dimensions:

Dimension	Target Solution
Accuracy	Moderate
Explainability	Moderate
Response Speed	Moderate
Scalability	Moderate
Flexibility	High
Embeddability	High
Tolerance for Complexity	High
Tolerance for Noise in Data	High
Independence from Experts	High

A mainstay of many asset management firms are statistical analysis, charting, and visualization techniques. LBS also makes use of these techniques to try to understand trends within the financial markets better. In LBS's case, however, this analysis is augmented and, the firm feels, focused by systems that search through volumes of data, performing portions of the analysis and looking for patterns of interesting activity and persistent predictability.

In the mid-1980s, LBS began to pursue expert systems technology as a way of supporting investment decisions. In large part, its curiosity about the technology was driven by the successes of expert rule-based systems (RBS) in areas such as medicine and engineering. In these areas, researchers had demonstrated the feasibility of capturing human expertise in the form of rules. Systems that encoded these rules showed levels of performance comparable to, and often exceeding, that of experts. At that time, proponents of expert systems technology and vendors of development tools claimed that similar success might be achieved with many business problems.

In the late 1980s, the firm built a rule-based expert system for assisting in *market timing* decisions. The initial objective was to come up with a system that would be able to make buy and sell recommendations on the direction and characteristics of various markets as a whole and provide an indication of the relative strength of its recommendations, with confidence. A system, based on the reasoning processes and trading practices of one of its expert traders, was designed to combine various pieces of market data and to evaluate the direction of the market (as characterized by the S&P 500).

By the early 1990s, LBS also began to focus on other intelligent systems technologies such as neural networks and also undertook the task of modeling individual securities.

Each of the three approaches, traditional statistics, rule-based systems, and neural networks, offers a potential method for making sense out of the huge volumes of data that LBS has available to assist in its decision making.

Of these three, though, which one was most sensible for the prediction problem?

A rule-based system (RBS) is a type of model that uses "IF-THEN" rules to figure out how to solve a problem. Since these systems get their knowledge from experts, not from examining data, an RBS is not overly dependent on large amounts of data. In addition, an RBS can be designed to be tolerant to some kinds of data faults, so LBS would need to be careful to incorporate this fault tolerance into the rules it designed if it chose this approach.

An RBS excels at explaining its results since it can demonstrate the exact chain of reasoning used to reach a conclusion. On the other hand, due to the need to "chain" through many rules, RBS approaches become more time intensive than other approaches, especially in complex domains. However, with higher speed computers, the gap in speed is narrowing. Also, since an RBS relies on abstract qualitative rules it often deals best with ranges like "between 1% and 5%" rather than exact quantitative values like "3.27%," and its results reflect this looser accuracy; however, this would be acceptable since LBS didn't need an exact result.

What are some other implications of the rule structure of an RBS? Due to the need to consult experts and manage the interactions of the various rules, an RBS can be rigid when it comes to adding new rules to deal with new situations. These interactions can also make it difficult to model complex domains and cause RBS performance to degrade gradually as the number of rules is increased or as the environment changes. Also, as a result of the special rule overhead, the systems usually require proprietary software and are often self-contained systems that may be hard to integrate into established environments. LBS would need to make sure that whatever shell it elected to use would be open enough to allow them to hook into their current systems.

Finally, as you'd expect, rule-based systems require a great deal of access to experts. These experts must "teach" the system how to behave and how to make predictions. After all, an expert system's rules are generated . . . by experts.

How about traditional statistical analysis?

Statistical analysis (and its cousin technical analysis) is by far the most commonly used method to model financial markets. The entire field of econometrics has grown out of the need to apply statistical theory to quantifying economic and financial processes. The domain of statistical tools is incredibly broad and deep, ranging from regression and time series analysis to complex kernel smoothing and survival analysis techniques. Accordingly, we will limit our discussion to some of the more generally used techniques for stock prediction, such as multiple regression and ARIMA. The points we raise generally apply to many other techniques as well.

Statistical techniques generally work by calculating a set of parameters from a particular data set. The resulting parameters form coefficients (or other types of parameters) in mathematical equations. For example, an OLS regression analysis of historical stock prices and volumes might be used to fit coefficients to data resulting in a simple summation equation to model data. By summing the coefficient-weighted variables, the user would get a prediction for future prices.

In general, the accuracy of these types of equations depends on the quality of the data used to develop them and the complexity of the process you are trying to model. In general, though, statistics provide an efficient method for modeling data. However, you usually cannot use too many variables at once.

In developing a statistical model, it is useful to know beforehand which variables and relationships might be significant in predicting the outcome. A conversation with someone who understands what you are trying to model is useful, but you do not need to spend excessive amounts of time with an expert.

Because the resulting equations are generally simple, they can usually be computed quickly once the data have been fit.

Since statistical models are based on certain mathematics principles, you can use knowledge of mathematics to explain the results. It is usually very easy, for example, to quantify not only which variables are significant in a model, but also the *degree* to which each is significant.

However, on the downside, you pay a price for this explainability. Statistical models are only valid if the assumptions that underlie them are not violated too severely. Unfortunately, many real-world problems, like LBS's, offer data that do, in fact, violate these assumptions.

There are often methods for getting around these limitations, but they generally require some thought and planning and they must be reevaluated each time a model is changed. LBS would need to consider whether the time that would be required to ensure the accuracy of these models was feasible, given the volume of analysis the firm hoped to do and the time frames in which it hoped to do it.

In addition, many statistical models are designed to highlight *linear* relationships, not complex non-linear ones. Here again, there are methods for dealing with non-linear processes, but these must be undertaken on a case-by-case basis. In order to use many non-linear statistical methods you need to know a bit about the *type* of non-linearity and the ways in which variables interact. But remember that LBS felt that there were many unknown types of relationships in its data.

Consider neural networks:

Neural networks are systems based on the neural structure of the brain. They involve networks of connections between simple processing units. They essentially "learn" from data. What they learn is stored in the connections.

Neural networks share many of the features of certain statistical analysis methods. The ID profiles for many statistical models along the lines of *accuracy, scalability, response time, embeddability,* and *independence from experts* look quite similar to those of neural nets.

However, where statistical modes and neural networks begin to diverge is in the other areas. Neural networks produce equations whose behavior is difficult to understand. As a result, it is usually difficult to determine which inputs are affecting the output and how severely they are doing this.

On the other hand, neural networks are "universal approximators." They can, in principle, take the form of any function. This single characteristic has important implications for the behavior of neural networks.

For one thing, this feature means that you have to make almost no assumptions about the data you are using. If the data are noisy or distributed differently than you think, the ANN should be able to approximate them. This also means that if the process is very complex, the ANN should still be able to recover the underlying form from the data. Furthermore, it means that if you need to adjust your model later on down the line, say by adding new variables, you do not necessarily have to worry that the changes you make will change the fundamental structure of the model.

Statistical analysis, rule-based systems, neural networks—LBS certainly had several alternatives. We can combine the results of the analysis and summarize it in the following table:

Dimension	*Target Solution*	*RBS*	*STATS*	*ANN*
Accuracy	Moderate	✓	✓	✓
Explainability	Moderate	✓	✓	
Response Time	Moderate	✓	✓	✓
Scalability	Moderate	✓	✓	✓
Flexibility	High			✓
Embeddability	High		✓	✓
Tolerance for Complexity	High			✓
Tolerance for Noise in Data	High			✓
Independence from Experts	High		✓	✓

Solving the Problem

LBS's development efforts have been consistent with the analysis above. A rule-based system that the firm constructed based on knowledge in 1988, 1989, and 1990 when financial markets were relatively volatile didn't perform particularly well in the comparatively tranquil markets experienced during 1992 and 1993. The system was not really flexible enough to evolve with the changing markets. It also suffered from a typical expert system related problem: When the system tried to apply its abstract knowledge to real situations, it did not always get "correct" results. LBS realized that it would have to make "fixes" to the system by adding new rules and relationships and all of this patching would make the system more and more inflexible over time.

In response, LBS tried a neural network approach that has been more successful. Rather than trying to develop a model that would show analysts how *any* security would perform, LBS developed models for *each* of the instruments that the firm tracks. LBS took this approach because the firm's research revealed that each stock has its own performance footprint.

So, for example, LBS has a separate neural network model for IBM stock, a separate model for AT&T stock, etc. Each of these networks is retrained every week based on the most recent data. These models are also much more scalable and flexible than the rule-based models since they are entirely data driven. As a result, LBS feels that the neural net models adapt well to new market conditions over time.

But LBS does not take a hands-off approach to its modeling operations. Each of the neural net models is analyzed over time using sophisticated sensitivity analysis and modifications are made to architecture, types of input variables, and confidence measures. One of the most challenging aspects of neural network models is deciding which inputs to use in the model and how they should be preprocessed. This has proven to be the case for LBS as well.

LBS continually evaluates which inputs from a broad range of fundamental and technical indicators have the most predictive value in its models. In some cases, price and volume-derived information might be useful inputs, in others cash flow might yield better results. Volatilities, the ratio of price to sales, etc.: Clearly, the number of financial inputs that can be fed into a neural net is virtually unlimited, so how does LBS decide which ones are appropriate?

There is no simple answer. LBS evaluates dozens of standard technical and fundamental factors as well as many of the firm's own in-house metrics. Experience, market insight, experimentation, and hard statistical analysis all play into the process. In fact LBS makes use of many standard and exotic statistical analysis and visualization techniques in making these input factor determinations. Furthermore, while LBS analysts report spending much of their time preprocessing and analyzing data, they are understandably reticent to provide details of what this involves. After all, to LBS this is proprietary information and where the firm feels it earns its money.

Results

So does all of this hard work (and it is hard work) pay off? LBS feels that the answer is a resounding "Yes."

At the time of this writing, LBS had been ranked as one of the country's top risk managers seven years running by MoniResearch. The firm has consistently increased its assets under management by between 25% and 100% per year.

In terms of tactical asset allocation investment results, LBS has never had a loss year in bonds or stocks, and the firm has avoided every market decline of more than 7%.

As an example of the benefits of the firm's technologies, LBS points to its Mid Cap Portfolios which invest in the equity of mid-sized firms. In 1993, LBS's Mid Cap Portfolios outperformed the S&P Mid Cap 400 index by 3.94%. In 1994, LBS again outperformed the index, this time beating the market by 2.90%. It is interesting to note that LBS was able to show a positive return in 1994 even though the S&P Mid Cap 400 actually had a *negative* return (−1.03%) that year.

It is impossible to say with certainty whether these impressive results are wholly attributable to LBS's technology. Nonetheless, the firm feels that its models give it the edge it needs to consistently outperform the market. As a result, LBS continues to invest in advanced modeling and AI technology as part of its strategic effort.

Lessons Learned

LBS has learned some interesting things from its experiences.

First, neural networks' high levels of both flexibility and tolerance for complexity allow the firm to train and use a huge number of nets per week. Many types of traditional statistical modeling would not be feasible on this scale, particularly in such dynamic markets.

But note the way in which LBS scaled its system up. Rather than, say, training one master neural network to predict all 3000 stocks, the firm decided to break the problem up into 3000 smaller problems. This let the neural networks specialize on each stock, rather than having to settle for weights that had been averaged to predict on all of the stocks.

Second, in addition, LBS has developed a set of very rigorous testing procedures that helps ensure that the models have not been overtrained. These are augmented by a series of trading policies that is followed strictly to ensure that the environment in which the models were tested is the same one in which they are used.

Finally, LBS has found that the biggest benefit it achieves is not through tweaking the number of hidden nodes and learning parameters of a neural network, but rather from spending a good deal of time pre-processing the data to make it easier for neural networks to use. In fact, this is where much of the firm's research time is spent.

Suggested Reading

Barr, D., and G. Mani, "Using Neural Nets to Manage Investments," *AI Expert,* February 1994.

Barr, D. S., and G. Mani, "Neural Nets in Investment Management: Multiple Uses," *Proceedings of the Second International Conference on AI Applications on Wall Street,* New York, 1993.

-------------------------------- **C A S E** ----------------------------------

Customer Support
Compaq Computer Corporation, Houston, Texas

THE ORGANIZATION

Compaq Computer Corporation is a major *Fortune* 500 company that manufactures a range of personal computer systems. It established itself as a major player in the portable computer hardware market in the early 1980s, and has continued to offer increasingly powerful laptop and high-end products since then. The company founded its reputation as an aggressive price competitor in the mid-1980s by wresting away a big chunk of the PC market from IBM, the then dominant player in that market. Over the last few years, however, Compaq has in turn been the target of intense price competition by smaller companies such as Dell Computer and AST Research.

In the face of intense price competition and commoditization in the hardware arena, computer companies have been trying to differentiate themselves on other fronts besides price. Superior customer service is an area that has become more and more important to companies whose products are becoming increasingly commoditized. Improving customer support, where customers include both dealers and end users, is one of Compaq's major strategic objectives.

Compaq started by providing product support at the dealer level. This has now been extended to the retail level.

This case deals with a hugely successful intelligent system developed by Compaq to address its customers' support needs.

THE PROBLEM

Modern computing systems are complex machines with thousands of microcomponents, network protocols, and hardware/software interfaces. Providing effective online service for these devices can be a daunting task. It requires that customer support engineers gather information about a customer's problem, enter the call into a logging system, analyze the customer's data, resolve the problem, and deliver the solution.

In analyzing the data and resolving the problem, the engineer makes use of whatever resources are at his disposal: personal expertise, manuals and other information sources, and other support engineers.

Effective customer service also requires customer support staff to have a highly versatile set of skills: good listening and analysis skills and the tenacity to track, solve, and "close out" the customer's problem.

Providing effective support for Compaq customers is particularly challenging for additional reasons:

- The range of products that the company offers is increasing, requiring a wider breadth of expertise for support. Support staff face an increasing variety of questions. There is no "typical" request. In effect, the problem domain is a moving target.

- The networking environment is becoming increasingly complex with players such as Novell, Microsoft, Banyan, and networks into which Compaq's products must integrate. This Third-party hardware and software widen the scope of the problem domain. Thus, in addition to being a moving target, the domain is also widening.

- Because of the diversity and evolution of the problem domain, few support staff ever actually encounter the full range of problems. There are few "go to" people in the organization who can guarantee correct solutions for *all* problems. Rather, expertise is distributed across the entire support staff.

Compaq realized that it faced an explosion in the number and variety of customer calls given its growth rate and introduction of new products. It was apparent that unless something was done, the staff would need to grow dramatically, thereby increasing support costs. The alternative was to somehow reduce the number of incoming calls and to reduce the time taken to resolve a call, and to achieve this while still maintaining a high quality of service.

Compaq thought that an intelligent support system might be a solution. The system would need to be able to provide expert diagnosis and recommendations to users. But this was not so simple:

- To be successful any system would need to be able to bring together pieces of knowledge from disparate places in the organization. While as an organization Compaq knew how to resolve most problems, the information was too distributed. No one individual had the expertise to troubleshoot all products.

- The system needed to be able to handle the large and changing array of models, products, and configurations that Compaq produced. As client needs change, so do Compaq's products. As the market changes, Compaq's products are integrated with a more and more diverse range of third-party systems.

- Users needed to be able to find solutions quickly. Furthermore, if a particular type of problem had never been seen before, users needed to be able to get guidance as to where they might look for a solution.

- The system would have to be accessible to many different employees at different locations. In addition, it would need to be accessible to remote users, such as dealers.

A system that addressed these goals would not only keep the size of the support staff under control, but equally important, it would enable the staff to resolve problems without requiring deep knowledge about all problem areas.

In 1989, the service department started by installing a call-logging system. This provided a mechanism by which the company could record information about problems and their resolution. It also provided the necessary first step in ensuring better service quality: the ability to "close the loop" on each problem.

The next step was to build more intelligence on top of the call-logging system.

Given the nature of the domain, it was important that the new system be easily expanded since Compaq expected that the system's domain of expertise would have to grow over time. It would also have to allow new kinds of problems to be added easily without affecting the system's current behavior.

Most types of problems could be categorized quite easily into relatively non-interacting categories: hardware, network, software, and general information such as care and maintenance. Even problems involving interactions (such as the inability to print because of incorrect device driver software) could be identified with a specific category. On the other hand, trying to untangle a complicated network of third-party hardware and software still made the problem non-trivial.

The requirement that the system get the user into the ballpark and not perform exact diagnoses suggested that while the system would have to do some degree of pattern matching, this could be relatively crude. It would, however, be important to provide the user with good navigational capabilities for searching. In other words, low-to-modest accuracy was acceptable as part of the system's first cut; the user could then hone in on the right problem.

Nevertheless, the user needed to be able to have confidence that the system was in fact focusing on the right problem, so some indication of why a solution was appropriate would be helpful. Also, speed was important: The system should help the support staff get to the right ballpark with as few questions as possible, typically less than five. Also, the problem should be resolved in a few minutes over the phone without requiring the user to call back again.

Finally, the reality of help desks is that clients are often unable to describe their problems accurately. Accordingly, the system would have to be able to accommodate inexact input. Similarly, clients rarely provide *all* relevant information, which would require the system to operate with partial descriptions of problems.

THE SOLUTION

In summary, any option that Compaq considered needed to be compared on at least the following dimensions of intelligence density:

Dimension	Target Solution
Accuracy	Moderate
Explainability	Moderate
Response Speed	High
Scalability	High
Flexibility	High
Tolerance for Complexity	Moderate
Tolerance for Noise in Data	Moderate
Tolerance for Sparse Data	Moderate
Independence from Experts	Moderate

What alternatives did Compaq consider?

Compaq would need to build and grow a central repository of expertise on problems and how they were resolved, and use this knowledge base to solve similar new problems.

There were two obvious candidates for the problem. The first alternative was to use a rule-based system. An RBS approach would require formalizing troubleshooting expertise as rules. This raised several questions. Was the problem domain stable enough to enable experts to articulate rules with a high degree of confidence? How much longevity would these rules have? How long would the knowledge engineering effort take to gather and refine the rules?

Another choice was to use a case-based reasoning system. This approach raised its own set of questions. Would the experts be able to come up with enough prototypical cases to cover enough of the problem domain? Could enough information be gleaned from the call-logging system to help build prototypical cases?[1] Who would be responsible for actually authorizing the cases: the system designer or the expert? An

---

[1] This turned out to be not a consideration for COMPAQ since the system dealt with a new line of products.

important thing would be to come up with a meaningful structure for the cases, one that would capture adequately the richness of the problems encountered by the staff.

A third alternative would be to use a standard database system. However, Compaq felt that a database system would not allow a rich enough structure for representing problems. The firm thought that a standard database system would be too rigid to give users access to open-ended data.

How do RBS and CBR, the primary contenders, stack up against this set of requirements?

Given the nature of the problem domain, COMPAQ felt that an RBS might turn out to be particularly deficient on flexibility. The XCON[2] experience made it apparent that while the task of configuring computers could be specified in terms of rules, considerable tweaking of rules could be required as the underlying technology, namely, the electronic components, kept changing. Given the similarity in the DEC and Compaq domains, this was a red flag against the rule-based approach. Also, given the width of the domain, scalability was likely to be a weak point of this approach. An RBS also tends to be somewhat brittle in its ability to cope with noisy or incomplete data.

The RBS approach was also risky for the system, which dealt with a new product line. The Compaq team felt that the likelihood of covering most of the problems related to a new line of printers with a set of rules was low. Furthermore, it might be difficult to account for all of the possible interactions among different hardware configurations.

On the other hand, an RBS would provide an exact audit trail of the reasoning used to arrive at a recommendation. The support staff would like that. RBS would also be able to solve most problems quickly enough to satisfy most users.

In contrast, the CBR approach would not suffer from the same problems. CBR systems are designed with the expectation that the domain will change and that new cases will be added over time.

Given the highly open-ended nature of the domain, it seemed overly optimistic to hope that a system would be able to diagnose problems with pinpoint accuracy. Rather, it seemed more promising to help a support person to get into the most likely problem area and let him browse from that point to find additional information. In effect, the burden of finding the problem would still largely be that of the support staff. This seemed reasonable since the staff's level of expertise was modest: As long as they could be guided into the right vicinity quickly, they could take over from there. A CBR system would provide this.

CBR systems also degrade much more gracefully in response to noise or incompleteness in the data. Specifically, the similarity distance computation metric tends to be flexible in dealing with noisy or missing data; noisy data tend not to skew the match much as long as some "good" attribute values are also present in the case being matched. The main weakness of the CBR system is its response time as the number of cases increases.

Also, for COMPAQ, the CBR approach had the advantage that the experts felt much more confident that they could articulate a set of prototypical cases than a set of

---

[2]XCON was developed at Digital Equipment Corporation (DEC) in the early 1980s to configure computers corresponding to customers' orders. Since its inception, the system has required a dedicated support staff to keep its knowledge base up to date with the changing technology of computer components.

rules. They also felt that they could clean up or augment these cases as new problems were reported by customers.

We summarize the comparison among the ideal solution, RBS, and CBR approaches, in the table below:

Dimension	*Target Solution*	*RBS*	*CBR*
Accuracy	Moderate	✓	✓
Explainability	Moderate	✓	✓
Response Speed	High	✓	✓
Scalability	High		✓
Flexibility	High		✓
Tolerance for Complexity	Moderate		✓
Tolerance for Noise in Data	Moderate		✓
Tolerance for Sparse Data	Moderate	n/a	✓
Independence from Experts	Moderate		✓

Solving the Problem

In 1991, Compaq's customer service department developed the SMART system in conjunction with a vendor of a commercially available case-based reasoning tool. The system allowed customer support staff to resolve problems over the phone related to networks of computers involving Compaq's computers in Banyan, Microsoft, Novell, or SCO UNIX environments.

In March 1991, Compaq rolled out the SMART system, a knowledge-based system that was integrated with the call-logging system. The following year, Compaq decided to reengineer its support operations further in order to limit the burden on its support staff. The objective was to *bundle* new products with a software system that would provide information about how to resolve problems pertaining to these products.

Specifically, Compaq introduced a new line of printers along with a troubleshooting system called QUICKSOURCE. The system was available in a variety of versions: for the end user, the dealer, and internal support. Since the end user population was a very heterogeneous one, its version was a very basic and user-friendly one. The other versions incorporated more sophisticated functionality. What Compaq in effect did was to off-load a component of the support function on the customer!

Both systems use case-based reasoning, where prototypical cases of previous problems are recorded. New problems are compared to these cases for similarity. If a similar case is not found, the new problem is considered "unresolved." It gets passed on to experts who can solve it and structure a new prototypical case. The new case is put into the case base. In this way, the case base can grow to accommodate new kinds of problems.

The structure of each case was as follows:

1. A description of the problem specified in English.

2. A set of questions. The questions could have answers of the form yes/no, text, numeric, or an item from a list. Each question also has a *match weight* and a *mismatch weight* which indicate respectively how heavily the answer to the question should be weighted in each case in determining similarity.

3. A set of actions (its solution).

SMART and QUICKSOURCE work as follows: A customer support associate first collects customer or dealer problem information, along with a textual description of the problem. The associate resolves simple problems right away, whereas the associate invokes the CBR system for those problems requiring further analysis.

The system performs an initial search for neighboring cases based on keywords from the textual description of the problem. A list of questions relating to the problem pops up on the screen. A list of matching cases is also displayed along with their distance scores. As questions get answered, the list of cases and their scores change. If a perfectly matching case is found, the problem is solved. If a matching case is not found, the case is marked as unresolved and passed on to the case builder experts. It is reviewed, researched, and solved.

The system gets refined as new cases are added to the case base.

While the ability to grow a knowledge base is a major strength of CBR systems, early in the life cycle of the SMART system the developers realized that they had to be very careful about adding new cases to the system. This was particularly important given the volume of calls; unless there was a systematic methodology in place for keeping the domain under control, the case base and the questions would explode. This would dilute the discriminatory power of the system. To prevent this, specific experts were trained and appointed as case builders early in the development life cycle. It was these experts' responsibility to add new cases only if they were judged to be unique after a careful review.

In addition to the distance computation procedure, QUICKSOURCE provides a *hypertext*-oriented navigational facility. This lets users click on keywords to get more information on them. A help module is also available that launches other applications containing information about hardware components or problem-solving information that is too loosely structured to fit into a casebased format.

When QUICKSOURCE was being tested, the support staff remarked that the system often asked what appeared to them to be dumb questions. For example, if the user specified "blurs" as part of the "print quality" in the initial problem description, it seemed "dumb" for the system to be asking any questions relating to print quality. To fix this problem, rules were added to the system to enable it to make whatever inferences it could based on the initial problem description. In effect, rules preprocess the initial data before the CBR system begins its distance computation.

Results

While it is difficult to quantify precisely the results of introducing the SMART and QUICKSOURCE systems, some benefits are obvious.

First, a larger number of cases are resolvable during the customer interaction with the system than without it. On test cases, it was observed that the success rate using SMART was more than 50% higher with it than without it. The fact that support staff have access to information they couldn't otherwise have also makes it likely that they will search more actively for relevant information instead of passing on the problem to other specialists.

Second, it is estimated that QUICKSOURCE has resulted in 20% fewer calls at the Compaq support center because of the use of the dealer and end user versions. Only the harder problems are directed to Compaq staff. This results in a savings of approximately $10 to $20 million per year in operations costs. It also elevates the job of the customer support beyond answering mundane questions repeatedly.

Third, the CBR systems serve as a valuable memory bank for Compaq. The fact that customer service interactions are analyzed systematically gives the organization a much better feel for how its products are doing, and a closer contact with its customers. The fact that Compaq can use its previous knowledge makes it much more of a "learning organization." The organization is less susceptible to shock if support staff members with specific areas of expertise leave the firm since the collective expertise of all the staff is captured by the CBR systems.

Lessons Learned

CBR has provided Compaq the infrastructure for increasing the sophistication of its support operations. It requires the organization to think clearly about the kinds of things that are important in providing good customer support. Developing a system has forced the help desk personnel to describe and categorize user problems to turn them into meaningful cases. Compaq now has a better understanding about how to structure a case, that is, what knowledge to include, how to compute similarity, what to do when the system can't find a matching case, etc. As new products are introduced, it should become easier to offload more parts of the customer service function to the customer as was done with QUICKSOURCE.

Second, CBR is particularly helpful when "similar" problems are encountered frequently, but each variation cannot be dealt with mechanically due to the open-endedness of the problem domain. Such problems are common to business. The customer support function is typical of such situations since the problems to be resolved are similar, but they evolve slowly over time. For such problems, it can make sense to use systems to capture prototypical cases into a case base and let this case base evolve as the problem domain (the organization's products and/or services) changes over time. CBR systems are well suited to such problems, enabling organizations to become more intelligent about the way they use prior experiences.

Suggested Reading

Acorn, T., and Walden, "SMART: Support Management Automated Reasoning Technology for Compaq Customer Service," *Proceedings of Innovative Applications of AI,* 1992.

Nguyen, T., M. Czerwinski, and D. Lee, "COMPAQ Quicksource: Providing the Customer with the Power of AI," *AI Magazine,* Fall 1993.

-------------------------------- **C A S E** --------------------------------

Pattern Directed Data Mining of Point-of-Sale Data

A.C. Nielsen, Chicago

THE ORGANIZATION

A.C. Nielsen is a division of the Dun and Bradstreet (D&B) corporation. While Nielsen is perhaps best known for its ratings of television shows, it is in the "information business" in a variety of areas. In particular, it collects point-of-sale data in supermarkets, which Nielsen stores in a very large database called SCANTRACK. It also collects a variety of other data related to buying behavior: demographic (household) data with buying behavior, television viewing-related data, magazine subscription data, etc. Nielsen's strategic goal is to eventually integrate these databases into what it calls "one source," which can provide comprehensive analyses of products, markets, and consumers.

In the late 1980s, Nielsen began to experience strong competitive pressures from its main rival, the Information Resources Institute (IRI). IRI had introduced a system called Coverstory, which performed a very rudimentary analysis of scanner data from supermarkets. It was rudimentary in the sense that it only provided simple graphs of share changes, and a boilerplate text and layout into which computed numbers were plugged.

While rudimentary, Coverstory filled a crucial market need. Nielsen had no such system.

THE PROBLEM

Nielsen's objective was to package analyzed data and sell the information to buyers, such as supermarkets. Buyers derive tremendous value by knowing how products or product categories performed last week, last month, last quarter, or last year in a particular region such as a borough, city, state, or nationally. More generally, they need various kinds of summaries of the data, by product or product category, or by market. These analyses can be in terms of variables such as volume, market share, price, promotion, and so on. Essentially, the analyses boil down to running standard queries against a database.

But there's a lot more in the data that can be gleaned by people who have experience in the consumer products industry. Because of their experience, they know what to look for. An organization such as Nielsen has several such people, who can eyeball various kinds of reports and come up with a story that is not apparent to a less experienced person. This experience is based on products or markets. An expert would just "know" that New Yorkers are more price sensitive to sourdough bread than Californians; if the expert saw a price increase in both states and volume declined in New York, this would be consistent. On the other hand, if volume did not decline in New York after a price increase, this would raise a flag, causing the expert to dig further in order to find the reason for the anomaly.

Nielsen's strategic objective was to leverage its expertise in consumer products and markets by making it available to its sales representatives. With this knowledge, the representatives would have a system focusing their attention to interesting consumption activity in the marketplace. Based on this information, the sales rep could fashion an appropriate sales pitch for the customer.

Nielsen's objective, then, was to understand how experts analyzed sales data, package this expertise into a system, and make it available to its sales reps across the country.

There were several key organizational and logistical issues that shaped Nielsen's approach to the development of the system:

- The system should provide a significant advance over IRI's Coverstory, otherwise Nielsen would merely be playing catch-up. Marketing representatives felt that Coverstory lacked the intelligence as a decision aid on two fronts.
  - The first had to do with the look and feel of the system which made people feel it was a reporting system more than an "intelligent decision aid": all of its reports, regardless of product or context, looked identical. It used a standard boilerplate, where numbers were simply plugged in. If you'd seen one report, you'd seen them all.
  - The real drawback of the boilerplate approach was its limited ability to emphasize different things about different products or markets, including *how* the results were presented. As a consequence, it was limited in its ability to *focus attention* on the relevant data. As a simple example, Nielsen experts felt that text (bullets, paragraphs), graphs, charts, spreadsheets, etc., could be used judiciously depending on what turned out to be interesting in the data. In this way, it would provide more customized and *varied* reports that would prove to be more useful for sales reps.

- The system should work with the "lowest common denominator" database, that is, on data that existed for *every* Nielsen customer. The objective here was to provide a service to every Nielsen client in order to maximize market coverage, and not cater to clients selectively.

- The system should not require any new databases or database technology, but work with Nielsen's existing databases. The costs associated with building a new platform to support the sometimes idiosyncratic needs associated with advanced technology were not deemed economical.

- The system should provide high-quality outputs that would be usable as is by sales reps. In order to accomplish this, the system should use vocabulary that is commonly used by the sales reps. Also the reps should not have to invest time in *analyzing* and *interpreting* the outputs. Rather, they should allow the rep to put together a clear and unambiguous story for the customer.

- The system should be distributable to sales reps across the country and it should run on low-end personal computers of the day since this constituted the installed base in the company. The objective was to allow the sales reps to access the central database over phone lines and have the system on their personal computers analyze the data and produce "the right reports," showing exceptional market activity and possible reasons for this activity. The marketing experts also felt that the reports should be produced in under 5 minutes (not counting printing time) in order to be acceptable to the user base.

- last but not least, the system had to be developed in six months. Top management wanted the system to be unveiled at the Food Marketing Institute (FMI) convention on May 5, 1991. It was late in November 1990 that the project, initially referred to as *Nielsen Performance Exception Review* (NPER), was approved. No prototypes or experimental versions were affordable in order to verify requirements: Nielsen needed the full-blown system within 6 months, otherwise the project would be a failure.

The overall objective was to have a system that could provide a user, the sales rep, a comprehensive answer to the question: *What is happening in the marketplace?* To the extent possible, the system would also provide the user with outputs that directly or indirectly point to the *reasons* for the observed market activity.

While the overall strategic objectives (i.e., catch-up and leapfrog IRI in the marketplace) and logistical constraints (system should run on a PC) were crisply defined at the outset of the project, the specific *outputs* the system was expected to produce were less apparent to the experts and technologists. In particular, would the system use a numerical scheme like probabilities to perform its analysis and present results? For example, would the systems say things like "there's *strong* evidence that X caused Y?" With such outputs, would the users then want to know *why* there was *strong* evidence as opposed to *weak* evidence? What would constitute *strong, weak,* etc.?

Nielsen decided that it was unwise to expect a system to provide meaningful probabilities or strengths of associations between variables, but that the outputs would be somewhat coarse. The domain was not well enough defined nor was the data adequately detailed or complete to support conjectures of this sort. The conclusion: Keep it simple—provide outputs that show exceptional market activity with commonly used concepts such as market share, volume, distribution, promotion, and price. Accompanying such reports would be *associated factors* that could directly or indirectly explain the observed market activity.

For example, a chart showing unusual sales volume changes of products belonging to some product category might be accompanied by charts showing shifts in the promotional activity for the same products, and charts showing changes in pricing. The idea was that such outputs would *focus attention* on these areas, making it easy for the sales rep to piece together the story behind the numbers.

Nielsen also felt that the problem domain was fairly decomposable, with limited interactions among the problem variables. Analysis of different categories of products could be done reasonably independently. For example, promotion and sales data for carbonated beverages have nothing to do with market share analysis for detergents. So, even though the sales database might have millions of records, it could be sliced into segments that could be analyzed independently.

Nielsen also felt that while the problem domain was not particularly complex, it was hard to nail down principles that would apply *universally* across products or markets. For example, it is well known that price has an impact on volume (in economics this is referred to as *elasticity*). However, elasticity varies across products: People might be much more sensitive to price for carbonated beverages than for cereals. Besides this sensitivity might vary across regions, even seasons. Similarly, while distribution and price are related to market share in general, a *competitor's* distribution and price might be more weakly related to *your* share. Knowing about these kinds of subtle variations among the variables is one of the sources of expertise in the consumer products area.

For these reasons, the experts felt that the system had to be specified in a way that allowed it to be "parameterized." So, while one could safely state that promotion would affect volume, the specifics of the relationship had to be parameterizable so they could be altered to specific circumstances.

The logistical constraints were clear. The speed of development had to be high. This was a *hard* constraint. The system simply *had to work* at the end of six months; there was no time for prototypes and experimentation. The system would also be critically dependent on access to expert knowledge. Fortunately, top management was committed to providing access. Nielsen also felt that these were high quality experts who would be able to articulate their strategies in evaluating market data.

Since the system had to produce directly usable output, it had better put things on the report that had a high chance of being related. Even though the sales rep would construct a story around the reports, the output information had to be really high quality for the rep to do so quickly and easily. So, even though the system wasn't required to provide cause-effect explanations per se, its explainability had to be high in the sense that the rep could look at the output and be confident about constructing explanations from it. On the other hand, the system wasn't required to be highly accurate in specifying which of the pieces of data were more important than others in explaining some unusual market activity: The sales rep could do that. In other words, it only had to be moderately confident that two things were related in order to display them along with its reasons. The speed of response had to be high since the rep would only be willing to wait for a few minutes for it; the response time also had to be highly predictable. Again, this was a hard constraint.

The system also had to be highly embeddable into existing systems such as databases and word processors. Finally, the system had to be moderately flexible in allowing users to change certain parameters of the system, for example, to tell it that a certain market was about twice as sensitive to a promotion as another. This was because it was impossible to state the relationships between variables precisely.

The market data were felt to be of high quality since Nielsen put in a lot of effort in ensuring high data quality at the source. Finally, one of the most important dimensions, the problem variables were felt to be relatively independent.

THE SOLUTION

The problem requirements are as follows:

Dimension	Target Solution
Accuracy	Moderate
Explainability	High
Response Speed	Moderate
Compactness	High
Flexibility	High
Embeddability	High
Tolerance for Complexity	High
Tolerance for Noise in Data	Moderate
Tolerance for Sparse Data	Moderate
Ease of Use	High
Development Speed	High

At the time that the project got off the ground, artificial intelligence had yet to "prove itself" at Nielsen. Given the extremely aggressive schedule, this presented the designers with even more of a challenge.

On the one hand, it seemed that the knowledge for data analysis, the relationships among the relevant variables, could be conveniently expressed in terms of rules. Experts thought of the problem in terms of rules, so there was a real advantage to the approach. Besides, if you think about it, the problem was really one of pattern recognition on a large dataset. Rules are ideal since each expresses a pattern and the interpreter figures out when it matches the data.

The other approach was to go the "traditional" route, using a standard procedural language like C. This approach did have some merits on the surface: Given the extremely tight memory requirements for the system, maybe standard procedural programs would prove to be more efficient. Concerning this issue of efficiency, however, as one of the developers later remarked:

> Basically we wanted to do pattern matching to see which of the heuristic rules expressed by the expert matched the data. The RETE algorithm is the fastest way to do pattern matching. There's this implicit assumption people make that procedural languages are more efficient than high level languages. This is generally true, but it really depends on what you're trying to do. If it's pattern matching you want, coding all the conditions that you express in rules in terms of IF/THEN statements wouldn't buy you anything. In fact, the system would be less efficient, less general, and less compact than the RETE algorithm which is optimized for pattern matching.

The major drawback of AI technology as far as top management was concerned was that it was still unproven. Would it be wise to risk such a critical system on an unproven approach? While the technologists felt that *they* were far enough up the learning curve with AI technology, they had still to prove themselves.

The traditional approach was well understood. But on several dimensions, it ended up looking inferior to the rule-based approach. The comparison can be summarized as follows:

Dimension	Target Solution	RBS	High level prog. language
Accuracy	Moderate	✓	✓
Explainability	High	✓	
Response Speed	Moderate		
Compactness	High		
Flexibility	High		
Embeddability	High		✓
Tolerance for Noise in Data	Moderate	✓	
Tolerance for Sparse Data	Moderate	✓	
Ease of Use	High	✓	✓
Development Speed	High	✓	

Solving the Problem

Work on NPER started early in December 1990. The system was eventually named SPOTLIGHT.

SPOTLIGHT was implemented in Eclipse, a small, efficient rule-based interpreter with an implementation of the RETE algorithm. Eclipse was written in C and allowed the access routines to the database and communications software to be written in C. In this respect, the rules were fairly integrable with existing technology. However, a fair amount of effort was required to architect the rule-based system so that it was compact enough to function with tight memory requirements.

SPOTLIGHT produced a set of formatted reports showing unexpected changes in market share. It used whatever data it had in its database to account for the unexpected changes. For example, as exceptional market activity, it might display a bar chart showing changes in market share of major brands in some market (called a competitive set) over two periods of time. It might then display a list of bullets, with each bullet describing promotion and price changes for members in the competitive set. A spreadsheet might also be included showing top and bottom performing cities or states for brands in the competitive set.

The sales database was *much* too large to be handled all at once. Further, memory constraints were extremely tight. For this reason, the database was split up into 15 smaller units, corresponding to various kinds of analysis (market share, trial and repeat, etc.). Accordingly, the knowledge base was also split up into 15 segments that had to be loaded up one at a time. The results of running each knowledge base on each set of data were saved and integrated into the final output report. In this respect, the efficiency requirement for a fast system dictated that the developers split up the rule-base, which was otherwise too bulky to run on the system.

The other difficulty posed by the rule-based approach was the fact that while it is possible to state broad rules such as "promotion will tend to increase sales volume," the degree to which such a rule applies to various classes of products varies considerably. For this reason, the designers spent a considerable amount of effort setting up rules that could be parameterized for different products, markets, etc. by users. In this respect, they really had to stretch the representation to fulfill problem requirements.

Given the extremely tight schedule, experts were brought into the evaluation cycle very quickly. While the final system would ultimately produce outputs in a word processor format, the experts had to read a somewhat more terse output during testing since the software drivers required to integrate the system with word processors was not yet developed.

SPOTLIGHT was completed on time and turned out to be a tremendous success with marketing reps. It did indeed provide them with the kind of reports that they could take straight to a customer.

Results

SPOTLIGHT turned out to be overwhelmingly popular with sales reps and clients. Nonetheless, it still had some limitations. Its analyses were limited and not interactive. In particular, it didn't answer a very important question that clients wanted answers to, namely, what *actions* should they take to remedy a certain situation? While SPOT-LIGHT offered insights into what was happening in the marketplace, it did nothing about telling the user what actions might *change* what was happening out there.

Also, a lot of work had gone into tweaking the knowledge base to make it work (in terms of parameterizing the rules). This was not a good long-term solution to the problem of making rules sensitive to the marketing context.

To improve the system, Nielsen felt approaching the problem from an object-oriented perspective would produce a more flexible and powerful system. In September 1991, Nielsen started work on a new system called Opportunity Explorer (OE).

Like its predecessor, OE was rule-based, but it also became more object oriented. This approach eliminated the need to parameterize rules since the rules could now, in effect, be attached to classes of consumer goods. So, the analysis would automatically depend on the context in which it is carried out.

On the interface front, OE was a considerable advance over SPOTLIGHT. It is Windows™-based and makes more use of GUI objects, making it possible to construct customized reports on the fly (reports are composed of objects) instead of a limited number of predefined reports. The interface also makes it easier for the user to navigate through the database, generate summary statistics on demand, and to specify the form of the outputs.

Overall Nielsen has been pleased with the results of both SPOTLIGHT and its subsequent replacement Opportunity Explorer.

Lessons Learned

The SPOTLIGHT experience resulted in several important lessons. From an engineering standpoint, it demonstrated the feasibility of implementing an expert system using conventional technology. This was novel at the time.

More importantly, however, it demonstrated the power of rule-based pattern recognition as an industrial-strength technique, where human expertise could be packaged into patterns that were used to continually monitor and mine a large database.

As databases become more accessible and stable, significant benefits can be derived by specifying patterns that can be used to monitor the data. Indeed, database technology is moving in this direction. Newer databases are equipped with the ability to define rules that trigger off activity depending on the contents of the database.

Since SPOTLIGHT, there have also been several applications of heuristic-based pattern recognition in the financial services industry.

Suggested Reading

Anand, T. and K. Kahn, "Focusing Knowledge-Based Techniques on Market Analysis," *IEEE Expert,* Vol. 8, No. 4.

Anand, T. and K. Kahn, "Making Sense of Gigabytes," in *Innovative Applications of Artificial Intelligence 4,* Scott, C., and P. Klahr, eds., AAAI Press, 1992.

------------------------------ **C A S E** ------------------------------
Improving Personnel Dispatching
NYNEX Inc., New York

PREFACE

The following case study is somewhat different from the others we presented. The other cases focus primarily on how a particular type of system solved a problem. This one emphasizes the learning process that one organization is going through in trying to make improvements to an existing knowledge-based system. In trying to make improvements, the organization is learning about the limitations of its existing customer support process and the complexity of the problem, and how these can be better addressed. The goal is ongoing process improvement.

THE ORGANIZATION

NYNEX came into existence as the result of the divestiture of Bell Telephone in 1982, which separated the long-distance and local telephone service into separate businesses. Following the divestiture, AT&T retained the long-distance business and Bell Labs (the research arm of the original company), whereas the local telephone business was spun off into seven regional companies. New York Telephone and New England Telephone were two such regional companies, which later became NYNEX

New York and NYNEX New England, respectively. NYNEX is the parent company of these two companies. NYNEX currently employs about 60,000 people.

Like many technology companies with a large customer base, a critical business process for NYNEX is customer service. Telephone lines break down all the time. Given the central role that telephones play in our lives, telephone outages are a nuisance for residential customers and simply unacceptable to businesses. Customers want them fixed immediately. While more reliable technology is the ultimate objective, a more pressing short-term goal for the telephone company is to fix these problems more cost effectively by doing a better job of understanding the nature of the problem and the skills required to resolve it.

THE PROBLEM

NYNEX handles about half a million customer reported troubles each month across 55 service centers. Out of an employee base of approximately 60,000, about 50% are devoted to maintenance and repair. Erroneous maintenance calls are costly. In fact, it is estimated that a 1% reduction in dispatching errors contributes to an annual savings of approximately $3 million dollars.

What happens when a customer calls the telephone company with a problem? First, a service representative collects information from the customer and initiates electrical tests on the customer's line referred to as the *mechanized loop test* (MLT). The MLT system was designed by and is maintained by AT&T. Results from this test, which consist of between one and two dozen readings of voltages, currents, resistances, etc., and some analysis, are put into a "trouble report" that is sent to a *maintenance administrator* (MA). Based on this report, the MA makes a high-level diagnosis about where a technician must be dispatched or whether additional data need to be collected.

After a problem is fixed, the technician who fixes it enters a four-digit code that best describes the resolution or what was done to fix the problem. This information goes into a database.

A large part of the repair problem is determining where in the network path to the customer's site the problem lies. There are four possible actions:

- dispatch to distribution wiring
- dispatch to the cable
- handle in the central office
- or do further testing

A wrong decision is very costly: Sending a technician to the wrong place can blow away a significant portion of the day, which is why a small improvement in this part of the business process results in such huge savings. Also, given the sheer volume of calls handled, even smaller improvements through better dispatching add up to large savings.

In 1990, the NYNEX Science and Technology center implemented a rule-based expert system to determine the location of malfunctions for problems reported by customers. Specifically, the expert system was designed to perform the job of the MA. It focuses on the "local loop," which connects the customer to the central office. Like the MA, the system determines roughly where the problem lies and the type of technician required to fix it. It does so based on expertise that is programmed into it in the form of rules. A rule is of the following form:

IF Voltage (across X) > *Threshold1*
AND Voltage (across Y) < *Threshold2*
THEN Dispatch to cable

where the voltages are taken across specific parts of the line and the thresholds define boundaries that distinguish between normal and pathological states of the system.

The expert system handles about a third of all calls across 55 service centers. While it is hard to measure specifically how accurate the expert system is, ballpark estimates rate it at between 60 and 70%. While these results are not bad, NYNEX felt that there was significant room for improvement.

On the surface this seems like a straightforward problem. The rules, in general, were performing well. Improving the system just required making the rules more accurate! And the problem involves measurements and a simple theory relating the measurements. In other words, the domain has structure, which can be articulated clearly by people familiar with it.

But this turns out to be difficult.

Why? First, measurements mean slightly different things depending on the geographic location. "High voltage" in rural Maine is quite different from Manhattan. Recognizing this problem, the designers of the expert system allowed for customizing the system by defining certain parameters, which were to be tweaked by local experts depending on their geographical area. But this ended up being a lot harder than anticipated.

One problem is that different experts have slightly different ways of diagnosing problems. Even with an identical set of measurements, different experts might disagree about their interpretation. Because the *process* of arriving at a conclusion is different, an expert at one location might not be totally comfortable with the reasoning process of an expert at a different location. Tweaking rule parameters is therefore not as natural to the experts as the designers had hoped it would be. The expertise just isn't standard enough.

The second problem is that the domain is inherently non-stable. A year ago, a set of readings that would have been considered normal might now seem pathological because the equipment on the line has become more sensitive. With the constant change in equipment, such as FAX machines, modems, and new telephones, interpreting readings can be a creative exercise with ample room for judgment. Because of this, rules require continuous monitoring and tweaking to be accurate. This is time consuming and painful.

Last but not least, the quality of the data is bad. Measurement errors creep into the data when the measuring device itself isn't working correctly! When this happens, you end up with a bad set of data. Unless you know exactly when the device began to malfunction, you have no way of finding and throwing out the bad data. There are even more serious problems at the human end, when the technician enters the diagnosis. We'll discuss this in more detail later.

THE SOLUTION

The following table summarizes the problem requirements. It also provides a scorecard for understanding how NYNEX's rule-based expert system stacked up on these requirements. A check mark for an attribute indicates that the system met or exceeded the requirements for that attribute.

Dimension	Ideal Solution	RBS	Acceptable
Accuracy	High	Medium	
Explainability	High	High	✓
Response Speed	Moderate	Moderate	✓
Scalability	Moderate	Moderate	✓
Flexibility	High	Low	
Tolerance for Noise in Data	Moderate	n/a	
Tolerance for Sparse Data	Moderate	n/a	
Independence from Experts	Moderate	Low	

As the table indicates, the company felt that it could do better with respect to accuracy than the current system. Also, the rule-based system wasn't flexible enough. This was a major drawback for two reasons. First it required a lot of time and patience from experts to tune the system to specific locations. Second, the problem domain was inherently non-stationary: Tweaking the rules was necessary from time to time anyway. In general, the more unstable or dynamic the knowledge, the greater the degree of effort required to overcome the lack of flexibility of a rule-based system.

NYNEX felt that the system was basically sound. Given the somewhat dynamic nature of the problem area, it seemed reasonable to try and make a system tune itself automatically to local conditions instead of requiring local experts to try and understand the knowledge base and make modifications to it. In other words, let the data build the model. The company had been collecting data about faults and how they were resolved. After all, the database contained the problem description as specified by the mechanized loop test and the customer. It also specified what the problem had turned out to be, as specified by the technician. And the data were abundant.

A number of techniques can be used for generating models to fit data. Neural nets are one obvious candidate since nets can learn patterns from data. Neural nets are particularly good at classification kinds of pattern recognition problems. This would make ANNs a candidate for this situation since problems are classified into four basic types of faults. With four output nodes and about 15 or so inputs, this would be a relatively small net. Certainly enough data were available for training and testing a net of this size.

The other obvious candidates would be recursive partitioning algorithms such as C4.5 and CART. These would explicitly find the combination of attributes that would classify the cases into the four types. The output is a decision tree where each node in the tree splits the data on an attribute. In this case, the splits would be of the form "if voltage across X is greater than y." A series of such splits should lead to a fault category.

For NYNEX's problem, a rule-based system would probably not be very accurate unless an inordinate amount of time was spent on keeping their parameters up to date. NYNEX's experience bore this out. The machine-learning techniques and neural nets are more advantageous in this respect: Both can usually achieve fairly high accuracy given good and plentiful data.

Both of these techniques also tolerate some noise in the data, assuming, of course, that there is some underlying pattern in the data in the first place, and the data are abundant. In general, though, neural nets are less forgiving than recursive partitioning when the data are sparse.

Both ML and ANNs are also highly flexible. Adding more variables is not a problem for either approach: They can automatically generate models that correspond to local conditions. This also eliminates the excessive reliance on experts required by the rule-based approach (more on this later).

An important distinguishing feature between neural nets and recursive partitioning algorithms, however, is their explainability. Neural nets are, for the most part, black boxes. In contrast, recursive partitioning produces decision trees that can be used to generate explanations as long as the trees don't get large and complicated. If they do get large and difficult to interpret, the penalty factor associated with each node can be increased, resulting in smaller trees. However, the smaller trees are not as accurate. In any case, recursive partitioning algorithms give more control in exploring the trade-off between explainability and accuracy.

While neural nets and recursive partitioning algorithms are highly independent from experts in terms of building the model (they both construct a model from the data), experts play much more of a role in interpreting the more explainable rule-like models generated by the partitioning algorithms. In this case, the fact that they are less independent from experts is a good thing: It gives the expert something simple and tangible to critique, and hence provide further insight into the problem.

Being able to understand the recommendations was important to NYNEX. It is vital to know why a specific diagnosis is being reached, especially since the data being used are not clean and hence conclusions can be suspect. It helps to see why the system is reaching a certain diagnosis. The implications of a wrong decision are also serious in terms of dollar costs. Finally, since a rule-based system was already in place, it would be reassuring to end up with decision trees that resemble the rules of the expert system, since it would support both methods' validity to some degree.

The table below compares neural nets and recursive partitioning algorithms for their suitability in this case. The rule-based system is also included as a "baseline" comparison since the objective is to try and improve on it. Again, a check mark indicates that a technique meets or exceeds the requirements on an attribute for the problem. Attributes on which all techniques meet the requirement are excluded from the table.

Dimension	Ideal Solution	RBS	ANN	ML
Accuracy	High		✓	✓
Explainability	High	✓		✓
Response Speed	Moderate	✓	✓	✓
Scalability	Moderate	✓	✓	✓
Flexibility	High		✓	✓
Tolerance for Noise in Data	Moderate	n/a	✓	✓
Tolerance for Sparse Data	Moderate	n/a		✓
Independence from Experts	Moderate		✓	✓

Solving the Problem

NYNEX decided to test the feasibility of the machine learning approach, particularly given the high premium the firm placed on explainability.

The research team first tested whether a machine learning approach could mimic the expert system. That is, given a set of data already used by an expert system to perform diagnoses, check whether a learning algorithm could learn to produce the same results with the same data.

It did. The learning algorithm NYNEX used was C4.5, and the results the firm got gave them comfort that the algorithm was working correctly. The firm applied C4.5 to the data in its database and used the system to both derive new rules and diagnose data problems.

Since this case deals more with organizational learning, readers will get a better feel for how the system is used if we now move directly to system results.

Results

When the system was given a set of measurements, it would categorize a problem into the same category as the expert system more than 90% of the time. For the cases in which it disagreed, human experts who analyzed these discrepant cases thought that the machine-learning algorithm's diagnoses were more accurate about 60% of the time. Theoretically, anyway, the machine learning approach worked.

However, when the machine learning algorithm was applied to data obtained from the field, the results were poor. The algorithm never got more than 56% accuracy.

The disappointing performance of the system was not, however, viewed by NYNEX as a failure. Rather, this system had discovered a number of non-trivial problems with the customer service process, and some subtle measurement and control problems that needed to be fixed in order to make significant improvements.

By examining the trees generated by the C4.5 algorithm, NYNEX learned about the types of data problems that exist in its database and about the procedures that the firm followed that might have led to these data problems. The firm also learned more about the nature of the *technical problems* themselves (line failures, cable problems, etc.) that its technicians fix.

Even though NYNEX's data were leading the model astray, the ML algorithm, in essence, diagrammed the data problems. NYNEX needed to determine how the errors in its database could be reduced.

Assuming the firm could spot the bad data, NYNEX had two options: either clean them up or throw them away.

Clearly, it would be better to clean up the data since there would be a larger training and testing data set, from which more powerful statistical conclusions can be drawn. But this didn't seem like a promising approach to NYNEX for several reasons. There was not enough of a concurrence among experts with data from different locations. Experts disagreed about 40% of the time. The same was true of comparisons across technicians, and between the expert system and technician, and the expert system and experts! In short, there was simply too much disagreement. In retrospect, this isn't surprising given the kinds of data quality problems enumerated above, the local differences among geographical locations, and the non-static nature of the problem domain.

The alternative was to somehow identify bad data and throw them away. While still difficult, this turns out to be an easier problem to solve. NYNEX's goal became to pull out the data that are maximally reliable and still end up with a large enough set of data that can lead to statistically significant results. The firm has been using several heuristics to identify the bad data.

For example, NYNEX started by looking for data on faults where the technicians would have no motivation to misrepresent the actual data. The firm also tried to identify cases where there is a large degree of agreement among the experts and technicians as a group. NYNEX generally throws out fault data that seem borderline or combines them into a single larger class. For example, dispatch to cable and dispatch to the distribution wiring are both "dispatch out" problems. Sometimes a technician dispatched to fix one can fix the other if it's a simple problem. By combining these two categories, the learning algorithm generated significantly better results.

A major problem was that fault codes reported did not seem to correspond well to the symptom patterns with which they were associated. NYNEX interviewed some of the technicians who report the codes. It turned out that many of the technicians did not realize the importance of the codes and had simply memorized a few of the more common ones, using these for most problems.

Furthermore, even when technicians tried to pick the correct code, the fault codes themselves were ambiguous; a single problem often mapped to several codes. Finally, there was a surprise: Technicians would sometimes report complicated problems as simpler ones to avoid charging customers high repair fees. This could happen for a number of reasons ranging from sympathy for the customer, fear of charging too much in a poor neighborhood, and so on.

While inaccuracies in mapping symptoms to fault codes sometimes occurred due to bad fault code data, there were also cases where the symptom data were corrupted. NYNEX's measurement instruments would sometimes become miscalibrated. But this isn't just noise. It's worse, because it might give the appearance of a completely false pattern.

On other occasions, a technician might even come to realize that measurements taken by tests such as the mechanized loop test are bad after he goes to a site and re-takes his own measurements. In this case, the technician would fix the problem correctly based on the new data. But the old data would never get fixed because the business process did not require it (and in fact made it difficult to do even if a technician wanted to do so). This would result in a corrupted case with the database.

What all of these discoveries point to is the fact that, although the machine-learning approach did not initially perform as well as expected, the system led to a great deal of digging into the reasons for the inaccuracy and, ultimately, to a better understanding of the problem. NYNEX was able to use the data "roadmap" provided by the ML algorithm to track down data problems. But translating this better understanding into concrete actions is still a challenge.

The net result of NYNEX's approach has been a significant increase in classification and data accuracy, as well as the discovery of many new rules.

Lessons Learned

There are several lessons to be learned from this experience. One general lesson is that machine-learning techniques are good for problems where the domain is non-stationary and where expertise is non-standard. They are not only useful for the *outputs* they produce, but in raising the level of consciousness about the problem area. In this example, the performance problems arose for a number of reasons having to do with the data quality, measurement errors, and ambiguities about the problem itself.

Furthermore, a benefit that was realized by applying machine learning in this case was the ensuing focus on data quality. Poor data plagues organizations. Historically, this hasn't been regarded by most organizations as a very serious problem since much of the data were recorded for limited operational purposes (such as order matching, delivery, etc.) for which they were adequate.

However, as organizations begin to recognize the decision-aiding power of clean data, the limitations of the poor data they have been collecting in the past are becoming clear. This is forcing organizations to invest in data clean-up efforts and putting into place systems and business processes where higher quality data can be collected going forward. It is an important way for an organization to learn more about its customers and internal processes. At the end of this exercise, NYNEX has a much better idea of where to start attacking the problem.

Finally, NYNEX learned about the service faults themselves. It turns out that some faults are transient: Sometimes a problem disappears between the time it was reported and when a technician gets to it. For example, a short circuit may be caused by water that dries up by the time a technician gets to it. The technician would report the problem as "No problem," which can be misleading since the problem could recur the next time it rains.

These nuggets of knowledge have helped NYNEX improve its service and understand how to address its customers' problems.

Suggested Reading

Danyluk, A., "A Comparison of Data Sources for Machine Learning in a Telephone Trouble Screening System," *IJCAI-95 Workshop on Data Engineering for Machine Learning,* 1995.

Danyluk, A., and F. Provost, "Adaptive Expert Systems: Applying Machine Learning to NYNEX MAX," *AAAI-93 Workshop on AI in Service and Support,* 1993.

Provost, F., and A. Danyluk, "Learning From Bad Data," *Workshop on Applying Machine Learning In Practice,* IMLC-95, 1995.

Index

A

A.C. Nielsen, pattern directed data mining of point-of-sale data case study, 244–51
Abstract data types, 191
Access databases, 74
Access paths, 38
Access paths data, 37
Access to experts, 20, 29
Accuracy, 17, 18, 26, 74
 of case-based reasoning, 166
 defined, 27
 of fuzzy system, 148
 of genetic algorithm, 75
 of machine learning algorithm, 181, 186
 of neural networks, 99
 of OLAP/data warehouse, 50
 requirements, 16
 test data vs. training set data, 100
Aggregation, 48
AI software products, 199–200, 248
AI technology, to manage invest-ment portfolios, 228–36
Algorithms, 34
ARIMA, 232
Artificial intelligence techniques, 2
Artificial neural networks (ANNs), 19, 77, 80, 81–83, 234
 as non-linear functional equations and mappings, 98
 for personnel dispatching system, case study, 254–55

"taking stock" phase, 85
Attribute deck, 161
Attributes, 151–53, 156, 165
 combination of, 157
 discriminatory power, 158, 159
 in high-dimensional space, 161
 numeric, similarity, 157, 158
 symbolic, 159
Audit planning, 105
Audit trail, 119

B

Back propagation algorithm, 101–3
Back propagation (backprop), 92
Back-propagation neural network, 197
Backward chaining, 109, 110, 150
Batch mode, 1–2
Bias, 100
Birth-rule, 138
Business requirements, 12

C

C4.5 learning algorithm, 170, 176, 254, 256
Call-logging system, case study, 236–43
CART family of algorithms, 170–71, 180, 182, 254
Case, 150
 complete, 152, 154
 defined, 151
Case-base, 149, 152, 153, 157